HISTORICAL
ATLAS
— OF —
Religions

HISTORICAL
ATLAS
OF
Religions

Karen Farrington

Checkmark Books™
An imprint of Facts On File, Inc.

HISTORICAL ATLAS OF RELIGIONS

Checkmark Books
An imprint of Facts On File, Inc.
132 West 31st Street
New York, NY 10001

For Library of Congress Cataloging-in-Publication data, please contact
Checkmark Books.
    ISBN 0-8160-5069-4

Checkmark Books are available at special discounts when purchased in bulk quantities for businesses, associations, institutions or sales promotions. Please call our Special Sales Department in New York at:
(212) 967-8800 or (800) 322-8755.

You can find Facts On File on the World Wide Web at:
http://www.factsonfile.com

For Thalamus Publishing
Project editor: Warren Lapworth
Maps and design: Roger Kean
Illustrations: Oliver Frey
Four-color separation: Proskanz, Ludlow, England

Printed and bound in Italy

10 9 8 7 6 5 4 3 2
This book is printed on acid-free paper

PICTURE CREDITS

AKG London: 19; AKG London/Erich Lessing: 117; AKG London/Gilles Mermet: 83; James L. Amos/CORBIS: 186–187; Archivo Iconografico S.A./CORBIS: 14, 39, 54, 82, 100, 109, 113, 120; Tony Arruza/CORBIS: 71 (top); Arte & Imagini srl/CORBIS: 10, 27; Yann Arthus-Bertrand/CORBIS: 49; Baldev/CORBIS SYGMA: 173; Nathan Benn/CORBIS: 16, 160; Dean Bennett/CORBIS: 134–135, 170–171, 176; Bettman/CORBIS: 2–3, 21, 32, 62, 70, 71 (bottom), 84 (left), 115, 124, 125 (bottom), 128 (top), 129, 158, 161, 172 (bottom), 177; Chris Bland/CORBIS:188–189; Michael Bodycomb/CORBIS: 89; Barmabas Bosshart/ CORBIS: 153; Marilyn Bridges/CORBIS: 58–59; National Gallery, London/CORBIS: 26; Gary W. Carter/CORBIS: 122; Elio Ciol/CORBIS: 35; Dean Conger/CORBIS: 11; Richard A. Cooke/CORBIS: 58 (top); CORBIS: 42, 64, 67, 69, 101; CORBIS/SYGMA: 73 (left); David Cumming/Ubiquitous Eye/CORBIS: 142–143; Howard Davies/CORBIS: 97 (right); Arnaldo de Luca/CORBIS: 30; Stephen Dupont/CORBIS: 178; Robert Essel/NYC/CORBIS: 183; Jack Fields/CORBIS: 6–7; Kevin Fleming/CORBIS: 159; Werner Forman Archive: 79, 88, 91, 107; Harry Foster/CORBIS: 60 (bottom), 61 (top); Michael Freeman/CORBIS: 162 (inset), 164; Oliver Frey/Thalamus Studios: 58 (bottom), 59 (right), 61 (bottom), 92–93, 104, 106, 114, 128 (bottom), 135, 156, 157 (bottom), 172 (top); John Garrett/CORBIS: 126; Philip Gould/CORBIS 85; Dallas and John Heaton/CORBIS: 121; Lindsay Hebberd/CORBIS: 139, 140, 141, 145; Georgia Lowell/CORBIS: 65; Julien Hekimian/CORBIS SYGMA: 66; John Heseltine/CORBIS: 12; Arne Hodalic/CORBIS: 41 (inset), 60 (top); Robert Holmes/CORBIS: 150, 154 (top), 154 (bottom); Angelo Hornak/CORBIS: 51, 137; Colin Hoskins/CORBIS: 95; Hulton-Deutsch Collection/CORBIS: 68, 97 (left), 179; Zen Icknow CORBIS: 174; Image Select International: 17, 20, 21 (top), 25, 37, 53, 55, 63, 72, 110, 123, 152, 155, 175, 185; Mimmo Jodice/CORBIS: 111; Wolfgang Kaehler/CORBIS: 80, 91 (left), 146; Christine Kolisch/CORBIS: 148, 149; Otto Lang/CORBIS: 77 (right); David Lees/CORBIS: 33, 103, 119; Danny Lehman/CORBIS: 52, 78; Charles Lenars/CORBIS: 92; Philippa Lewis/CORBIS: 125 (top); Chris Lisle/CORBIS: 138, 169; Araldo de Luca/CORBIS: 116; Francis G. Mayer/CORBIS: 112 (left); Shandiz Mohsen/CORBIS SYGMA: 46; Richard T. Nowitz/CORBIS: 93; Gianni Dagli Orti/CORBIS: 102; Christine Osborne/CORBIS: 165, 168; Tim Page/CORBIS: 157 (top); Caroline Penn/CORBIS: 84 (right); Ezio Petersen CORBIS: 176; David Read/CORBIS: 22 (bottom); Roger Ressmeyer/CORBIS: 23, 100–101; Bill Ross/CORBIS: 13 (top), 15; David Rubinger/CORBIS: 44; Leonard de Selva/CORBIS: 94; Lee Snider/CORBIS: 73 (right); Stapleton Collection/CORBIS: 112 (right); Kurt Stier/CORBIS: 36–37; Keren Su/CORBIS: 40–41; Chase Swift/CORBIS: 118; Thalamus Publishing: 13 (bottom both), 47, 48, 77 (left); Arthur Thévenart/CORBIS: 43; Alessandro Tiarini/CORBIS: 29; Peter M. Turnley/CORBIS: 50; Penny Tweedie/CORBIS: 182; Underwood & Underwood/CORBIS: 96, 127; Gian Berto Vanni/CORBIS: 76; Ruggero Vanni/CORBIS: 105; Sandro Vannini/CORBIS: 90; Brian A. Vikander/CORBIS: 45, 147, 151; David H. Wells/CORBIS: 24; Nik Wheeler/CORBISL 1; Peter M. Wilson/CORBIS: 18; Roger Wood/CORBIS: 156 (bottom); Alison Wright/CORBIS: 81, 143; Michael S. Yamashita/CORBIS: 162

PAGE 1: A Dogon star chart (see pages 90–91). Diviners of the Dogon people of Mali, West Africa, who worship the Dog Star Sirius, draw "questions" in the sand for the Sacred Fox to answer during the night. In the morning, the diviner interprets the footprints left behind by the fox. The Dogon are an eminently practical people. To ensure a fox will come, offerings of milk, millet, and peanuts are strategically placed on the star chart.

PAGES 2–3: Primitive religions around the globe display a sense of fusion between man and nature, exemplified by the famous late Palaeolithic Age cave paintings at Lascaux, Dordogne, France. The so-called "Chinese Horse" seen here was painted approximately 15–17,000 years ago, and it is hard, if not impossible, for modern scholars to define its exact meaning for the prehistoric artist.

Contents

6 Introduction—*A Common Human Psyche*

8 Chapter 1—*The Middle East*
10 *The Story of Judaism*
12 *Moses and the Exodus*
14 *The Promised Land*
16 *The Creation of Israel*
18 *Maimonides—Traveler and Doctor*
20 *Persecution of Jews*
22 *Jewish Tradition*
24 *Focus of Faith—the Synagogue*
26 *The Story of Christianity*
28 *The Death of Christ*
30 *St. Paul and the Spread of Christianity*
32 *Christian Persecution*
34 *Schism in Christianity*
36 *The Story of Islam*
38 *Succession to the Prophet*
40 *The Spread of Islam*
42 *The Koran—Teacher of Man*
44 *Islamic Worship*
46 *A Lifetime's Journey—the Hajj*
48 *Centers of Prayer—Mosques*
50 *The Selected Ones—Sufism*
52 *Bahá'í—a Refuge from Orthodoxy*
54 *Religious Conflicts in the Middle East*

56 Chapter 2—North America
58 *Gods of the Moundbuilders*
60 *Shamanism—the Healing Seers*
62 *The Pilgrim Fathers*
64 *Mormonism—a New Mission*
66 *Jehovah's Witnesses*
68 *Out of the Dark—Spiritualism*
70 *Christian Science*
72 *Scientology*

74 Chapter 3—Central *and* South America
76 *The Maya—Order from Chaos*
78 *The Aztec—Divine Fire of Sacrifice*
80 *The Inca—Time and Space*
82 *Jesuits—Missionaries Abroad*
84 *Voodoo—Africa meets America*

86 Chapter 4—Africa
88 *The Terracotta Gods*
90 *Star Worshippers—the Dogon*
92 *Gods of the Nile—Ancient Egypt*
94 *Missionaries in Africa*
96 *Rastafarianism*

98 Chapter 5—Europe
100 *The Dawn of Man*
102 *Gods of the Greeks*
104 *The Roman Empire*
106 *Old Norse Religion*
108 *Christianity in the Middle Ages*
110 *The Crusades and Papal Control*
112 *The Reformation in England*
114 *The Reformation in Europe*
116 *To Reach God—Cathedrals*
118 *Greek Orthodox Church*
120 *Russian Orthodox Church*
122 *Methodism—a Precise Approach*
124 *Quakers—The Society of Friends*
126 *The Salvation Army*
128 *Theosophy*
130 *Religious Conflicts in Europe*

132 Chapter 6—Asia
134 *The Story of Hinduism*
136 *Sacred Texts—the Vedas*
138 *Hindu Tradition*
140 *Reincarnation and the Caste System*
142 *The Story of Buddhism*
144 *Buddhist Belief*
146 *The Buddhist Lifestyle*
148 *Buddhist Texts*
150 *Buddhist Sects: Zen, Rinzai, Soto, and Tantric*
152 *Persecution of Buddhists*
154 *Jainism—Faith of Sympathy*
156 *Zoroastrianism—Faith of Fire*
158 *Taoism—the Way to Confucius*
160 *Confucianism—a Civil System*
162 *Shintoism—Way of the Kami*
164 *The Story of Sikhism*
166 *The Sikh Gurus*
168 *Sikh Religious Texts*
170 *Sikh Worship—the Gurdwara*
172 *Persecution of Sikhs*
174 *Krishna Consciousness*
176 *The Unification Church*
178 *Religious Conflict in Asia*

180 Chapter 7—Australasia
182 *Spirits of Dance—Aborigines*
184 *A Fierce Spirit—Maori Religion*
186 *Easter Island—Mystery in Stone*

188 Conclusion—Is there a God?
190 Glossary *and* Index

A Common *Human* Psyche

God—or rather, belief in God—still drives human affairs. In Heaven, God is the ultimate power. On Earth, religion is the ultimate tool to power. This is evident in any study of historical conflict. Few leaders go to battle without God on their side and no struggle is quite so righteous as that which seeks to defend His will. To truly win a soldier's heart and mind, rulers and politicians must invoke clear, simple ideas: right and wrong; good and evil; salvation in death. Here religion is the perfect conduit. What better way to persuade the young to die for the cause?

Here lies the cynic's creed and it conveniently ignores the fact that today's mainstream religions are demonstrably forces for good; teaching mutual love, respect, protection of the weak, and a moral code for life. In assessing them, there is danger in making comparisons. To do so pre-supposes that they share similar components and concepts. Such thinking is fundamentally flawed. It can be partly blamed on early European explorers, who readily stamped religious labels onto foreign cultures, assuming they possessed the same structures as Christianity.

Defining the nature of religion is equally problematic. Convention confines the term principally to Judaism and its legacies of Christianity and Islam. Yet this ignores so-called "primitive" religions that have equally valid claims to spirituality and the truth of creation. Primitive beliefs found in parts of Africa and the Pacific islands carry no clear boundary between the spiritual and material world or between dreams and reality. There is a strong sense of fusion between man and nature, which some scholars have likened to a mystical version of the science of ecology.

The third main religious category concerns typically Asian belief systems such as Hinduism, Buddhism, and Taoism. Followers do not denounce the idea of God but focus on ways of liberating human consciousness from the boundaries imposed by social factors. They attempt to explore beyond thought and language to higher planes in which everything in the Universe is interdependent.

Within these categories—and within our limited understanding of the ancient religions—there are surprisingly similar

RIGHT: A worshipper lights incense at the altar in front of the reclining Buddha at Wat Lokaya Sutha in Ayutthaya, Thailand.

religious myth, and burial rites and has been explained by the Swiss psychiatrist Carl Jung as the product of a common human psyche. Jung argued that just as all people possess similar physical traits, so their unconscious being stems from similar psychological influences.

The following pages give an overview of religious practice from the time more than emergence of today's great global faiths, to modern beliefs. It avoids moral judgments and the competing claims of differing traditions and instead looks to the origins of religious practice and the development of doctrine. It is written for anyone who has ever questioned the meaning of spirituality and the power of belief.

CHAPTER 1

The Middle East

SPAIN

Barcelona

Seville ○   ○ Cordoba

ATLANTIC OCEAN

Tangier   Ceuta

Canary Islands

Corsica

Balearic Islands

Sardinia

Genoa   • Venice

• Ravenna

Pisa

Rome ○

Naples •

AFRICA

Tunis •

• Kairouan

• Palermo

Sicily

MEDITERRAN

• Tripoli

This carved relief from the Golan Heights shows the nine-branched menorah used on the holy feast of Chanukah and called a Hanukiyah. Oldest of all Hebrew symbols, the menorah is usually a seven-branched candelabrum constructed according to the instructions in Exodus 25: 31–40. Originally, it was lit every evening in the sanctuary of the Temple to remind Israel to be a "light unto the nations."

The earliest symbol of Christianity was not the cross, but a simple outline of a fish. It symbolized Christ's mission to be a "fisher of men." It was also a secret sign. For Christians fearing persecution, a fish idly drawn in the sand with a staff could be passed off as nothing more than a doodle to anyone except a fellow Christian.

One unremarkable corner of the globe brought forth three great religions. Although centuries separate them, Judaism, Christianity, and Islam were fashioned in a similar environment and share essentially the same threads. This mighty triumvirate worships one God, embraces piety, charity, and love in His name, and characters like Abraham and Moses are pivotal to all three. With so much common ground, it is perplexing that these faiths are so disparate and mutually hostile today.

Wrestling with the wealth of material yielded by this fascinating trio, it is easy to overlook other religions that have flourished in the Middle East. But these alternatives—some admirable, some bizarre—were equally valid in the era. Occupied by one empire then the next, the people of the region were exposed to paganism, Zoroastrianism, Manichaeism,

classical deities, and more, not to mention a host of cults that mushroomed and then melted away over the ages. A sizeable number loved these religions, lived by their tenets and died for them. The collective experience of the region has helped to shape world religion.

For the dispassionate observer, today's religions of the Middle East have chinks in their armor. We know what was included but are left wondering what the Old Testament, New Testament, and the Koran left out. These abstract scripts are open to interpretation. As such none of the three faiths can be identified by a single recognizable face. They are multi-faceted— and usually at war among themselves, as well as with each other.

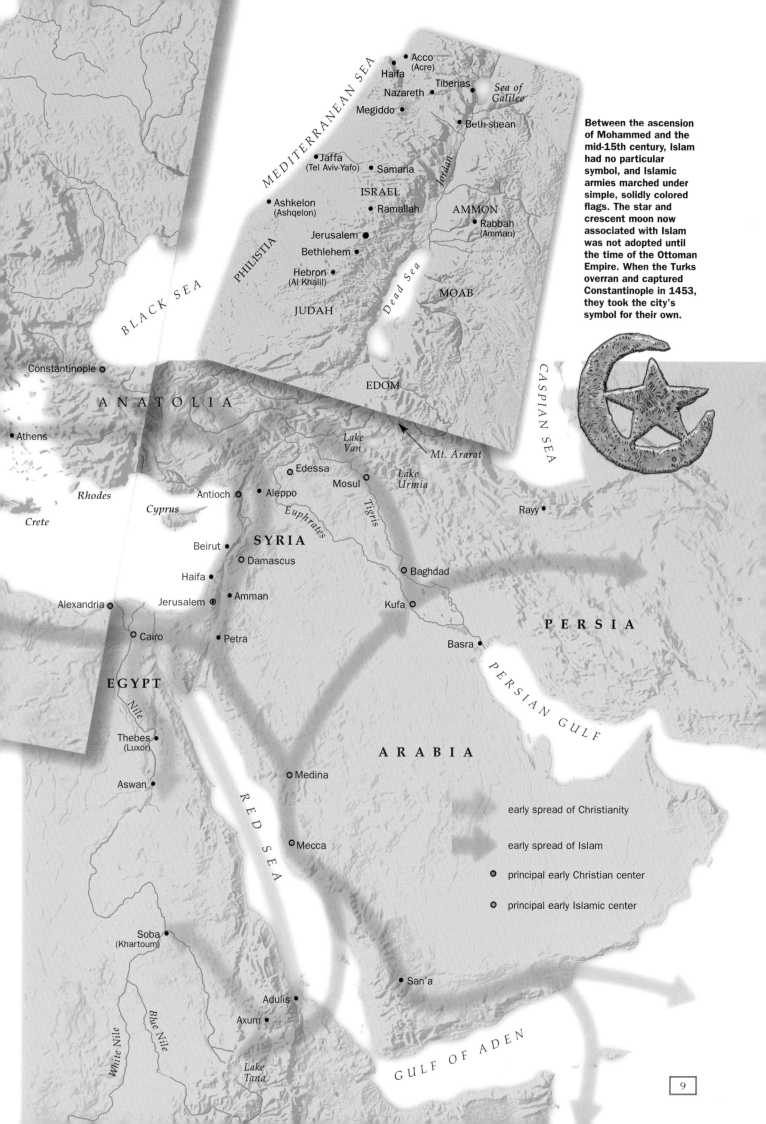

Between the ascension of Mohammed and the mid-15th century, Islam had no particular symbol, and Islamic armies marched under simple, solidly colored flags. The star and crescent moon now associated with Islam was not adopted until the time of the Ottoman Empire. When the Turks overran and captured Constantinople in 1453, they took the city's symbol for their own.

MEDITERRANEAN SEA

Acco (Acre)
Haifa
Tiberias
Nazareth
Sea of Galilee
Megiddo
Beth-shean
Jaffa (Tel Aviv-Yafo)
Samaria
ISRAEL
Jordan
Ashkelon (Ashqelon)
Ramallah
AMMON
Rabbah (Amman)
Jerusalem
Bethlehem
PHILISTIA
Hebron (Al Khalil)
Dead Sea
MOAB
JUDAH

BLACK SEA

Constantinople
ANATOLIA
EDOM
CASPIAN SEA

Athens
Lake Van
Mt. Ararat

Rhodes
Edessa
Lake Urmia
Cyprus
Mosul
Antioch
Aleppo
Crete
Euphrates
Tigris
Rayy

Beirut
SYRIA
Damascus
Baghdad
Haifa
Jerusalem
Amman
Kufa
PERSIA
Alexandria
Basra
Cairo
Petra

EGYPT
PERSIAN GULF
Nile

Thebes (Luxor)
ARABIA
Aswan

Medina

RED SEA

early spread of Christianity

early spread of Islam

Mecca
principal early Christian center

principal early Islamic center

Soba (Khartoum)

San'a

Adulis
White Nile
Blue Nile
Axum

Lake Tana
GULF OF ADEN

9

The Story *of* Judaism

The history of the Jewish people is told in the books of the Hebrew Bible—also known as the Old Testament. It is likely they were written no earlier than the sixth century BC, sometimes cataloging events from centuries before. Tales of this age must be viewed with caution, but there is archaeological evidence that roots the Old Testament in fact.

FACING: A silver padlock and gate guard the tombs of Abraham and Sarah in the Cave of Machpelah, Hebron, now covered by a combined mosque and synagogue.

RIGHT: In the Old Testament's Book of Genesis, we are told that Abraham was ordered to sacrifice his beloved son Isaac (Ishmael in Arabic) in order to prove his obedience to the word of God. As Abraham was about to do so, God sent an angel to stop the ritual killing and provided a sacrificial lamb in Isaac's place. The story documents a moment when the Hebrews made a covenant with a single deity, one with a kinder outlook than they were accustomed to. To their Caananite neighbors, child sacrifice to cruel and demanding gods was common. In Caravaggio's painting, the lamb has been replaced by a ram.

At worst the Old Testament is a mix of myth and mysticism alongside parables, parallels, and eyewitness accounts. Modern publishers have named the genre "faction." But to know the stories of the Bible is to understand how Judaism came into being.

Abraham, father of the faith, lived some 1,900 years BC. He had a special agreement or covenant with God and spoke with Him on several occasions. Abraham was told to leave his home for a new land. According to the Book of Genesis, God promised, "I will make of you a great nation, and I will bless you, and make your name great, and you will be a blessing. I will bless those who bless you, and curse him that curses you, and by you shall all the families of the earth be blessed."

One of Noah's descendants, Abraham, Abraham's wife Sarah, and nephew Lot summoned considerable courage to leave their familiar environs and kinfolk for the unknown. They eventually settled in Canaan, a fertile strip of land bordering the Mediterranean Sea. God made a pledge which He repeated several times: "Unto thy seed will I give this land."

In their old age, Abraham and Sarah had a son, Isaac. Before then they endured childlessness in an age when having a son and heir was of paramount importance. When God promised him a son, He made "an everlasting covenant" with Abraham, that boys would thereafter be circumcized at the age of eight days. Later, Abraham proved his faith in God by preparing to sacrifice the much-loved child. The grisly ritual was halted only by the last-minute intervention of an angel. The incident is believed to have taken place at Mount Moriah in Jerusalem, where Solomon's Temple was later built.

The agreements between God and the

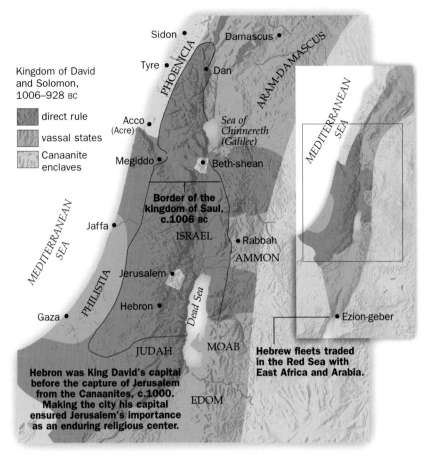

Kingdom of David and Solomon, 1006–928 BC

- direct rule
- vassal states
- Canaanite enclaves

PHOENICIA

ARAM-DAMASCUS

Sidon •

Damascus •

Tyre •

• Dan

Acco •
(Acre)

Sea of
Chinnereth
(Galilee)

Megiddo •

• Beth-shean

MEDITERRANEAN SEA

MEDITERRANEAN SEA

Border of the kingdom of Saul, c.1006 BC

Jaffa •

ISRAEL

• Rabbah

AMMON

Jerusalem •

Dead Sea

Hebron •

Gaza •

PHILISTIA

JUDAH

MOAB

Hebron was King David's capital before the capture of Jerusalem from the Canaanites, c.1000. Making the city his capital ensured Jerusalem's importance as an enduring religious center.

EDOM

• Ezion-geber

Hebrew fleets traded in the Red Sea with East Africa and Arabia.

with the powers of the natural world—summoning lightning, thunder, earthquakes, and so forth—but was always deemed above and beyond such phenomena.

Judaism as we know it today did not exist. The faith evolved from the time of Abraham, through Moses and his descendants to a more familiar form by the era of the Roman Empire. After the death of Sarah, Abraham took another wife and had more children. According to Genesis his death came at the age of 175 years and he was buried alongside Sarah in the cave of Machpelah. The site in Hebron is today marked by a building split between a synagogue and a mosque. The 12 tribes of Israel are descended from the 12 sons of Isaac's son, Jacob. His sons were Reuben, Simeon, Levi, Judah, Issachar, Dan, Naphtali, Gad, Asher, Zebulun, Benjamin, and Joseph (the latter two did not found tribes, but their sons did).

obedient Abraham are fundamental to Jewish people. Through it they have laid claim to the land roughly equivalent to Canaan. Today it is known as Israel.

SODOM AND GOMORRAH

There were other religions in evidence at the time. In Canaan—where the world's first alphabet was created—the god Baal was widely adored, a symbol of order against chaos, of abundance above drought and of regeneration. There was a god more powerful than Baal known as El, but both were remote from the people. Hebrews believed in one creator god. One of the key transitions between early Hebraism and emerging Judaism was the acceptance that this was not just a local god but a universal one.

Abraham witnessed God's rule first-hand with the destruction of two cities, Sodom and Gomorrah, by fire and brimstone in retaliation for the depraved behavior of their inhabitants. Abraham's nephew and his family narrowly escaped, although Lot's wife was allegedly turned into a pillar of salt after disobeying a command to not look back at the infernos.

The notion of God was kept alive by Abraham's family. Their God was invisible—no idols were fashioned or pictures drawn. He was sometimes imbued

Moses *and the* Exodus

Although the rule of the pharaohs lasted almost 3,000 years, it is described in the Bible in a matter of sentences. But the Egyptians loom large in the story of Moses, who led the Hebrew people out of slavery in Egypt during the 13th century BC. The story of Moses remains fundamental to the Jewish faith.

Just how the Israelites were taken into bondage to build new cities for the Egyptians remains unclear. In 1468 BC Egyptians led by the pharaoh Thutmose triumphed against the Canaanites in a battle at Megiddo. It is tempting to believe this event is pivotal, yet the Bible says Israelites were in captivity for 430 years, which places them in Egypt much earlier. Hebrew workers may have settled in Egypt as early as 1640 BC in order to secure employment.

According to *Exodus*, the Hebrew people continued to thrive and their hosts became fearful that they could destabilize the Egyptian empire. An unnamed pharaoh commanded that every Hebrew male baby should be tossed into the river. Affected families would be deprived of the future income brought by sons but still had to bear the cost of bringing up daughters.

One mother hid her baby boy for three months then took him to the Nile, made an ark of bullrushes, and left him to float by the bank. He was discovered by the pharaoh's daughter and coincidentally his real mother was chosen to wet-nurse him. He was eventually brought into the royal household and called Moses.

One day, after witnessing the abuse of a Hebrew worker, Moses killed an Egyptian. Knowing the pharaoh would seek revenge, he fled and became a shepherd. His existence remained inconspicuous until years later, when God spoke to him through the flames of a burning bush. Armed with a rod given mystical power by God, Moses confronted the pharaoh. His identity is not revealed in *Exodus*, but the pharaoh is thought to be Ramses II (c.1290–1224 BC).

THE PLAGUES STRIKE

In the company of his brother, Aaron, Moses begged the pharaoh, "Let my people go." Moses' plea was denied. Time after time Moses brought down a plague upon Egypt, including frogs, lice, locusts, and a three-day spell of darkness. Only after the tenth plague, in which the firstborn son of every Egyptian was killed, did the pharaoh agree to demands. On the night of the tenth plague, Hebrew families were told to slaughter a lamb, mark their doorposts with its blood, and eat the meat with bitter herbs and bread. The plague miraculously skipped their houses, an event marked ever since by the religious festival of Passover.

The Hebrews made a hurried departure. In *Exodus* a figure of about 600,000 men is mentioned, as well as women and children, cattle and sheep. Today that number seems

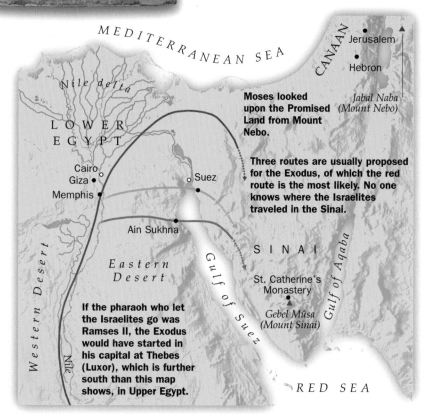

Moses looked upon the Promised Land from Mount Nebo.

Jabal Naba (Mount Nebo)

Three routes are usually proposed for the Exodus, of which the red route is the most likely. No one knows where the Israelites traveled in the Sinai.

If the pharaoh who let the Israelites go was Ramses II, the Exodus would have started in his capital at Thebes (Luxor), which is further south than this map shows, in Upper Egypt.

MEDITERRANEAN SEA

CANAAN

Jerusalem

Hebron

Nile delta

LOWER EGYPT

Cairo
Giza
Memphis

Suez

Ain Sukhna

Eastern Desert

Western Desert

Nile

Gulf of Suez

SINAI

St. Catherine's Monastery

Gebel Mûsa (Mount Sinai)

Gulf of Aqaba

RED SEA

unfeasibly large. The difficulties of watering and feeding this number would have been immense. Although their exact route is not known, the caravan led by Moses and Aaron would have traversed desolate country.

The pharaoh, grieving for his son lost in the tenth plague, had a change of heart and decided to pursue the Israelites. His forces trapped them before the Sea of Reeds—incorrectly translated for many years as the Red Sea. Moses used his rod to part the waters, creating a safe, dry passage for the escapees. When the last Hebrew had crossed, two walls of water crashed down, engulfing the pursuing Egyptians.

After traveling in the desert for three months, the Israelites made camp at the foot of Mount Sinai, which Moses ascended and famously received the Ten Commandments on two stone tablets. He also received extensive laws-for-life from God, and the framework of the faith was wrought.

Traditionally, thanks to this divine authority, Moses has been accepted as the author of the first five books of the Bible: *Genesis*, *Exodus*, *Leviticus*, *Numbers*, and *Deuteronomy*. These are collectively known as the *Pentateuch* or *Torah*. Recently, scholars have cast doubt on this assertion, believing the books to be the work of various authors.

The Promised Land

For 40 years the Israelites wandered in the wilderness, drinking from springs miraculously created by Moses' rod and eating food—or manna—provided by God. In one of their regular dialogs the aged Moses offended God by expressing doubt. His punishment was severe: Moses would not be allowed to lead his people into the Promised Land.

Although he saw it from Mount Nebo before his death, Moses never reached the Promised Land of Canaan. The site of his tomb is unknown; claims that his body lies at the desert monastery of Nebi Musa are strongly disputed. The honor of leading the Israelites into Canaan fell to his successor, Joshua, a feisty soldier undaunted by the array of fortified towns in the region.

According to the Bible, Joshua laid siege to Jericho, the world's oldest city, with eerie military tactics dictated by God. For six days the Israelites marched silently around the city walls, led by priests bearing the Ark of the Covenant, containing the Ten Commandments. Those within heard only the tramping of thousands of feet and the passing blasts of trumpets blown by priests. On the seventh day, after seven circuits of the city, the walls of Jericho tumbled down to the cries of the Israelites, who forged through and killed the inhabitants.

Archaeological evidence shows otherwise, since excavations in Jericho revealed it was not fortified with high walls at the time of Joshua (c.1230 BC). It is thought that city walls were in place some 300 years earlier but were torn down by unknown invaders. Nevertheless, Jericho would have been key in the campaign to occupy Canaan, for it boasted a productive spring. History proves that another city, Hazor, was destroyed at the end of the 13th century BC, which concurs with the continuing Old Testament story of Joshua.

After his death, Joshua's people lapsed in their worship of God, although there were notable heroes in the subsequent years, including Samson and Samuel, who helped Saul become the first king of Israel. Saul's star began to wane while David, a local shepherd boy employed as Saul's harpist, enjoyed better fortunes. He shot to fame through killing the enormous Philistine Goliath, an enemy of the Israelites. Ultimately Saul killed himself and David inherited the crown.

HOUSING THE ARK

Uniting Israel and Judah, David was both powerful and pious. He displayed uncharacteristic avariciousness when it came to Bathsheba, the wife of one of his generals. They had an affair and, when she fell pregnant, David plotted the death of her husband. The result of their liaison was Solomon. Granted the gift of wisdom by God, Solomon is remembered for his sage judgments and for the building of the first immense Temple dedicated to God in Jerusalem.

BELOW: The story of how the youthful David slew the Philistine giant Goliath has been an inspiration for artists throughout the centuries. "David with the head of Goliath" is one of two paintings on the subject by Caravaggio (1573–1610), probably painted about 1605.

In 597, Judah rebelled against Babylonian rule. King Nebuchadnezzar captured Jerusalem, the capital of Judah, plundered the Temple of Solomon, and sent many of the citizens in captivity to Babylon. During this period of exile, Jewish introspection in the face of disaster led to much of the Old Testament being written in a form close to what we have today.

The population of Jerusalem was deported to Babylon for a second time after the rebellion of 587. The Jews stayed there until 539, when Achemenid Persians overthrew the Babylonians and allowed the Jews to return home.

The Middle East, 1000–500 BC

- kingdom of Israel at greatest extent
- kingdom of Judah at greatest extent
- kingdom of Egypt, 920
- Assyrian Empire, 720
- Babylonian Empire, 590

dedicated to God in Jerusalem. However, he gathered a number of foreign wives who led him into idolatrous worship. As a result the kingdom was weakened and, following his death in 922 BC, once again split into Judah and Israel.

One of the women Solomon courted was the Queen of Sheba, who traveled from her native Ethiopia to "test him with hard questions." She was evidently impressed with his answers, for she gave him considerable gifts, including gold, precious stones, and spices. In return, the Bible declares that he gave her "all that she desired, whatever she asked."

Rumors have long persisted about the existence of the Ark of the Covenant, closely guarded in a remote monastery in Ethiopia, presumably inspired by the Sheba/Solomon liaison. Officially, for 400 years the Ark, the most sacred object of the Hebrew people, was housed in the Temple built by Solomon. It was kept in a sanctuary called the Holy of

Holies, entered just once a year by the High Priest, until the marauding Babylonians destroyed the temple and took the Israelites into exile in 586 BC. Its whereabouts since then are unknown.

The Persians overwhelmed the Babylonians within 50 years and the Jews were permitted to return to Jerusalem, where they built the Second Temple. Although they succumbed to the Greeks under Alexander the Great, the Israelites finally rebelled in 164 BC under the charismatic leadership of Judas Maccabeus to establish independence. By this time the Israelites were recognizably Jewish.

ABOVE LEFT: Another of Lorenzo Ghiberti's Gates of Paradise depicts the fall of Jericho. At the top, Hebrew priests circle the city walls, blowing their trumpets, while in the foreground soldiers tramp silently around, revealing more priests bearing the Ark of the Covenant on their shoulders.

The Creation *of* Israel

The glories brought by Judas Maccabeus were short-lived and in 63 BC the Jews, like many, fell to the might of Rome. At first the Romans diplomatically installed a Jewish king, Herod the Great, to rule Jerusalem. However, Rome soon took the reins of power.

Despite a considerable degree of religious tolerance, a brooding resentment festered among the Jews, who were compelled to pay heavy taxes and adopt Roman ways. By AD 66 the Holy Land was ripe for rebellion. Rome responded to the uprising with great resolve. Jewish people fought with ardor but were no match for disciplined Roman troops. By AD 70 Jerusalem was in Roman hands and the Temple had been destroyed.

The remaining Jewish insurgents were at Masada, a mountain fortress looming over the Dead Sea, with a thousand men defending the impressive complex against 10,000 legionnaires. It took the Romans more than two years to breach the walls—when they found the Jews had chosen to commit mass suicide rather than submit. Archaeological excavations of Masada, in tandem with texts from the era, tell us what occurred. From this point, the Bible bears no

relevance to Israel's history.

A second Jewish War broke out in the region in 132 with Simon bar Khokhba leading the rebels. The Roman emperor Hadrian (r.117–38) renamed Jerusalem Aelia Capitolina and forbade Jews to enter. While some Jews were sold into slavery across the empire, others fled across Europe and Africa. This was a repeat of the Diaspora (dispersal) Jews experienced in the eighth and sixth centuries BC, but this time it had a more lasting effect.

RETURNING HOME

Those who headed through northern Africa and settled in Spain are known as the Sephardim, from the word Sepharad, which is Hebrew for Spain. Those who became centered in Germany were known as the Ashkenazim. Both strands of Judaism developed distinct customs and cultures.

The land of Israel came into the sphere of numerous empires and monarchs and its name was abandoned in favor of the geographical term of Palestine. The broad distribution of Jews, together with the changing face of the Holy Land, made it impossible for a nationalist movement to gather momentum. Israel and the Temple had been erased but there was a set of scriptures and laws and a series of festivals, which took on increased significance. Jews assimilated reasonably well into new societies, including those ruled by Islam after its inception in the seventh century. The continuity that has been the hallmark of the Jewish faith remained unbroken despite a bleak outlook.

One Asian empire adopted Judaism and flourished for several centuries. The faith prevailed among the Khazars after their leader heard in detail from an Arab mullah, a Christian priest, and a rabbi on the merits of each religion. The date may have been as early as 740 or as late as 861. This emperor made his choice with multitudes of Islamic Arabs to the south and Christian armies to the west. His decision critically stalled the progress of Islam across Asia.

When the Khazarian empire collapsed in the 11th century, the Jewish population is thought to have gone to East European countries like Hungary and Bulgaria, or even to the eastern Caucasus. It is probable that many of the Jews converted to Islam.

Organized pursuit of a Jewish homeland was hardly evident until 1897, when the First Zionist Congress was held in Basel. One of the leading lights at the occasion was journalist Theodor Herzl, who went on to become first president of the World Zionist Organization. A fund was established to buy land in Palestine, then part of the weakened Ottoman Empire. In 1909 the city of Tel Aviv was founded, then a suburb of Jaffa, which would be home to thousands of Jews returning from all parts of the globe.

ABOVE: Budapest-born journalist Theodor Herzl, seen here in 1900, became the first president of the World Zionist Organization. In Europe the Zionist movement had gathered strength since the late 18th century, until by the 1860s funding was becoming available to send Jewish colonists to Palestine. The movement was another manifestation of the nationalism sweeping through Europe at the time, except that Zionism had no home to call its own. Herzl (1860–1904) was only the first of a long line of political activists who would change this and ensure that, after almost 2,000 years, Jews would be able to return to Eretz Israel.

Maimonides – Traveler *and* Doctor

Twelfth century Europe was fraught with fundamentalism. The Crusades, stained with blood and bigotry, were a potent feature of religious life, and Christianity was shaping up for the Inquisition. Against this vivid religious backdrop, one of Judaism's most eminent thinkers set to work.

BELOW: Maimonides is honored in Cordoba, Spain by this statue. Prior to the arrival of the Berber Almohad dynasty, Al-Andalus (Andalusia) had been one of the glories of the Islamic world and its capital of Cordoba one of the most important cities of Europe.

Moshe Ben Maimon (1135–1204) was born in Cordoba, Spain and forced into exile when the Almohad dynasty stormed to power in 1148. These Islamic Berbers had no time for tolerance toward Jews and Maimonides and his family were forced to flee. They went to Morocco then to Egypt, where the Islamic rulers permitted Jews to live openly.

Plans to study were sidelined when his brother David went down on a ship in the Indian Ocean, along with the family's riches. Maimonides embarked on a career in medicine and became physician to Saladin (1137–93), the scourge of the crusaders in Palestine. Saladin became wazir of Egypt in 1169, and sultan of Syria, Palestine, and Egypt in 1174. Maimonides' schedule was demanding. Attending to Saladin, his family, harem, and chief officers in the morning, Maimonides returned home in the afternoon to find his surgery filled with Jews and Gentiles needing treatment. At night he was exhausted by the constant interviews. He spent the Sabbath instructing Jews on matters of faith and law. "We study together a little until noon, when they depart," he wrote. "Some of them return and read with me in the afternoon service until evening prayers. In this manner I spend that day."

All the more remarkable, then, that alongside his medical work he produced one of the most authoritative books on Jewish Law, the Mishna Torah. In addition he wrote in *Arabic Commentary on the Mishna* and *Guide to the Perplexed*, and summarized the principles of Jewish belief in his famous Thirteen Articles.

The Mediterranean region at the time of the Third Crusade, 1160–90

After wandering around Christian Spain for some 12 years, Maimonides' family settled in Fez in 1160 for five years before being driven out by the Almohad authorities.

Almohad Emirate
Ayyubid Emirate
Crusader States
Byzantine Empire

likely route of Maimonides
possible alternative route

MODERNIZING THE JEWISH CODE

Maimonides believed it was primitive to scrupulously adhere to some of the Jewish scriptures set down thousands of years earlier. His aim was to marry the mystical elements of Judaism with rational thought to modernize and strengthen the faith. He wanted to re-interpret the Talmud, the Jewish code compiled in Palestine in about AD 200 dealing with the rules and rituals for everyday life, from diet to worship and beyond. Troubled by the literal translation by scholars of the Bible, he was dismissive of and even mocked traditionalists. Soon he was marked as a dangerous radical and his books were burned in the streets.

But his message left a mark on mainstream Judaism, so much so that when he died Egyptian Jews observed three days of mourning. He had worked in the wake of Rabbi Shlomo Yitzchaki, known as Rashi (1040–75), who produced definitive commentaries on the Talmud and the Bible. Together Rashi and Maimonides, also known as Rambam, are still hailed as among the brightest stars in the Jewish firmament.

The appeal of Maimonides' philosophy is clear from quotes like this one: "God is like a king in his palace and his subjects were trying to find him. Those who merely obeyed the Torah had not even set eyes on the palace. Those who read the Talmud but failed to apply reason to their faith were walking outside the palace walls. It was the faithful who read and understood philosophy that won access to the palace antechamber—and only when they understood the limit of what can be learned did they enter the palace itself."

His reputation is further enhanced by the wide appeal of his writings. At conference called in 1985 to mark the 850th anniversary of his birth, a Soviet scholar said, "Maimonides is perhaps the only philosopher in the Middle Ages, perhaps even now, who symbolizes a confluence of four cultures: Greco-Roman, Arab, Jewish, and Western." A Jewish expression of the Middle Ages asserts: "From Moses [of the Torah] to Moses [Maimonides] there was none like Moses."

BELOW: The first page of a commentary on the Talmud by Rabbi Shlomo Yitzchaki (Rashi), writing at the end of the 11th century. The page also contains comments added in the 13th century by another hand.

Persecution *of* Jews

main concentration of
Jews in the medieval era

Jewish Pale of Settlement
1880–1907, subject to
pogroms

☐ concentration camp
1935–45

⬚ death camp
1943–45

**Spain's
substantial
Jewish
population
co-existed
with ruling
Muslims for
almost 700 years.
In 1492, having
finally taken Granada, the last Muslim
stronghold, King Ferdinand and Queen
Isabella's first act was to expel
thousands of Jews who refused to
convert to Christianity.**

GERMANY
Warsaw
RUSSIA
Cologne
Rouen
Paris
Mainz
Auschwitz
Ratisbon
FRANCE
Kiev
Arles
SPAIN
Toledo
ITALY
Seville
Rome
Granada
Constantinople
*BLACK
SEA*
MEDITERRANEAN SEA
Alexandria
Palestine
EGYPT

**From 1835, Jews in Russia
(and part of Poland) were
legally required to live within
the designated Pale of
Settlement. Commencing in
1881, a series of pogroms
forced millions to flee in order
to avoid massacres which the
authorities did little to
prevent. Some of the worst
occurred around Kiev.**

**At the outset of the First
Crusade in 1096 and again
during the Black Death,
1347–8, Jews were
massacred along the Rhine,
Main, and Danube rivers.**

**More than two million Jews fled from
Russia to the U.S. and over 60,000 to
Palestine during the 1880s.**

In 1917 Britain's foreign secretary, Arthur Balfour, pledged a homeland for the Jews in Palestine. This famous declaration, backed by a military campaign, heralded hope for Jewish people everywhere and despair for resident Arabs, who had their own plans for the region they had occupied for centuries.

In the early 20th century some 85,000 Jews lived in the Holy Land, compared with an estimated 500,000 Arabs. About 4,000 Jews moved their every year. However, Jewish immigration would accelerate with the ascendancy of Hitler. Much has been written about the World War I corporal and failed artist who found a fertile breeding ground for his extreme politics in Germany. He hated minorities, Jews in particular.

Those feelings were nothing new. Anti-Semitism existed in Europe in medieval times, when Christian crusaders killed thousands while *en route* to Jerusalem to expel Muslims. Jews were massacred in Germany and blamed for the spread of the Black Death, which claimed the lives of an estimated 75 million Europeans after its outbreak in 1347. In 19th-century Russia there were pogroms in which Jews were killed and ousted from their homes. The Russian word *pogrom* is literally translated as "devastation." At the end of the century anti-Semitic feelings in France were revealed with the trial and imprisonment on bogus charges of a young Jewish army officer.

For centuries the Catholic Church held Jews responsible for the death of Jesus. The fact that only a few Jews sought the crucifixion, at a time when conniving politics were prevalent, was overlooked. Only in 1965 did the Vatican officially clear Jews of responsibility for His death.

Arabs had long competed with Jews for spiritual sites sacred to both faiths. Prior to 1917 Arabs were accommodating to Jewish settlers. They were persuaded by the sentiments of luminaries like Dr. Chaim Weizmann, the future first President of Israel, who pledged to safeguard the interests of the Arabs. "Not a hair of their heads shall be touched," he wrote. However, the Balfour Declaration appeared to fly in the face of promises made by Britain to the Arabs, making them resentful of both the British and Jews.

THE HOLOCAUST

As Hitler enforced anti-Jewish policies in Germany, immigration began to rise, to some 30,000 during 1933 and more than doubling to 61,800 by 1935. Britain began immigration controls in the region, which prevented numerous Jews reaching a safe haven in subsequent years.

Concentration camps—the first, in Dachau, opened in 1933—were packed to bursting point all over Germany and its occupied territories. It wasn't just the Jews who were incarcerated. Homosexuals, Romanies, Jehovah's Witnesses, and political opponents were all made slaves. Yet special venom was reserved for Jews, who once again became Europe's scapegoats. When Jews from all over eastern Europe were dispatched to Germany, there was no room to accommodate them. From the summer of 1941, Nazis instituted the Final Solution—mass killings in specially constructed gas chambers.

Architect of extermination policy Reinhard Heydrich made no secret of his aim to eliminate the Jewish race. In 1942 Hitler was steeling the German people for just this when he said, "The war will not end as the Jew imagines it will, with the uprooting of the Aryans, but the result will be complete annihilation of the Jews. Now for the first time they will not bleed other people to death but… the old Jewish law of 'an eye for an eye' will be applied."

In the madness that prevailed until the collapse of the Third Reich, an estimated six million Jews lost their lives. International sympathy for them was immense—yet in the years following the war Britain still refused Jewish refugees entry into the Holy Land. Unpopular with both Arabs and Jews, Britain finally realized her position was untenable. In 1947 the United Nations took over government of the region. On the eve of the withdrawal of British troops on May 14, 1948, to the fury of Arabs around the region, the state of Israel was declared.

FACING: A 1934 issue of Nazi newspaper Der Stürmer says, "Jewish Murder Plans against non-Jewish humanity uncovered!" and at the bottom, "The Jews are our Misfortune." Edited by Julius Streicher, the Gauleiter of Nuremberg, Der Stürmer aroused furious hatred (and fear) of the "Jewish pollution." Exposure to such a livid cocktail of propaganda inevitably dulled common German sensibilities to the horrors that were about to unfold.

BELOW: This German photograph of Jews being herded from the Warsaw Ghetto after its fall in 1943 was exhibited at the Nuremberg War Crimes Trials.

Jewish Tradition

Judaism not only defines faith but also a way of living. Jewish people draw a huge sense of identity from their religion that binds and strengthens. Underpinning worship, laws, and daily life is a wealth of tradition to which devotees can cling in troubled times.

RIGHT: The most holy day of the Jewish year is Yom Kippur, heralded by the symbolic blowing of a ram's horn.

BELOW: The ceremony of Bar Mitzvah, usually celebrated on a boy's 13th birthday, marks his coming to adulthood, after which he may partake in the full religious life of the community. For Jews living in Israel, the Wailing Wall in Jerusalem is the most popular place for Bar Mitzvah.

Perhaps the most powerful Jewish tradition is that of study. Jews set so much store by the words of the Hebrew Bible that they have often been branded "people of the book." One Jewish saying urges the faithful to pick up the Bible and "Turn it, and turn it, for everything is in it; contemplate it, and grow old and gray over it, and do not stir from it. You can follow no better course than this." To know the Bible and all its interpretations is a tall order. For Jews there is much more to learn in the form of the Talmud, a compilation of all aspects of the wide-ranging Jewish tradition. This schedule detailing ritual, religious, and legal correctness is an essential constituent of Judaism.

One element of the Talmud is the *Mishna*, which supplements the laws laid down in the scriptures. For centuries this was an oral tradition, until the era of Rabbi Akiba ben Joseph (c.AD 15–135). Although born into poverty, he emerged as an eminent nationalist and scholar and began to impose a system on these additional laws, setting it down for future generations. The active support he lent to the Jewish uprising headed by Simon bar Khokbha led to his execution by the Romans. Within a generation, the task he began was completed by Rabbi Judah Ha-Nasi (c.135–219), a Jewish patriarch.

There is further discussion of Jewish ethics in the *Gemara*, a commentary on the *Mishna*. It exists in two forms, the first and most authoritative from Babylonia and the second, smaller version from Palestine. In addition, a host of texts—including those by Maimonides—have mushroomed down the ages, dealing with all aspects of law and morality in minute detail. One of the most notable books is the *Halakhah*, which dates from medieval times, rooted in the oral tradition and dealing primarily with the law.

CALENDAR OF CELEBRATION

Emerging from this rich written heritage is a rhythm within Jewish life, highlighted weekly by the observance of Shabbat, or the Sabbath, beginning on Fridays at sunset—which in Biblical terms is the start of the day—and ending 24 hours later. This is a day of rest, gladness, and family togetherness. The aim is to renew the covenant between God and the Jewish people, a valued connection.

Some of the Jewish celebrations have their roots in ancient Canaanite festivals, highlighting the slow transition from ancient Hebraism to modern Judaism. Annually, the most holy day in the religious calendar is Yom Kippur, a solemn mark of fasting and penitence occurring ten days after the start of the Jewish New Year, Rosh Hashanah, symbolized by the sounding of a ram's horn. At Passover God's salvation of Hebrew children during Egypt's final plague is reverently remembered, along with the ensuing flight to the Promised Land. It coincides with a past barley harvest celebration.

During the two-day Shauvot celebration—also known as the Feast of Weeks—special contemplation is given to the Ten Commandments and the giving of the law to Moses. It also shares dates with the ancient wheat harvest thanksgiving. Sukkot is likewise linked to the Biblical episode of Moses, to give thanks for the deliverance of the Israelites from 40 years in the wilderness.

The Temple in Jerusalem, destroyed for the second time in AD 70, still figures prominently in Jewish thinking, and each year it is remembered on Tisha B'Av. A more joyful celebration is Hannukah, an eight-day festival of lights marking the re-dedication of the Temple in 165 BC following the military campaign of Judas Maccabeus.

BELOW: Seder is celebrated on the first two days of the Passover, the feast commemorating the Jews' exodus from Egypt. The meal's constituents have various symbolic meanings and are centered around the Seder plate. This often elaborate dish holds five tiny saucers with portions of Charoset (a mixture of apples, walnuts, raisins, and wine), horseradish, parsley, egg, and a roasted bone.

Focus *of* Faith — *the* Synagogue

Until its destruction, the religious devotion of Jewish people was focused on the Temple in Jerusalem. The number, role, and significance of synagogues expanded to replace it and they became a vital part of Jewish life all over the world.

The Temple was a majestic building of colonnades, archways, and flights of steps, extended and glorified by Herod the Great. Here the high priests carried out sacrifices, the Torah was cherished, and the people were at one with God.

Jewish historian Flavius Josephus told how the Temple was set ablaze: "When the flames rose up the Jews let out a terrific cry and, heedless of mortal danger, ran to put it out." Their efforts were in vain and the Temple was razed—only the western wall survived. Without the focus of the Temple, the Jewish people scattered across the globe.

While the spiritual importance of the Temple remained, Jews were compelled to seek a practical alternative and the role of the synagogue, hitherto a low-key feature of

BELOW: Children learn how to handle the Torah with a scaled-down model in a synagogue in Philadelphia, USA.

Jewish life, assumed far greater importance. There is evidence of synagogues operating in Palestine, Rome, Greece, Egypt, and Babylonia by the middle of the first century AD. Synagogues are for prayer, meetings, and study of the Torah and Talmud. Their function as schools was vital when Jews lived in the shadow of anti-Semitism and their children were denied mainstream education. Today Hebrew is studied so the vitality of psalms and scriptures in their original form can be appreciated. Worship takes place in a synagogue every weekday so long as at least ten men attend.

Externally, synagogues usually reflect local architectural styles. Inside, however, they have common themes. All have an ark, a special cupboard or box in the wall facing Jerusalem that houses a hand-written scroll bearing the words of the Torah. The scroll is protected in ornately decorated velvet coverings and has a silver pointer to prevent the manuscript from becoming too well-thumbed (*see picture on page 22*).

ORTHODOX AND REFORM GROUPS

Outside the ark is the Perpetual Lamp, an echo of Temple days when the central candle of the *menorah*—the seven-armed candlestick identified with the Jewish faith (*see picture, page 8*)—was always alight, symbolizing the eternal presence of God. The *menorah* is designed to house a candle for each day of creation, plus an additional "servant" light for kindling the others.

In most synagogues prayers are led and sermons preached from a raised platform or *bimah* in the center of the room. The congregation usually sits on three sides of the *bimah*. A rabbi (literal translation, "teacher") usually leads worship but a synagogue and its services can function without one. Sometimes there is a ritual bath on the premises, a *mikvah*.

Like other faiths, Judaism has divided into cults, creeds, sects, and splinter groups. Broadly speaking there are two umbrella groups, Orthodox and Reform. In Orthodox synagogues the sexes are segregated in the congregation. Prayers are in Hebrew and sung without accompaniment. Sermons are spoken in Yiddish.

ABOVE: In this oil painting of 1892 by Jan Styka (1858–1925), a rabbi is seen wearing the tefillin (phylactery) on his head, a black leather cube containing four texts from the Torah.

In Reform synagogues, congregations are mixed and the sermon is given in the local language. There is frequently music to back the singing voices. In essence, Reform Jews concentrate more on the ethics of the faith, taking into account contemporary scholarship, while Orthodox followers adhere to Biblical laws.

Whatever their inclination, synagogues are essentially democratic institutions run by the local community. Each is independent of its neighbor.

HASIDISM

One of the most notable offshoots of Judaism is Hasidism, which has its roots in eastern Europe. It is associated with the innovative Ba'al Shem Tov (1700–60), the acknowledged "Master of the Good Name" known as Besht for short. From his home in the Ukraine, Besht revitalized Judaism by re-introducing elements of the Jewish Kabbalah, the mystical branch of worship popular in the medieval era. The Hasidim became known for making their connection with God through ecstatic dance. This both terrified and alarmed mainstream Jews and Hasidism became marginalized.

The Story *of* Christianity

BELOW: In Christian iconography, the birth of Christ is a central theme, most pictures elaborating on what must have been an essentially homespun affair. In this painting by Piero della Francesco (c.1415–92), the three wise kings watch shepherds serenading mother and child under a cool Italian light.

Jesus lived in the Holy Land, became a Jewish teacher, and met his death on a cross in about 30 AD. These facts are supported by several reputable historical sources and banish the far-fetched argument that Jesus was the creation of fervid Christian imaginations. However, it is difficult to state much more about him with certainty.

For many years it was said that Jesus was born in a stable in Bethlehem. His parents Mary and Joseph went there as part of a census. Today we know it is more likely that Jesus was born in a cave—and that no census was taken in the region until Jesus was about nine years old.

The sources for much of our information about Jesus's life and death are the Four Gospels of the New Testament, all written by his followers. Mark is credited with the first of the Gospels, probably in the latter part of the first century—at least 30 years after the death of Christ. Next comes

Matthew's version, which partly mirrors Mark's events and furnishes extra detail and new information. In this Gospel Jesus is portrayed as the Messiah, long awaited by Jews to usher in the kingdom of God.

The lyrical words of Luke weave the most popular version of the nativity. Apparently writing for a patron c.AD 85, he based much of his work upon the previous Gospels. Collectively these are known as the Synoptic Gospels because of their similarities in material and message.

The Gospel according to John is distinct from the others by its absorption with the divine nature of Christ. Scholars once held that it was the work of John, Christ's disciple. The author is surely a different John, working about 60 years after the death of Jesus.

Oral traditions were strong at the time so it is reasonable to assume the Gospels reflected what was known about Jesus. There is no evidence that Jesus committed his teachings to papyrus, therefore a source that would prove the authenticity of the Gospels is absent. To the modern reader, the idea of Jesus' miracles as related in the New Testament seems far fetched, yet how else would he have generated such a following? Moral teaching held only so much appeal in Palestine at the time.

CHRIST'S NOTORIETY SPREADS

As a child it seems Jesus lived in Nazareth. There are no details of his childhood, apart from one story that puts him in the Temple in Jerusalem at the age of 12, debating matters of faith with religious leaders. He came to prominence after being baptized in the River Jordan by his kinsman John. As the waters of the Jordan trickled over Jesus, a voice from Heaven said: "Thou art my beloved son. In thee I am well pleased."

There followed a ministry lasting some three years, during which Jesus performed numerous miracles. He calmed stormy seas, gave life to the dead, restored sight, speech, and hearing, healed lepers and epileptics, fed 5,000 people with five loaves and two

fishes (leaving a dozen baskets of scraps), and turned water into wine.

Astonishing activities like these, coupled with simple "love thy neighbor" philosophies, inevitably grabbed the attention of the masses and earned him a sizeable following. Jesus was Jewish, as were the vast majority of those in the crowds that gathered around him. He was hailed as the Messiah at a time when Jews were eager for someone to release them from the yoke of Roman rule.

But unlike the Pharisees and Sadducees, two prominent Jewish sects of the day, Christ was not hide-bound by the intricacies of Judaic law that governed every tiny aspect of daily life. Chastised for picking a few ears of corn on the Sabbath—technically construed as reaping—Jesus replied, "The Sabbath was made for man and not man for the Sabbath."

He kept company with society's "outsiders," including prostitutes and tax collectors, supported parity for women, and treated friends and strangers with equal respect and compassion. This radical attitude with which Jesus challenged the Jews religiously and the Romans politically—in an era when meek obedience to accepted laws was the norm—attracted powerful enemies.

ABOVE: Jesus gathered around him 12 disciples who—with the exception of Judas, Christ's betrayer—became the first apostles (a person sent out on a special mission). In this 15th-century painting by Joos van Ghent titled "The Communion of the Apostles," Jesus breaks bread and shares wine with his disciples and teaches them about the love of God the Father.

The Death *of* Christ

The air was heavy with dramatic tension as Jesus walked the streets of Jerusalem during the week prior to his crucifixion. He knew a select few were plotting to have him killed. His betrayal, death, and resurrection are fundamental to Christianity.

Jesus did nothing to modify his responses or curry favor. He overturned traders' tables in the Temple precincts. "Is it not written: 'My house shall be called a house of prayer for all the nations'?" he cried. "But you have made it a den of robbers." His campaign against the hypocrisy of the Jewish elders continued. He urged his followers to love God totally and secondly to "love your neighbor as yourself." This was not the way Moses told it and traditional Jews were outraged.

At a meal celebrating Passover, the reason for their visit to Jerusalem, Jesus told how one of the disciples would betray him. He broke bread and said, "Take, eat: this is my body." He passed around a cup of red wine, declaring, "This is my blood of the New Testament, which is shed for many." Thus the Jewish Passover became significant as the Christian Last Supper and the Eucharist (the bread and wine of Holy Communion) was established. The embryo of a new faith came into being, although all the main players remained Jewish for the time being.

After the meal Christ went to the garden of Gethsemane on the Mount of Olives for solemn and heartfelt prayer. The burden of his imminent betrayal, trial, and death was immense. Shortly after, the disciple Judas Escariot approached amid an armed gang. Judas kissed Jesus, giving the signal to the armed men in league with the "chief priests and the scribes and the elders" to arrest him.

STATIONS OF THE CROSS

Jesus was charged with blasphemy, an offense that ranked alongside robbery and murder. Found guilty by the Jewish scribes, he was passed over to the Roman Pontius Pilate, who sentenced the prisoner to death by crucifixion.

Today pilgrims revere the route taken by Jesus from the Roman fortress, where he was condemned to death, to the site of his death at Golgotha, thought to be Calvary. Called the Via Dolorosa or Way of Sorrows, it is marked by the 14 Stations of the Cross, each significant for an event that happened *en route*. For example, the third station is where Jesus is said to have fallen for the first time, the fourth is where he met his mother Mary, and the eighth station was where he consoled the weeping women of Jerusalem. There is no historical basis for the trail, which has changed over time. Likewise the place of Christ's death— marked presently by the Church of the Holy Sepulcher—is hotly debated. Religious tradition transcends fact on this occasion.

The sufferings of Jesus were mighty, as they were for all those who endured this barbaric and commonly used punishment. He was flogged by soldiers, which would have weakened and bloodied him. Along the route, as he hauled the crossbeam, he was jostled, jeered, and abused. When he was pinned to the cross to await death, darkness covered the earth, although it was the afternoon. The Temple curtain ripped and the ground shook. The crucifixion occurred on a Friday between AD 29 and 33, after which Joseph of Arimathea claimed Christ's body. It was wrapped in a linen shroud and placed in a rock tomb, the entrance covered by a large boulder. Guards were installed to prevent Jesus' followers taking his corpse.

On Sunday Mary Magdalene went to the tomb to discover that the boulder had been rolled away and Christ's body was gone. The Disciples refused to believe he was raised from the dead until they saw him with their own eyes. Grief turned to ecstasy. Out of the jaws of public defeat came victory, in a most unexpected manner. Forty days after his resurrection, he ascended to Heaven.

FACING: Inspired by the chiaroscuro realism of Caravaggio (see page 14), 17th-century artists began to depict Christ's crucifixion in a less stilted style. In this painting (c.1630) by Alessandro Tiarini, the event is given a grim physicality as the soldiers haul the cross upright.

St. Paul *and the* Spread *of* Christianity

If the life of Christ is striking, the story that unfolded after his death is nothing short of extraordinary. His disciplines became the Apostles, beginning the process of spreading Christianity.

Immediately after the crucifixion, the number of believers amounted to little more than 11 disciples, Christ's female followers, his mother, and his brothers, all of them adherents to the Jewish faith. During his lifetime many other Jews were persuaded that Jesus was the Messiah, as promised in the Hebrew Bible. But when he proved unwilling or unable to save himself from a horrific, humiliating death, most were disillusioned or wavered and returned meekly to traditional Judaism.

Two thousand years later, there are an estimated 1,900 million Christians in the world, making it the faith with the most followers. This colossal figure is a tribute to the tenacity and talent of those few.

Jesus instructed his closest associates to make his name known throughout the world. According to the *Acts of the Apostles* (written by the same author as Luke's Gospel), Jesus had promised they would be given divine powers. "And suddenly there came a sound from Heaven as of a rushing mighty wind, and it filled all the house where they were sitting. And there appeared unto them cloven tongues, like as of fire, and it sat upon each of them. And they were all filled with the Holy Ghost. And began to speak with other tongues, as the Spirit gave them utterance." With these newly received powers, the disciples were able to mimic some of the work

After the emperor Constantine adopted Christianity as the Roman state faith some time after AD 312, the religion rapidly spread throughout Romanized Europe, Africa, and the Middle East, consolidating the earlier conversions made by St. Paul.

largely Christian areas

by 325

by 600

St. Paul's journeys
1st
2nd
3rd
4th

possible journey of Paul to Spain

possible journey of Thomas to India

of Jesus, assisted by seven specially appointed "deacons." The group's activities soon attracted the hostility of the authorities so they split up in order to spread the word of God.

The work of the majority of the Apostles goes unreported. However, we know that one of the deacons, Stephen, was stoned to death for blasphemy. James was killed "with the sword." Peter preached and healed, and was freed by an angel after being imprisoned in Jerusalem. Philip, another deacon, traveled extensively around the region.

CHRISTIAN LAW EVOLVES

The most remarkable character to emerge was Saul, an unlikely convert, having previously sworn vengeance on the disciples for undermining Judaism. On the road to Damascus Saul was blinded and heard the voice of Jesus. He became known as Paul, an ardent missionary, and his work became a cornerstone of the new faith.

Christians, named for their reverence of Christ, were still a Jewish cult at this stage. Humble residents of Jerusalem, already entrenched in the "one God" culture, responded well to the Apostles and the number of converts grew. The Jewish Diaspora played its part.

Missionaries went to the synagogues established all over the classical world to tell how Jesus had died and was born again. But there a dilemma loomed with those still absorbed in petty Jewish law that gave rigid instructions regarding non-association with non-Jews or Gentiles. Relentless opposition from some elements of the Jewish community meant the two could not abide under the same umbrella forever.

There was no single incident that split the Christians from the Jews, rather a series of events that heralded a parting of the ways. Peter was told in a dream that it was permissible to eat animal flesh hitherto deemed unclean in Jewish law. The next day he welcomed a Roman soldier, Cornelius, into the fold, realizing that the dream applied to more than just Jewish eating habits. Christ's message applied to all.

In AD 49 a conference among eminent Christians in Jerusalem decided that Gentiles and Jews could be admitted to the faith. Subsequently, missionaries traveled all over Europe, the Middle East, and North Africa to spread the "good news." They used the Greek language to broaden their appeal. Considerable momentum now propelled the movement, sufficient to overcome the prejudices and animosity encountered by individual Christians. By AD 64 there were churches in all main centers of the Roman Empire.

ABOVE: The cross, or crucifix, was not adopted as a symbol of Christianity in the first years of the faith. Jewish converts retained the menorah (the seven-branched candle-stick symbolizing Judaism), while Greeks and later Romans used the sign of a fish (see picture, page 8), which symbolized Jesus' function as the "fisher of men."

Christian Persecution

To some, Christianity was radical and refreshing. To others, it was dangerous, lawless, and immoral. Its appeal was particularly potent for slaves, women, and other under-valued members of society, thus the establishment was alarmed at the way it overhauled accepted frontiers.

ABOVE: An engraving after Jean Léon Gerome's painting called "The Christian's Last Prayer in the Circus Maximus" depicts events during the reign of the emperor Nero. Threatened by a released lion, the Christians huddle in prayer while their crucified fellows behind them are set on fire.

The story of Christianity now largely moves away from the Holy Land and into Rome, center of the civilized world at the time. Jesus' execution would have meant little to anyone in Rome. However, Christ's message spread rapidly along the excellent lines of communication established by the Roman Empire, so there were small Christian communities in existence even before the arrival of the first missionaries, Peter and Paul.

Already the violent manner of Christ's death and the consequent joyful resurrection was the central theme of the Christian faith, although the symbol of the crucifix was not adopted for several centuries. Clearly the missionaries were able to construct convincing arguments about the life and death of Jesus for those who never knew him. They did not dwell on what he had done in the past or his teachings but on the religious salvation he could offer in the present, as revealed by the resurrection, to those who adopted his tenets. There was an "open access" policy that freed converts from the rituals associated with Judaism.

Today it is tempting to believe that Jesus did not die on the cross and was revived afterward. It was common practice to attempt resuscitation on victims of capital punishment. Although vague notions of resurrection expressed in the Hebrew Bible might have prepared the Jewish faithful for the concept, nothing mirrored the events occurring on what we now know as Easter weekend. In any age, resurrection is a hard story to swallow, so the missionaries faced a monumental task.

Christian religious celebrations created confusion. At night Christians withdrew behind closed doors for prayer, leaving outsiders wondering what took place. Famously, they withdrew to the catacombs beneath Rome, where traces of the early Christian community can still be found. When it became known that "flesh and blood" (of Christ) was consumed at the Eucharist, opponents leapt to the assumption that Christians were cannibals. The elated nature of worship implied that orgies took place.

SALVATION THROUGH BATTLE

When Nero was made emperor of Rome in AD 54 he was competent and well advised. But his mental abilities rapidly faded and he sought to make scapegoats of the Christians following the great fire of Rome in 64. The conflagration spared only four of the city's 14 districts. Famously, Nero rounded up Christians and used them as human torches in his garden. As Tacitus reported: "Mockery of every sort was added to their deaths. Covered with the skins of beasts they were torn by dogs and perished; or were nailed to crosses; or were doomed to the flames."

It is believed that both Peter and Paul, later venerated as saints, died in Rome during this spate of persecution. Anti-Christian sentiments were by no means over, even when Nero committed suicide in 68. Roman historian Suetonius (c.70–140) recorded that "The Christians are a class of men given to a new and wicked superstition."

Persecution ebbed and flowed until the reign of Emperor Gaius Decius, 249–51, who was committed to bringing Roman gods back to the fore. He dispatched eminent Christians and forced numerous others to recant on their beliefs, under threat of death. The death of Christians at the sword of a gladiator or in the jaws of a wild beast was deemed wildly entertaining.

Only with the advent of Emperor Constantine the Great (r.306–37) were Christians at last assured of religious tolerance. Constantine was a devotee of the sun god until he had a vision featuring the letters "CH" and "R" and the words "In this sign shalt thou conquer" prior to a successful military campaign. He interpreted this as divine intervention from the Christian God.

His domestic policies soon encouraged conversion to Christianity and scheduled special penalties for those who did not profess the faith. Constantine—whose mother, St. Helena, was a devout missionary—was baptized on his deathbed.

BELOW: A monk examines a section of the catacombs in Rome. In some sections of the underground network of tunnels and rooms, the early Christians turned their secretive gathering places into churches. Examples of plastered and decorated walls still exist.

Schism *in* Christianity

When Constantine moved his empire's capital from Rome to Byzantium, which he renamed Constantinople, he created a third focus for the Christian world. With geographic separation came theological divisions, which eventually divided the Church.

Jerusalem was already crucial to the faith, as the place of Christ's death and resurrection. Rome was where St. Peter and St. Paul were reputedly martyred. Now Constantinople was graced with a raft of bishops and fabulous churches with domes, the insides of which were decorated to look like Heaven. All lay within the boundaries of the Roman Empire.

Politically, the Roman Empire had two rulers prior and subsequent to Constantine, one in the east and the other in the west. In AD 380 Eastern Emperor Theodosius declared his empire a Christian realm and began a tradition of intolerance toward other faiths. The western arm fell to invaders in the fifth century and did not come to glory again until the Holy Roman Empire, inaugurated in 800. In the east the Byzantine Empire, as it became known, was steadfast. If the vast region had remained fused by the might of Rome, Christianity too may have stayed united. Instead, there was a disastrous schism.

Not only were there great physical diversities between the three cities but also enormous theological differences. One of the issues was the nature of Jesus and his relationship to God. Jesus occasionally called God "Abba," which translates to "dad." But he often referred to himself as the "son of man." Was he divine or human, begotten or created—or both?

Christians, like Jews, worshipped one God and the prospect of dividing loyalties was an alien one. His exact whereabouts

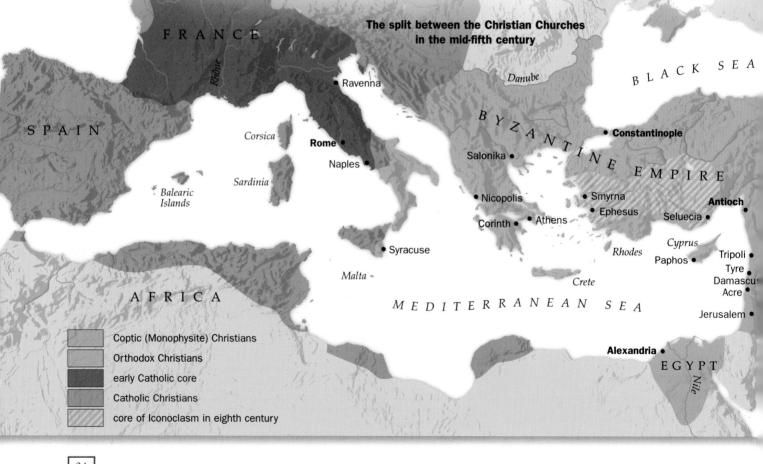

The split between the Christian Churches in the mid-fifth century

FRANCE

Rhine

Ravenna

Danube

BLACK SEA

SPAIN

Corsica

Rome

Naples

Sardinia

Balearic Islands

BYZANTINE EMPIRE

Constantinople

Salonika

Nicopolis

Corinth · Athens

Smyrna
Ephesus

Antioch

Seluecia

Cyprus

Rhodes

Paphos

Tripoli
Tyre
Damascus
Acre

Syracuse

Malta

Crete

AFRICA

MEDITERRANEAN SEA

Jerusalem

Alexandria ·

EGYPT

Nile

Coptic (Monophysite) Christians
Orthodox Christians
early Catholic core
Catholic Christians
core of Iconoclasm in eighth century

make unto thee any graven image, or any likeness of anything that is in Heaven above, or that is in the earth beneath, or that is in the water under the earth." In Rome the trend for smashing religious imagery was keenly embraced, which gave support to the powerful iconoclastic party in the Greek Church.

Differences over the Filioque, a creed devised to the satisfaction of the Roman Church regarding the relationship between Jesus and the Holy Spirit, caused outrage in the East. The spat came to a head in 1054 when the pope in Rome excommunicated the Patriarch of Constantinople. The Catholic (universal) Church and the Orthodox (correct) Church were permanently split.

LEFT: The Virgin and Child, a common theme for early medieval icons, is seen here typically displayed in an ornately decorated frame. The two-dimensional artform was also ideally suited to mosaics, of which thousands were made in Byzantium, Venice, Ravenna, and wherever the writ of the Byzantine Empire ran.

in the celestial hierarchy was defined in the first General Council of the Church held at Nicaea in 325. The Greek or Eastern Church agreed that God, Jesus, and the Holy Spirit were three entities in one being. The Latin or Western (or Roman) Church said there were three persons in one substance. This wordplay represented an uneasy truce.

DAWN OF THE ICONOCLAST

In 451, at the Council of Chalcedon, the structure of the Christian faith was decided. Rome, claiming authority from St. Peter, put itself at the head of the table, figuratively speaking, although seats of power were recognized in Constantinople, Jerusalem, Alexandria, and Antioch. The recurring discord over the nature of the Christ compelled a split in the Christian Church in the sixth century when the Syrian, Armenian, and Coptic churches sheered off to pursue a theological framework with which they were comfortable.

In the East great emphasis was placed on paintings of Christ and the saints: the holy icons (although three-dimensional representations of sacred figures had always been banned). Typically the icons were framed ornately and considered a channel of blessing from God. By the eighth century there was a backlash against the veneration of images, which found authority in one of the Ten Commandments: "Thou shalt not

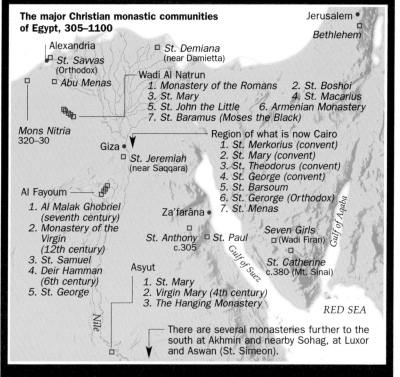

The major Christian monastic communities of Egypt, 305–1100

Jerusalem
Bethlehem

Alexandria
St. Savvas (Orthodox)
Abu Menas
St. Demiana (near Damietta)

Wadi Al Natrun
1. Monastery of the Romans   2. St. Boshoi
3. St. Mary   4. St. Macarius
5. St. John the Little   6. Armenian Monastery
7. St. Baramus (Moses the Black)

Mons Nitria 320–30

Giza
St. Jeremiah (near Saqqara)

Al Fayoum
1. Al Malak Ghobriel (seventh century)
2. Monastery of the Virgin (12th century)
3. St. Samuel
4. Deir Hamman (6th century)
5. St. George

Region of what is now Cairo
1. St. Merkorius (convent)
2. St. Mary (convent)
3. St. Theodorus (convent)
4. St. George (convent)
5. St. Barsoum
6. St. Gerorge (Orthodox)
7. St. Menas

Za'farâna
St. Anthony c.305   St. Paul

Seven Girls (Wadi Firan)

St. Catherine c.380 (Mt. Sinai)

Gulf of Aqaba
Gulf of Suez

Asyut
1. St. Mary
2. Virgin Mary (4th century)
3. The Hanging Monastery

RED SEA

Nile

There are several monasteries further to the south at Akhmin and nearby Sohag, at Luxor and Aswan (St. Simeon).

EARLY MONASTICISM

As power grew in the Church, so did corruption and hypocrisy. Monasticism developed as a result. St. Antony is regarded as the heroic founder of monastic principles. He was a hermit from Egypt who spent 20 years in the wilderness wrestling with temptation before emerging in 305 to found the first monastery, near Za'farâna. As the Christian system became abused, so the appeal of a life of meditation, prayer, and study became greater for faithful ascetics.

The Story *of* Islam

The arid wastes of Arabia seem an unlikely spot for the birth of a brave new religion. Tribesmen better known for derring-do than devotion appear a strange choice to receive a heavenly message. Yet it was among the rough-hewn desert nomads that Islam was brought into being by the prophet Mohammed.

Central to the fascinating story of Islam is Mecca, a city of outstanding wealth and quality, given its unpromising position in the midst of barren hills. At its heart lies the Ka'aba, a "house of God" reputedly built by Abraham and his son Ishmael, thus Mecca was already on the pilgrim trail by the time Mohammed (or Muhammad) was born.

Details about the prophet are sometimes conflicting, but we know he was born in about AD 570, orphaned at an early age, and a merchant by trade. During the course of his business Mohammed would have encountered monotheistic religions like Judaism—which was strong to the north in Palestine and to the south in Yemen—and Christianity, although the primary faith among his people was pagan polytheism. Accordingly the sacred Ka'aba was decorated with idols.

It seems he was the subject of divine events even at an early age. Mohammed's mother heard angelic voices while she was pregnant and he was born bathed in light. Two angels allegedly visited him as an infant and used pure white snow to erase a black clot of sin from his heart. There was a birthmark of darkened skin surrounded by hair on his back, identified as a mark of godliness by Jews, Christians, and Arab soothsayers.

Mohammed lived with his uncle, Abu Talib, and was then retained by Khadija, a wealthy widow for whom he acted as a commercial agent. Eventually he and Khadija married, considerably elevating his position in society. Yet still Mohammed lacked contentment. It became his habit to spend a month in each year on Mount

BELOW: Evening light sets the minarets and mosque roofs of modern-day Medina aglow. About 200 miles due north of Mecca, Medina gave Mohammed shelter while he organized the elements of the new faith and consolidated religious power ready for his return to Mecca.

Hira in contemplation, devoting some time to feeding the poor.

RECITING THE KORAN

It was during one of these spells away from home when, at the age of about 40, Mohammed was first visited by the angel Gabriel. At the angel's instruction, Mohammed found he was reciting verse as if in a waking sleep. In this way he received the text of the Koran (or Qur'an), the sacred book of Islam. At first he was terrified by the experience and doubted his sanity, but a local Christian reassured Mohammed that he was "the prophet of this people."

His family and immediate friends were persuaded by his experiences. It was on the direct orders of God that Mohammed finally made his revelations public and with remarkable foresight he feared the response. At first the local pagans were tolerant. Only when Mohammed began attacking the validity of the array of gods worshipped in Mecca did he earn the hostility of the people.

Mohammed sought protection for himself and his followers away from Mecca, firstly in Ethiopia and then in the oasis town of Yathrib, now known as Medina. The *hijra*, or the flight, from Mecca took place in AD 622, the first year of the Muslim calendar. He imposed a constitution upon Yathrib that provided for tolerance of the Jewish community. Only when the Jews felt they were unable to pay tribute to the Islamic God did relations fall apart. There were disagreements, too, among Mohammed's followers as men from rival tribes found themselves side by side in the congregation. A long-running campaign against Mecca led to victory for Mohammed after about eight years. He also took control of other important oases in the region. He probably would have continued with his expeditions had he not died of intestinal problems in 632.

The central theme throughout Mohammed's life as a prophet was that there was one God, known to the Muslims as Allah—a word without gender or plurals—and that the devout must submit to Him. The word "Islam" means making an act of "submission."

ABOVE: Detail from a 14th-century miniature showing Mohammed ascending to Heaven on his horse. According to some traditions, this event occurred in Jerusalem and the site is now where the Dome of the Rock stands. The prophet's face is left unrendered in accordance with Islamic law that forbids his representation or that of his mother.

Succession *to the* Prophet

On his death, Mohammed had no male heir. Successors spread the religion and documented its teachings but could not prevent division. The Muslims' search for a leader eventually split Islam into its two main sects, Sunni and Shi'ite.

FACING: An Arabic manuscript illumination of the 13th–14th centuries depicts a battle scene with Ali ibn Abi Talib and his adversaries. The emergence of Islam was not a peaceful one, and there was much bloodshed before the Umayyad dynasty brought a period of uneasy peace to the Middle East.

"Oye people, if anyone worships Mohammed, Mohammed is dead, but if anyone worships God, he is alive and dies not." By this pronouncement the people of Mecca learned that their religious leader had passed away.

By the time of his death Mohammed had wed ten times and taken two concubines. Although four daughters survived him, his only son had died in infancy. This presented a problem of succession, which proved enough to test even this most disciplined of religions. The man chosen to lead the Islamic faithful was to be known as the Caliph—guardian of the faith—and was supposed to be the best candidate for the task. There was nothing to say the title should be kept in the family. Ali ibn Abi Talib—Mohammed's cousin, husband of his youngest daughter Fatima, his closest male relative, and an aspiring Islamic leader—was initially overlooked.

The first incumbent, chosen by Mohammed's closest colleagues, was Abu Bakr, who had been mentor and father-in-law to the prophet. Kindly and pious, Bakr devoted much of his energy to caring for orphans and freeing slaves. He was, however, already an elderly man and outlived Mohammed by just two years.

He was followed by Umar, founder of the Umayyad dynasty. Umar—another of the prophet's father-in-laws—is remembered for imposing an organization on the community or *umma* Mohammed had founded, purposefully bringing Arabs to the fore. He was a noted empire-builder and added Palestine, Persia, and North Africa to the Islamic fold.

Umar took control of Jerusalem but paradoxically saved the Church of the Holy Sepulcher for Christianity. He was invited to pray inside and, had he done so, it would certainly have become as a mosque. Umar chose to pray on the steps outside, permitting it to remain a Christian site. He died in 644 at the hand of a Persian slave in Medina.

Umar's successor was Uthman,

Arab armies invaded the Frankish Kingdom in 713–25 and again in 732, when Charles Martel defeated them at Poitiers.

Within 120 years, the Arab caliphate had spread to encompass an area stretching from Spain to the borders of India.

The spread of Islam at:

■	death of Mohammed, 632
■	death of Abu Bakr, 634
■	death of uthman, 656
□	end of Umayyad dynasty, 750
▨	Jewish populations, 632–750

Arab raiders reached down the Nile to Dongola during 652.

Zaragoza • Narbonne
Seville • • Cordoba
Tangier •
• Rome
Carthage •
BLACK SEA
Constantinople •
ANATOLIA
ARMENIA
CASPIAN SEA
Bukhara • • Samarkand
Merv • • Balkh
Ardebil •
• Kabul
Herat •
MEDITERRANEAN SEA
• Edessa
Antioch •
• Rayy
PERSIA
Damascus •
Kufa •
Alexandria •
Basra •
• Persepolis
Heliopolis •
PERSIAN GULF
GULF OF OMAN
EGYPT
ARABIAN SE
RED SEA
• Medina
ARABIA
• Mecca
INDIAN OCEAN
Dongola •
YEMEN

responsible for gathering eminent scholars to produce an authoritative version of the Koran. The result was 114 chapters or *suras* in rhyming prose. The interpretations therein earned the antipathy of some Muslims. He also favored the Umayyad dynasty, of which he was a part, inspiring the enmity of others. The simmering discontent finally boiled over, with Uthman the target of a revolt in 656.

ISLAM DIVIDES

Ali claimed leadership of the Muslim people, in face of opposition from Aishah, Mohammed's third and favorite wife who was with him when he died. Within five years Ali was killed by the poisoned sword of a fellow Muslim in the mosque at Kufa, Mesopotamia. Ali's son Husayn—Mohammed's grandson and head of the prophet's family by this time—was killed in battle at Kerbala near present-day Baghdad on October 10, 680 by a sword wielded by an Umayadd. His grave at Euphrat remains a place of pilgrimage.

It proved impossible to unite Muslims after these fundamental differences had emerged. The era of the "rightly guided" Caliphs was over. Those who supported the Umayadd Caliphate, who moved their center of operations outside Arabia to the cosmopolitan city of Damascus, were thereafter known as Sunni Muslims. Today an estimated 85 percent of the globe's Muslims consider themselves Sunnis, with their beliefs rooted in the Koran and the sayings and actions of Mohammed.

The Shi'ites, accounting for some ten percent of Muslims worldwide, have distinct Islamic laws and believe the direct descendants to Mohammed, the Imams, are rightful heirs to his dominion. Shi'ites can be divided into different groups. Ismailis recognize the authenticity of seven Imams and as such are known as The Seveners. The Assassins (*see map note, page 111*), much-feared warriors in the medieval period, were Seveners, as are Druze Muslims and those who revere the Aga Khan.

Other Muslims heed a dozen Imams, otherwise known as The Twelvers. They believe the last of the Imams who

disappeared from public view in the ninth century will re-emerge as the *mahdi* to herald a new age. The Twelvers are in the majority and rule in Iran.

The Spread *of* Islam

In the first decades of Arabic expansion throughout the Middle East and North Africa, it was Arab warriors who brought Islam to their conquests. But the real widespread dissemination of the faith was due to extensive trading connections. Arab merchants traveled the Silk Road, **BELOW**, extending Islam's boundaries to the edge of China, and sailed the oceans to Africa, India, and the Indonesian archipelago in their redoubtable dhows, **FACING,** from a 13th-century manuscript illumination.

During his lifetime Mohammed never hesitated to brandish the sword in the name of God and conquest. After his death the tradition continued, with the result that Islam spread across the known world at breathtaking speed.

At first it seemed the death of the prophet might signal the demise of the faith he founded. Until Mohammed rose to power on the Arab peninsular, there was no strong government, empire, or state identity; instead a number of tribes traded and battled in equal measure. Mohammed and Islam gave them a unity hitherto unknown in the region. Upon his death some tribes felt the bond was broken and they were free to go their own way. The first four Caliphs worked hard to restore Islam's authority over residents of Arabia, taking up arms against former comrades where necessary.

At the demise of Ali in 661, Islam was split. The Umayyad dynasty appropriated the Caliphate and seasoned military campaigner Mu'awia—brother-in-law to Mohammed—became leader. Mu'awia had fought in opposition to Mohammed, until the latter won control of Mecca, and was instrumental in the rebellion against Ali, facts never forgotten by his enemies. Nevertheless, Mu'awia was at the Islamic helm for nearly 20 years, moving its headquarters from Medina to Damascus and extending its sphere of influence westward into North Africa and as far east as Afghanistan. At the Battle of Poitiers in 732 the armies of Charles Martel, ruler of the Austrasia kingdom in central Europe, prevented Mu'awia from taking Europe (*see map on previous page*).

Obedient to Mu'awia, the Umayyads were commendably tolerant when they came across Jewish and Christian colonies on their excursions. But among Muslims there was distrust as the regime grew ever more secular. The Umayyads were seen to enjoy high living, fine arts, and literature at a time when Muslims wanted to see humility, piety, and devotion to the faith. Rumblings of discontent finally erupted in open warfare and the Abbasid dynasty ejected the Umayadds from the Caliphate in 750.

This clan was named for al-Abbas, one of Mohammed's uncles, who assisted in administering the infant Islamic nation. One of his descendants, Abu al-Abbas as-Saffah, was the first of 38 Abbasid Caliphs. Retribution against the Umayadds was predictably fierce—the majority of the family were slaughtered. However, one man, Abd al-Rahman, escaped to Spain to establish a Muslim empire with the help of the North African tribes. The Moors flourished until the end of the 15th century, when they were driven from Spain by neighboring Christian kingdoms.

GOLDEN BUT FRAGILE

Initially Shi'ites—sworn enemies of the Umayyads—stood shoulder to shoulder with the Abbasids, but doctrinal divisions soon forced them apart. It resulted in a

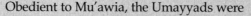

failed Shi'ite revolution in Mecca in 786, after which the followers of Ali retreated to West Africa to forge an empire of their own.

The Abbasids centered on the area today occupied by Iran and Iraq and founded a new capital in 762. It took four years to complete Baghdad, which quickly became a cultural oasis. Clerics completed the first written commentaries on the Koran here.

A golden age of Islam commenced with study not only of Muslim writers and thinkers, but also eminent and ancient Greek philosophers whose works were eagerly translated. One of the Abbasid caliphs, Mamun, promoted scholars to high rank and, according to one historian, "surrounded himself with learned men, legal experts, traditionalists, rationalists, theologians, lexicographers, annalists, metricians and genealogists." Consequently science and technology flourished; one of the triumphs was an irrigation system. Trade in spices, silks, and so forth was prolific.

Once again, doubts over the rulers' reverence to Allah and Mohammed crept in, sufficient to create fragmentation. In 969 Egypt came under the control of the Fatimids, descendants of Mohammed's daughter. Persia likewise broke away and Iraq itself fell under the control of the Buyid dynasty. In North Africa another Islamic regime knew greatness before it was condemned for becoming too wealthy and too remote from its professed religious purpose. The Almoravids were ousted by the Almohads in 1147, primarily Berber tribesmen devout in outlook. The era of the Abbasids finally ended in 1258 when Baghdad fell to the Mongol horde.

The Koran – Teacher *of* Man

The greatest miracle of all in the minds of Muslims is the Koran, containing the words of Allah as revealed to Mohammed. First recorded in 650, it is given much respect and study throughout the Islamic world.

RIGHT: The Cairo Koran— so called because it was a gift to Egypt from Morocco—was created for the Sultan of Morocco in the 18th century.

As we know, an angel appeared to Mohammed while he contemplated in isolation on a mountainside c.610. "Recite," the angel said, a command that is sometimes translated as "read." Mohammed protested that he was unable to understand the written word. Three times the order was issued before Mohammed understood the words were being delivered from God while he acted as a conduit.

Recite, in the name of thy Lord, who created—Created man from a blood clot. Recite, for thy Lord is bountiful, Who taught by the pen, taught man what he knew not.

By all accounts Mohammed was an uneducated man. It therefore appears unlikely he would have devised the lyrical wording of the Koran by himself. To Muslims this newfound literary finesse is proof of the Koran's divinity and gives it a mighty authority. (Some, however, are reluctant to accept that the Koran was uncreated and eternal for that suggests dualism rather than monotheism. They compromise by claiming God created it.)

From the first, Mohammed preached the messages he memorized, initially to his own family, then to a wider audience. He apparently made no attempt have the words written down. Only after his death did the ensuing Caliphs attempt to preserve the words of the Koran.

Mohammed's companions—notably his secretary Zayd ibn Thabit—compiled the sacred book from "scraps of parchment and leather, tablets of stone, ribs of palm branches, camels' shoulder blades and ribs, pieces of board and the breasts of men." In

650 Uthman dispatched an early version to all the major cities of the Islamic empire, regardless of differences on dogma, which enraged his opponents.

PRESERVING THE POTENCY

Rules within the Koran extend over every aspect of daily life, from worship to trade, marriage and charity, hygiene, and hospitality. In this breadth it resembles the Jewish Torah. Through the words of the Koran, Muslims learned that religious figures from the Torah remained sacred. Abraham, Noah, and Moses were to be revered by Muslims as prophets, as was Jesus. But the Jews had too often ignored their prophets. As for the Christians, they had made the cardinal error of apparently worshipping Jesus and his mother Mary alongside God. Consequently the Christian faith was littered with icons. Mohammed represented a last chance for mankind to listen to the word of God alone and obey.

The words of the Koran were earnestly pored over and the actions of the prophet analyzed. The result of this centuries-long study were the *Hadith*, sayings attributed to Mohammed that fall outside the Koran, and the *Sunna*, relating the custom and practice of Islam. Muslims always read the Koran in Arabic, the tongue of Mohammed. Translations are believed to dispel the charm and potency of the original version and would be inappropriate to use during worship. It is customary to keep the book wrapped in protective cloth and stored on a shelf higher than other books, indicating its superiority. Before reading it Muslims wash carefully as a mark of respect.

Muslims aspire to learn the Koran by heart, as Mohammed did, and the task begins in childhood. This is no mean feat, considering that there are 6,666 verses divided into 114 chapters, or *suras*. A benefit of speaking rather than reading the Koran is that ambiguities in the written text caused by misreading the vowels or consonants do not occur. The oral tradition provides a strong link with the original. The Koran presumes some grounding in the faith and can be obscure in its references. There are books to accompany the Koran containing explanatory notes, called *tafsirs*. Most famous among these is the one written by al-Tabari, who died in 923.

Analysis in the West found strong links to Christian and particularly Jewish theology of the era. The Koran itself denies that it was influenced by other sources and asserts that every word was God-given.

BELOW: Muslims reading their Korans. The task of learning the Koran by heart starts as soon as a child can read.

Islamic Worship

ABOVE: The tall, graceful minaret is as much a part of a mosque as is the campanile or steeple of a Christian church; although not every community can afford to build a minaret. "Minaret" translates as a light house or a fire tower, and the primary function of a minaret is to carry a light to guide the way of the faithful in darkness. Minarets are directly derived from the fire towers of Zoroastrianism (see pages 156–157). Minarets also provide a high vantage point for the muezzin, the call of the faithful to prayer, seen here in Istanbul, Turkey.

"There is no God but God and Mohammed is the messenger of God." This is the central theme of Islam, the first of five fundamental rules of the faith. Those words, known as the shahadah, are frequently repeated during the course of a day.

Another of the five rules of Islam governs prayer or *salat*, which occurs five times daily, as prescribed by Mohammed himself. His aim was not to achieve a display of piety but to assure each worshipper of a time for reflection during the course of a busy day. At first prayers were said facing the direction of Jerusalem. In 624 Mohammed changed the direction to Mecca and the Ka'aba (*see pages 46–47*).

Prayers are preceded by ritual washing and are performed by standing, bowing, kneeling, and prostration. At the start and end of prayer the *shahadah* is spoken, to reiterate personal faith. The first session of prayer comes between dawn and sunrise, the second soon after midday, the third is before sunset, the fourth between sunset and darkness, and the fifth said as the last act of the day. Worshippers do not need to attend a mosque, although most gather there at least once a week, on a Friday.

For the third rule, Muslims are expected to give alms or *zakat* to the needy each year. *Zakat* is like a tax designed to spread wealth, striking a balance in society. The word translates to purification and growth, thus the giver is cleansed of sin, emerging a better person, while envy among the "have-nots" is diminished. No one is expected to go hungry in order to fulfill this religious obligation. Those who do not have sufficient wealth to give away are expected to think and act in a charitable way.

The fourth duty of Islam is *sawm*, a fast during daylight hours during the month of Ramadan. By any standards it is a rigorous process of self-denial with food and drink—even water—barred from sunrise until dusk. Bear in mind that the Muslim calendar is lunar and that Ramadan moves through the seasons. Muslims must comply even during the hottest months, forbidden even to swallow their own saliva. Tobacco and hurtful words are also prohibited.

RAMADAN AND EID-UL-FITR

Mohammed initially instituted a 24-hour fast in 623 to mark the first anniversary of his flight from Mecca. Ramadan is also the month that the Koran was given to mankind through Mohammed so it is a joyful rather than a solemn celebration. Today Muslims look to the Koran for authority on the issue.

"You who believe, fasting has been prescribed for you, just as it was prescribed for those before you, so that you may do your duty on days that have been fixed." The verse goes on to excuse those who are ill or traveling. They are expected to feed a poor person for every day of fasting that is missed. Children are excused, although they are expected to exhibit some degree of abstinence.

Fasting unites the Muslim community by once more redefining the faith. At the end of Ramadan a festival called Eid-ul-Fitr is sometimes marked by the giving of presents, the wearing of new clothes, gifts to the poor, and congregational prayers. In the words of Mohammed, "A fasting person will have joy and happiness twice; when he breaks the fast he will be full of joy because it is at an end, and when he meets his Lord on the Day of Judgment, because he has kept his obligation."

The fifth and final duty is the *hajj* or pilgrimage (*see pages 46–47*). Together these rules are called the Five Pillars. If the faith is thought of as a large building, it is these five pillars that hold it up. Every Muslim knows that if religious observances are broken, the edifice of the faith may come tumbling down.

BELOW: Before prayers, Indian Muslims wash their feet at the Jama Masjid (literally, "Friday Mosque") in Delhi, India. Because the faithful must remove any unclean traces from themselves before entering a holy place, water for cleansing is a vital element of any mosque, and supplies vary from region to region. Here in northern India, water is plentiful and fills a large pool. In drier conditions, small fountains might serve or, as in Andalusia, Spain, narrow water channels laid under the shade of orange trees may provide for the washing of feet.

A Lifetime's Journey – *the* Hajj

Every year several million Muslims flock to Mecca to perform one of five religious duties demanded by Islam. The significance of the obligatory pilgrimage—the hajj—to each of the travelers is profound, no matter what their age, gender, or home country.

Muslims must make the *hajj* once in a lifetime, although repeated journeys are permitted. Performed in the 12th month of the Islamic calendar, the streets of this Saudi Arabian city teem with the faithful, all unified in a display of devotion to Allah. With this single religious observance

Muslims can put their history and heritage into context, while simultaneously achieving intense spiritual satisfaction. It is an ambition to which many aspire for years and from which supreme comfort is drawn.

It is not the magnificent Masjid Al-Haram mosque in Mecca that the pilgrims seek but

RIGHT: After circling the Ka'aba seven times, concentric rings of the faithful pray before the holy stone. The sheer press of numbers means that most pilgrims will be unable to touch the stone. Among Muslims, even the great make at least one pilgrimage to Mecca, in this case the Iranian president Khatami, who visited Saudi Arabia in May 1999.

the Ka'aba that lies within its walls. The Ka'aba is a strikingly simple building for one invested with such profound importance. It is a black cube with dimensions of 30 by 36 by 45 feet housing a sacred stone, reputedly white in ancient times but believed by Muslims to have blackened through the centuries due to the sins of mankind.

The Ka'aba was reputedly built by Adam after he was ousted from Paradise, using stones from Mount Sinai, Mount Lebanon, and the Mount of Olives. It fell victim to the same floods that Noah survived, but it was reconstructed by Abraham and his son Ishmael (the Christian Isaac) more than 4,500 years ago.

A spring that bubbled up beneath the infant Ishmael's feet as his mother Hagar pleaded an angel for water is also a feature of the *hajj*, along with a trip to Mina. By visiting these places each pilgrim feels he or she is walking where the prophet Mohammed walked, seeing the sights he saw, and even drinking from the same source of water.

The *hajj* is a clearly defined ritual and there are scores of official guides in Mecca to help out first-timers. Male pilgrims wear a white robe, the *ihram*, out of respect for Abraham and Mohammed, who both wore such garments, and to ensure equality among pilgrims. Women wear their own ankle-length clothes.

CASTING OUT EVIL

From Mecca the pilgrims go to Mina, an uninhabited village, for contemplation, then to Arafat for a sermon. After sunset they walk to the plain of Muzdalifah for prayer. Here they collect bean-sized pebbles for the symbolic "stoning of the devil" at Mina the following day. Three pillars at Mina represent the devil, who reputedly tempted Abraham here, and pilgrims throw seven stones at each pillar in a gesture of casting out evil.

The next stage is an animal sacrifice, the meat of which is given to the poor. For speedy distribution the Saudi authorities have established a meat-packing plant nearby. By this stage much of the *hajj* is complete. The pilgrims can return to

wearing regular clothes and many will cut or shave their hair as a sign of humility.

All that remains are the seven circuits of the Ka'aba, for which the faithful must return to Mecca. Prayers are said and the aim is to touch the stone, although sheer weight of numbers mean that most people must be satisfied with saluting it from a distance. Next the pilgrims drink water from the Zamzam spring. They may complete their *hajj* by re-enacting Hagar's desperate search for water.

The above is a simple outline of a crucial ceremony through which Muslims can feel at one with Allah. In 1934 Lady Evelyn Cobbold became the first English woman to experience the *hajj*, and she wrote enlightening words about its prayers: "The shining eyes, the passionate appeals, the pitiful hands outstretched in prayer, moved me in a way that nothing had ever done before and I felt caught up in a strong wave of spiritual exaltation."

ABOVE: A sprawling camp of Hajj pilgrims sits under the slopes of Arafat-Jebel-Ur-Rahma (Mount Arafat). Later, the mountain will swarm with pilgrims attending sermons before the stoning of Mina.

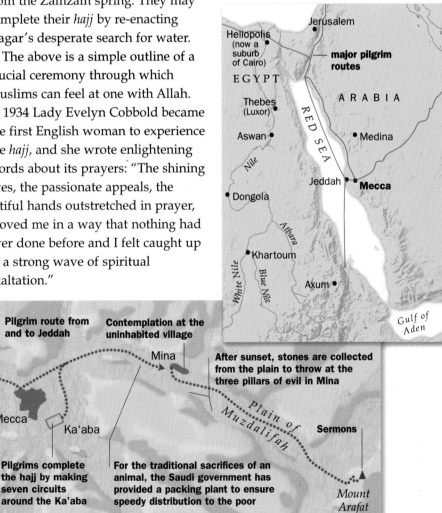

major pilgrim routes

Jerusalem

Heliopolis (now a suburb of Cairo)

EGYPT

ARABIA

Thebes (Luxor)

Aswan

RED SEA

Medina

Nile

Jeddah • Mecca

Dongola

Athbara

Khartoum

White Nile

Blue Nile

Axum

Gulf of Aden

Pilgrim route from and to Jeddah

Contemplation at the uninhabited village

Mina

After sunset, stones are collected from the plain to throw at the three pillars of evil in Mina

Mecca

Ka'aba

Plain of Muzdalifah

Sermons

Pilgrims complete the hajj by making seven circuits around the Ka'aba

For the traditional sacrifices of an animal, the Saudi government has provided a packing plant to ensure speedy distribution to the poor

Mount Arafat

Centers *of* Prayer – Mosques

The location of the first purpose-built mosque was chosen not for its fair view or verdant garden but as the first stopping point of a wandering camel. Mosques are not a vital part of Islamic worship but are popular sites of prayer and study.

FACING: At 656 feet above sea level, the minaret of the Grand Mosque of Hassan II is the tallest in the world. Built between 1987 and 1993, the magnificent building stands on the sea shore at Casablanca, Morocco.

BELOW: The orangery at the Mezqita of Cordoba sits in a secluded walled enclosure before the mosque's doors. Here, under the shade of these orange trees, the faithful washed in the numerous water channels before entering the mosque for worship and prayer. After the reconquest of Cordoba from the Moors in about 1238, the vast area of the Mezqita was pierced at its center by a tall Christian cathedral, which can be seen here rising above the battlemented exterior wall of the mosque.

When it came to picking a venue in Medina, Mohammed was overwhelmed with offers of land from the rich, the pious, his family and friends. To resolve the issue he set his favorite camel loose and would site the building where it stopped. It happened to halt on some undesirable wasteland. Undaunted, Mohammed led community prayers on the spot and it became the first mosque.

The mosque is not a vital facet of the religious life of Muslims. Anywhere is suitable for prayer, once a clean prayer mat has been laid down, so Muslims in remote regions can still pursue their religious obligations. At first the courtyard of Mohammed's house served as a mosque.

However, Muslims cherish the opportunity for congregational prayer, and of course the mosque plays a vital role here. It is also a meeting house for the community, a shelter for travelers, and a place in which to study the Koran.

A mosque can usually be pinpointed on the skyline by its towers or *minarets*, which became a familiar part of Islamic architecture during the Umayyad dynasty. From atop the tower a lone crier or *muezzin* calls the faithful to prayer five times daily (*see page 44*)—although sometimes his voice is heard through amplifiers or from a recording. His earnest invocation rings through the streets: "God is most great, I bear witness that there is no god but God. I bear witness that Mohammed is the Messenger of God. Hasten to Prayer, hasten to success. Allah is most great, there is no god but God."

Inside the mosque a fountain (*fauwara*) allows worshippers to fulfill the obligation to purify themselves prior to prayer. The faithful proceed into a main hall for prayer in rows, side by side, the poor man next to the rich. Women do not join men in the hall but sit in a separate area, often a screened gallery. Integration between the sexes is considered highly unorthodox. Ahead of the worshippers is a *mihrab*, or niche, which indicates the direction of Mecca. There is also a *minbar* (reading desk, *see page 51*) from which Friday's sermons are given by the prayer leader or *imam* (sharing the name Shi'ites give Mohammed's successors).

THE TALLEST MINARET

Mosques frequently reflect local architecture but, wherever they are in the world, none are adorned with images of God, Mohammed, or any of the other recognized prophets. Muslims abhor idolatry, including the depiction of sacred figures. It has meant patterned mosaics and calligraphy assume a decorative significance.

The most religiously imperative mosque is the Masjid Al Haram in Mecca. Another important religious sanctuary lies in Jerusalem in the site of the old Jewish Temple. Properly called the Haram esh-Sharif but commonly known as the Dome of the Rock, it dominates the city. There's double significance here for Muslims as it is allegedly

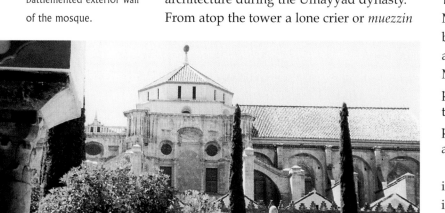

the site where Abraham displayed supreme
faith by preparing to sacrifice his son Ishmael
(Isaac) and also the point where Mohammed
left Earth for his night ride to Heaven.

Men labored day and night to complete
the Great Hassan II mosque in Casablanca,
Morocco, which boasts the tallest minaret in
the world, standing at 656 feet above sea
level. It took seven years and 50 million
man-hours to complete the magnificent
building in 1993, named for the Moroccan

king. Measuring 600 feet in length, 300 feet
wide, and 180 feet high, it has a retractable
roof. It can accommodate 20,000 people
inside and a further 80,000 in its courtyard.

Istanbul possesses some of the world's
most photographed mosques. The Hagia
Sophia is a former Christian church
converted into a mosque in 1453 after the
Ottomans took over the city. The Mosque
of Suleyman and the Blue Mosque are both
architectural splendors.

The Selected *Ones* — Sufism

BELOW: Many Sufi sects are characterized by their use of repetitious physical movement and chanting to achieve a state of ecstasy in which the word of God is more easily assimilated. In this trance state participants lose any sense of pain to the extent that a follower can plunge a sword through the side of his body.

As a prophet Mohammed is said to have traveled from Arabia to Jerusalem on the back of a winged mule and from there he was conducted to seventh heaven by the Angel Gabriel where he prayed with Moses, Abraham, and Jesus. This episode is at the heart of Sufism, a more spiritual division of Islam.

Some Muslims have understood Mohammed's heavenly journey to be a vision, significant because it served to reinforce Mohammed's celestial ranking. To others it indicated a deeper mysticism in Islam that came under threat after the death of the prophet, when Islamic rulers appeared to be predominantly worldly in

translated to "the selected ones."

The Sufi seeks a mystical union with God, usually achieved in a state of ecstasy through a series of devotional deeds. One of the key techniques upon which a Sufi depends is *dikhr*, the recitation of the name of God or Koranic phrases. This helps to achieve a loosening of the bonds with

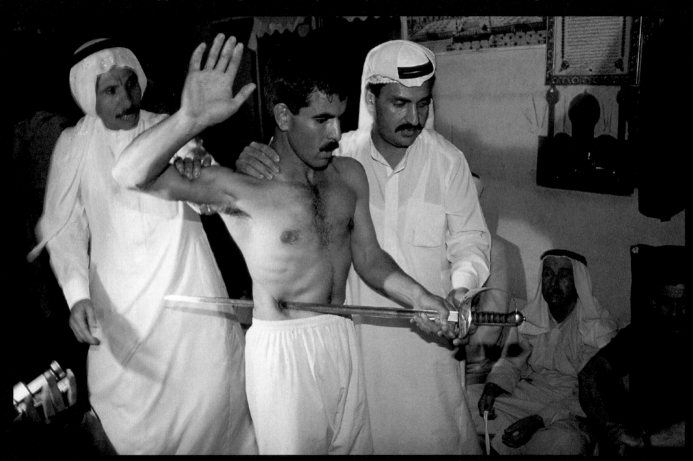

their aims and aspirations.

The result was Sufism, a grass roots move to return Islam to its purest form through inner enlightenment. Sufi is usually associated with the Arab word *suf*, which means wool, and denotes the humble garments worn by the early Arab ascetics. Yet it might have been derived from *safa*, meaning purity, or *safwe*,

earthly life and encourages a personal experience of God's realm.

Sufism has been variously defined over the years. According to one tenth-century imam prayer leader it means "adopting every higher quality and leaving every low quality." Nine centuries later Shaykj Ibn Ajioba wrote: "Sufism is a science by means of which you learn how to behave in order

Lord through purifying your inner being and sweetening it with good actions."

The movement began in the early eighth century by men like Hasan al-Basri, who was born within ten years of the prophet's death. He was responding primarily to the decadence attached to the Umayyad dynasty that ruled the Islamic world at the time. Another early Sufi, Rab'iah al-Adawiyah, who died in 801, is remembered by this devout prayer: "O God! If I worship Thee in fear of Hell burn me in Hell; and if I worship Thee in hope of Paradise, exclude me from Paradise; but if I worship Thee for Thine own sake, withhold not Thine Everlasting Beauty."

MUSLIM SAINTS

Al-Adawiyah's natural successor appears to have been al-Hallaj (857–922), a wandering preacher who was revered by many disciples. However, he became an object of hatred after he appeared to place himself on a par with God by declaring "I am the Truth." He was jailed for eight years and finally crucified.

In common with other regimes around the world, Caliphs were generally brutal, oppressive, unjust, and intolerant. The way Sufis questioned the rituals and strict theology of orthodox Islam often highlighted them as targets. But Muslims with serious concerns about manipulation of the faith had no realistic opportunity to rebel. Thus many turned to the inner self in search of spirituality and Sufism flourished, despite objections among the most orthodox.

Eminent Sufis would spring up and gather together a group of supporters. But on the death of the Sufi the group inevitably disbanded. Only after the 12th century did such orders endure, after founders learned the habit of naming a successor.

approach, they broadly believed in a network of saints or *walis* who acted as teachers and passed down secret divine knowledge to pupils. A student who graduated to teaching was dispatched to distant lands to help spread the word. The belief in saints inspired persecution over the centuries from Muslims offended by the free use of divine issues. Several orders based in

BELOW: A minbar (see page 48) presented by Qait Bey in 1483 stands in part of the Khankah (Sufi monastery) of Fraga ibn Barquq, built 1399–1409 in the City of the Dead, Cairo.

Turkey disappeared after 1925, when Kemal Ataturk took control and installed a secular government. However, Sufis successfully converted many Turkish tribes of Central Asia to Islam.

Bahá'í—*a* Refuge *from* Orthodoxy

ABOVE: One of seven of the Bahá'í faith throughout the world, the temple near Panama City conforms to strict architectural requirements. All Bahá'í temples have nine sides, which symbolizes world unity, and a centrally placed dome. Other temples are situated in: Haifa, Israel; near Chicago at Wilmette, Illinois; Apia, West Samoa; Sydney, Australia; outside Frankfurt, Germany; and the newest, which opened in 1986, at New Delhi, India. A further 120 sites have been identified for use.

Unity, parity, and harmony are bywords for the Bahá'í faith, a religion emerging just 150 years ago. Foretold by an alleged descendant of Mohammed, its founder wrote much of the faith's modern, peace-loving texts.

Bigotry and prejudice are loathed by Bahá'ís, while democracy and free debate are fostered. According to Bahá'í credo, if religions are a cause of war, it is better to have no religion at all. No wonder the Bahá'í movement has become a refuge for those disgruntled with the less enlightened attitudes of orthodox faiths.

The prophet of the faith was Mizra Husayn Ali Nuri (1817–92), whose coming was foretold by a radical Muslim known as the Bab, meaning "the Gate" (to the truth). The Bab was Sayyid Ali Mohammed (1819–50), who claimed descent from the prophet Mohammed. His followers—the Babis—believed him to be significant to the

hidden Imam in Shi'ite tradition. However, his declarations amounted to heresy as far as most Muslims in his native Persia were concerned, a pardonless crime. Before his death by firing squad in Tabriz the Bab predicted the advent of a messianic figure.

Thousands of his supporters were massacred. One who escaped the slaughter but was nevertheless incarcerated in a filthy jail in Teheran was Nuri. While he was in prison suffering all its privations, a revelation from God occurred. He described it like this: "I was but a man like others, asleep upon my couch, when lo, the breezes of the All Glorious wafted over me and taught me the knowledge of all that hath been. This thing is not of me but from the One Who is Almighty and All Knowing."

He kept the nature of the revelation to himself for a decade, during which time he was exiled from his homeland and moved to Baghdad in the Ottoman Empire, to be reunited with other Babi refugees. He shaped a religious movement and once again inspired alarm in the authorities, who decided to move him on. Before he left Baghdad for Constantinople Nuri revealed his divine mission to followers and became known as Baha'u'llah, meaning "Glory to God."

REFRESHING THE DIVINE MESSAGE

Baha'u'llah continued to spend considerable tracts of time behind bars, finally being jailed in Acre, a walled city known for its primitive cells and appalling environs. In jail and afterward, he received visits from the faithful, many of whom traveled miles to be in the company of the religion's founder. They were rewarded with an audience of someone both charismatic and imposing. One Englishman who met Baha'u'llah wrote: "The face of him on whom I gazed I can never forget, though I cannot describe it. Those piercing eyes seemed to read one's very soul; power and authority sat on that ample brow."

Baha'u'llah did not deny the sacred status of Moses, Jesus, or Mohammed. His contention was that a modern prophet appeared to refresh the divine message after it had become stale over the years. Without a new, invigorating presence, the rituals of religion became nothing better than window dressing, he preached.

After his release from prison Baha'u'llah spent the rest of his life in Acre and was buried nearby. Bab's body is interred in a spectacular gold-domed temple at the port of Haifa (Hefa), which has become the spiritual center of the Bahá'í faith.

Unlike the major religions, at least some of its sacred texts were written by the founder. His works extend to more than one hundred volumes. The remainder were penned by the Bab and Baha'u'llah's son Abdu'l-Baha, who administered the religion in 1892. There is no priesthood and areas are administered by elected boards. The Bahá'í faith is reasonable and rational, believing faith and science are like the two wings of human intellect. It is not possible to fly on only one wing. Bahá'í also teaches that universality is key. "It is not for him to pride himself who loveth his own country, but rather for him who loveth the whole world. The earth is but one country and mankind its citizens."

BELOW: The center of the faith is in Haifa, Israel, where all the records and papers are stored. The first temple was completed in 1908 in Ashkhabad, Central Asia. It was closed when the Soviet government seized it in 1938, after which the faith's spiritual center moved to Israel. Bahá'í temples are more than places of worship to the faith's eight million adherents. They also act as centers of community life and incorporate social, scientific, educational, medical, and humanitarian services.

Religious Conflicts *in the* Middle East

Just as the Middle East has spawned three of the world's great faiths, so it has been the focus for some of its bitterest interdenominational wars. Although the trio acknowledges there is one supreme God, there is no agreement on how to worship Him. The result has been two thousand years of conflict.

BELOW: Detail from a medieval manuscript illumination depicting Christian knights of the First Crusade battling for Antioch. Two centuries of Christian fanaticism and greed during the Crusades (1096–1291) brought three religions that had sprung from similar foundations into cruel conflict in the Middle East. The repercussions still sound echoes today.

Feuds between Jews, Christians, and, later, Muslims have been a long-standing feature of life in the Middle East. Sometimes those conflicts involved terrible suffering and needless loss of life. But co-operation between the faithful was largely stable until the era of the Crusades, when the zealotry of Christians was unleashed upon Jews and Muslims alike. Bloodshed and cruelty across two centuries scarred

that not every Jew is a Zionist—that is, one actively seeking a Jewish homeland. Rabbi Eliezer Schach, one of the most influential Jewish leaders of the 20th century, thought Israel came at too high a price. "The existence of Israel is not dependent on land. Jews existed in the Diaspora, dispersed among the nations of the world, without land under their feet. But the people of Israel preserved in that condition the

the collective psyche of each religion. Unity of purpose was never fully achieved again.

But before we condemn any faith, we should examine the divisions within each. No religion can claim the united support of all that profess a following.

The complex history of modern Israel has already been outlined. We should not forget

strength of their faith and tradition."

Israel has pursued a policy of expansionism. Yet some Orthodox Jews oppose the settlement of lands in Palestine, as it distracts from scholarship of the Torah, as well as inspiring foreign condemnation.

Debate over whether Israel is a religious or secular state is rampant. Jewish sects put religious laws above those of the state. Thus the Bratslav Hassidim permit marriage between girls and boys as young as 14 years of age, in contravention of national law. The government's decision to integrate women into the army's combat units has caused more ructions among the religious groups that sit under the umbrella of Judaism.

SPIRITUALITY OVER GREED

Nor is the Muslim world a model of rapport. Despite the tidal nature of Islamic fortunes, it still prevails in North Africa, East Africa, Arabia, southern Asia, Bangladesh, and Indonesia. However, the Caliphate—maligned though it was—disappeared when the Ottoman Empire collapsed at the beginning of the 20th century. There is no single head of the worldwide Islamic faith and Muslim countries veer from the secular to the devout.

The phenomena of Muslims seeking to overthrow lax or secular Islamic regimes has become characteristic of the faith. One important modern day example of this is the overthrow of the Shah of Iran in 1978, after which a religious leader, Ayatollah Khomeini, was installed.

Imperialism also re-invigorated Muslims who felt oppressed by a Western presence and an imposed culture. The result is that, following several centuries of decline, a healthy vein of fundamentalism has flourished during the 20th century. Given that the West appears ever-more consumed by materialism and money, Muslims take heart in their faith, which gives them the power of spirituality. Islam is perhaps

increasingly relevant and more dynamic than ever before.

Apart from its important pilgrimage sites, Christianity is now largely remote from the Middle East. The faith is riven with internal strife, for example, in Northern Ireland and the Balkans, but usually outside the Holy Land. Still, the West has become embroiled in the politics of the region. America's policy in the Middle East—interpreted as pro-Israeli and anti-Arab—was the reason given for the World Trade Center atrocity on September 11, 2001. The result was war in Afghanistan and Islam jumped to the top of the world agenda.

ABOVE: In earlier periods, religious conflicts were largely restricted to the areas of unrest. No longer. Religious zeal can have consequences across the whole globe.

CHAPTER 2
North America

Klo-kut

Great Bear Lake

KUTCHIN   HARE

TANANA   DOGRIB

HAN   Frank Channel

Chimi   Mackenzie   Great Slave Lake   YELLOW KNIFE

Nunivak Island   INGALIK   Beluga Point   Charlot River

Togiak   Yukon   TUTCHONE   BEAVER   Lake Athabasca   Reindeer Lake

Naknek   KASKA   Peace   CHIPEW'

ALEUT   Glacier Bay   Athabasca   Tailrace Bay

Port Moller   Kodiak Island   WESTERN WOOD

Edmonton   Saskatchewan

TLINGIT   TSIMSHIAN

Dodge Island   CARRIER   SARCEE   Calgary   Avonlea

Queen Charlotte Islands   KWAKIUTL   Nesikep   Fraser   SHUSWAP   BLACKFOOT   PLAINS CREE

Yellow

Vancouver   ASS

NOOTKA   Seattle   NEZ PERCE

Ozette   CHINOOK

Hoko River   Columbia   Wakemap Mound   Snake

Nearts Sand Spit   SHOSHONE   Grea   S

Hogup Cave

YUROK   KAROK   Alkali

POMO

Gunther Island   Sacramento   YOKUTS   PAIUTE

San Francisco Bay   Topoc

San Francisco   CHUMASH

PACIFIC OCEAN   Santa Barbara

Los Angeles

San Di

HUDS BAY

INUIT

Elaborate totem poles are a feature of the religious life of Native American tribes on the northwestern coast of the U.S. and Canada. This 200-year-old example stands in the Heritage Park, Ketchikan, Alaska.

Before the arrival of Europeans, the religious life of North America was rich and diverse. Native American tribes had roundly evolved faiths that lent a rhythm to daily life. It took into account their earthly requirements and thus was tailored to the needs of the hunter, warrior, child-bearer, and chief. In all its numerous forms, Native American religion gave the greatest respect to the natural world.

White settlers failed to appreciate the worth of tribal beliefs. One can only guess at how many sacred rites and rituals were obliterated in a largely destructive approach toward Native Americans. Only in New Age culture, which emerged in the second half of the 20th century, was due attention paid to the longstanding spiritual landscape of this mighty continent.

To European eyes, North America was a blank canvas, religiously speaking. Early settlers from Britain brought the churches of the old country, most famously the highly disciplined Puritan beliefs that held sway in England in the mid-17th century.

The frontier mentality of America in the 18th and 19th centuries was attractive to evangelists who delighted in causing a frenzy of excitement among largely uneducated audiences. Methodists and Baptists became the most vital churches. America also became a breeding ground for sects and cults, many becoming tied with capitalist ventures. With so much space and so many people invigorated by a sense of freedom, the continent had the capacity to host them all. Some cults became extinct, such as the German Pietists, who opposed marriage and procreation. Others flourished and survive today.

Later, a tide of immigrants from around the globe added their own colors to the religious map. For many, a new life in America was a chance to celebrate their faith openly, without fear of persecution. There were Jews from Russia, Protestants and Catholics from Ireland, slaves bearing the remnants of an African faith, Huguenots from France… the list is relentless. Religion in all its many forms became part of the fabric of society on the North American continent.

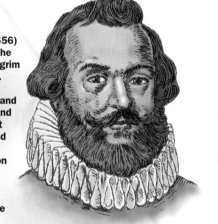

Miles Standish (1584–1656) was a serving soldier in the Netherlands when the Pilgrim Fathers settled in Leiden. He joined them on their voyage in the Mayflower and was among the first to land on American soil to scout out the bleak area around Plymouth harbor. The Puritan settlers relied on his military experience to protect them from the Indians, but his hot temper led to one of the worst incidents in the young colony's life. After a warning from friendly Indian Chief Massasoit (see page 63), Standish was called to protect the new colony of Wissagusset (Weymouth) from Indians furious at the settlers' continual stealing. Tricking the Indians into a parley, Standish had the chief and five of his followers slain.

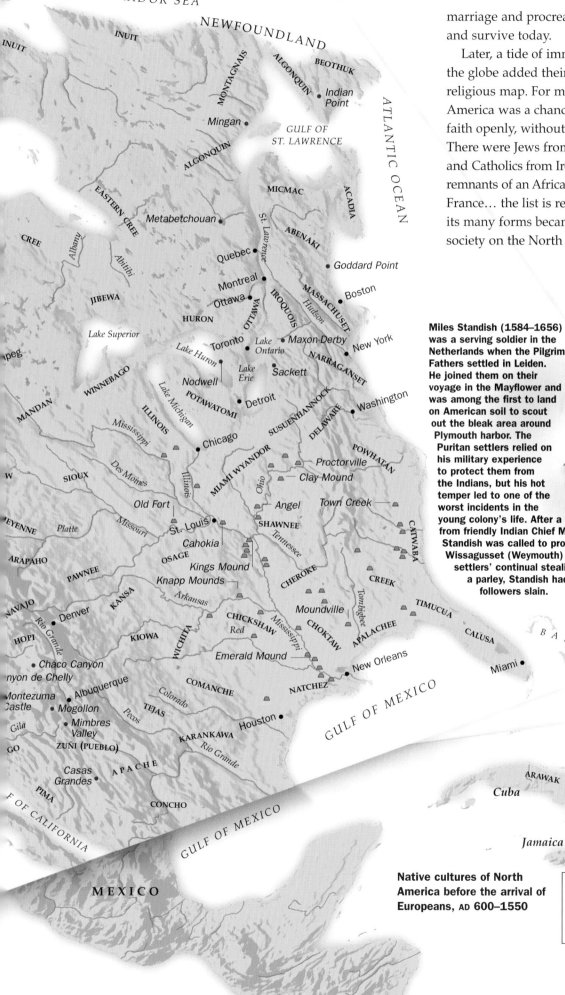

Native cultures of North America before the arrival of Europeans, AD 600–1550

- ▲ temple-mound
- ● important site
- ● modern city
- UTE Native American tribe

Gods *of the* Moundbuilders

For some 2,500 years the heartlands of North America were dominated by three distinct cultures. The stars, seasons, and a rich animal mythology drove the spiritual life of these people, known collectively as the moundbuilders.

ABOVE: Sightseers ascend Monks Mound, one of the largest Indian mounds, by the modern stairway. The Hopewell culture of the Mississippi region were skilled artists and many effigies of birds and animals exist. The hand, **BELOW,** is unusual in being human rather than animal.

Unraveling the moundbuilders' beliefs is a speculative business, but folk legends suggest there was deep religious rivalry between differing tribes. In times of war the vanquished were probably forced to worship the deities of their conquerors, though evidence suggests that forbidden gods were entombed in the earth to be venerated in secret.

The earliest of the cultures, the Adena, takes its name from a site in the Ohio Valley. These people colonized much of the upper Midwest between c.1000 BC and AD 200 and were responsible for many earthworks in the form of panthers, lizards, falcons, turtles, and, on a prominent ridge in Iowa, an entire group of bears marching single-file. The Adena were gradually subsumed into Hopewell culture, with its skilled artists and traders, and there was a trend toward even larger effigies and many fort-

like earth structures.

Between AD 600 and 1600 the Mississippian moundbuilders created vast and elaborate religious centers, such as Monks Mound, east of St. Louis. This

108-foot truncated pyramid is named after a community of 19th-century Trappist monks, though it was part of a 2,000-acre Mississippian complex known to native people as Cahokia.

The most spectacular of all the Midwest earthworks is the Great Serpent Mound at Peebles, Ohio, once attributed to the Adena but now thought to be Mississippian. This 1,200-foot snake effigy has an oval-shaped tomb in its open mouth, a feature which some academics believe relates to a global cultural tradition in which snakes symbolize major celestial events. In Asia, for instance, a snake swallowing an egg has for centuries symbolized lunar eclipses. Snake worship is also a feature of modern-day Native American worship—the Hopi or Moqui people of northern Arizona believe they are descended from the great Snake Hero and Snake Maid.

CELESTIAL TRIBUTE

Archaeological surveys of the Great Serpent in the mid-1990s indicate that it is aligned with the summer solstice sunset and, possibly, the winter solstice sunrise. Samples of wood charcoal recovered from the mound have yielded a radiocarbon date of AD 1070, which would place the Serpent in an era of two major astronomical events: the 1054 Crab Nebula supernova (so bright it was visible during daylight hours for two weeks) and the 1066 arrival of Halley's Comet (its brightest appearance). It is possible that the

Great Serpent was constructed as a response to these events, perhaps to appease a snake god. One theory put forward by Kansas University psychologist Thaddeus M. Cowan proposed that the earthwork mirrored the Little Dipper constellation, which ends at the North Star.

In 1840 one of America's first archaeologists, an itinerant trader called William Pidgeon, resolved to investigate the mounds more closely. On the Upper Mississippi he befriended an elderly Indian medicine man called Deecoodah who taught him snippets of tribal folklore. Deecoodah believed that serpent mounds were linked to star-worship, but only in a roundabout way. He told Pidgeon that "when the worshippers of reptiles were reduced by the fortunes of war, and compelled to recognize the sun, moon, and heavenly bodies as the only objects worthy of adoration, they secretly entombed their gods in the earthwork symbols which represented the heavenly bodies."

Sadly, the truth about the moundbuilders was lost forever during their annihilation at the hands of Spanish invaders in the 16th century. It seems likely that a shadow of their religion later re-emerged in the spiritual lives of Native Americans, many of whom recognize divine power in sunlight, fertility and strength in the earth, and wisdom and power in the hands of earthly "rulers" such as snakes, bears, and jaguars.

CENTER BELOW: The Great Serpent Mound at Peebles, Ohio is best viewed from the air. The serpent's mouth can be seen at the lower left of the picture, its gaping mouth closing on an egg-shaped mound. At the right, its tail appears coiled in a spiral.

BELOW: Mound City, north of Chillicothe, Ohio, is an archaeological site located on the west bank of the Scioto river. Many other mound sites have been irreparably destroyed by farming since the 1930s.

Shamanism—*the* Healing Seers

The word shaman comes from the Siberian language of Tungus and can be translated as "he who knows." Shamanism is a vocation and the extraordinary powers associated with it are inherited from dead predecessors.

ABOVE: Harrington Luna, a Pima medicine man, undergoes a purification ceremony in a sweat lodge. Traditionally, the Pima lived in the Salt and Gila river valleys of southern Arizona.

RIGHT AND FACING TOP: Shaman rattle with death face from the Tsimshian tribe and Shaman face mask. The Tsimshian lived in the Pacific coastal range of northern Canada.

which the spirits are invoked. The shaman is so charismatic he can keep an entire audience entranced by his movements and music. He may be possessed by a spirit, the symptoms being quivering, intense anger, unequaled knowledge, and superhuman strength. Alternatively, when externally he appears to fall into a trance-like state, the shaman's soul may leave for the heavens or a mysterious land beneath the waves.

Shamanism extends far beyond the boundaries of North America. It seems likely that North American Indians brought the concept with them when they emigrated from Asia thousands of years ago. The phenomenon exists among North and Central Asian tribes, as well as the peoples

Shamans are likely to be distinguished by extraordinary characteristics, like having six fingers, extra teeth, or strangely colored eyes. They are believed to possess an extra bone inside their bodies. Shamans may adopt various habits. They often imitate an animal by donning a skin. There may be a headdress adorned with animal bodyparts, including eagle claws and deer antlers.

The shaman is summoned to his calling by spirits during a dream or vision and must prove himself in a personal quest. In effect he dies and is resurrected in his new identity. Experienced shamans arm the novice with further lessons in technique.

A single-skinned drum, round or oval, is frequently used during dramatic rites in of South America, Malaya, and Oceania. Similar traditions exist in Africa, Australia, and Europe. Debate exists over whether tendencies among Shinto priests can properly be described as shamanistic.

In North America shamanism was typically associated with healing and the shaman was frequently dubbed a "medicine man." He was also deemed responsible for control of the weather and knowledge of the future. The onus is upon the shaman to know implicitly what humans need and want, what lies in the future, the whereabouts of lost articles, the prospects for a hunting expedition, and the outcome of a battle.

WILD CONNECTIONS

The shaman heals the sick and accompanies the dead to the next world. There are cherished tales of how shamen visited the heavens or the Underworld to retrieve the souls of people recently deceased, but these events are rare.

In tribal terms, the shaman commands great authority because of his contacts with the spirit world, thus his social ranking is second to none. While he generally uses his power to the good, he might also evoke evil, a threat that hangs heavy on a settlement.

Most people who were shamanistic were absorbed into other religions—for example, the Turkic people in Central Asia became Muslims and the Mongols converted to Buddhism. Evidence of their previous beliefs remains apparent in their folklore and mythology. Only from isolated communities can we glean details of societies dominated by a shaman.

For centuries Eskimos were in thrall of the shaman, known for taking an underwater journey to the Mother of Animals to appeal for bountiful catches of fish or seals. This semi-divine creature is said to be a young Eskimo woman tossed into an icy sea by her father. As she clung

to the boat, the cruel parent severed her fingers. Incorporated into Eskimo shamanistic practices is an element of prophecy and magic. Eskimo society is pinned down by taboo; forbidden territories that, if trespassed upon, might anger the spirit world. When a taboo is broken the shaman must venture into the spirit world to work out how to make amends. Eskimo shamans are thought to converse with animals, using a secret language, and similarly can talk to the dead in the celestial world above.

In Canada the Ojibway liken the shaman to an otter who can move gracefully between earth and water. Use of an otterskin pouch is also significant in the Winnebago tribe. Further south, the Algonquin are shamanistic and totemic, paying special heed to their own totem animal. Here the shaman might use a sweat lodge as a device to purify the soul and harmonize the elements of earth, air, fire, and water.

ABOVE: Serenity and certainty combine in the face of this Shaman figure from the Nayarit or Jalisco cultures of Mesoamerica, dated to betwen c.200 BC and AD 250.

The Pilgrim Fathers

In the early 17th century a determined group of Puritans in rural England became overwhelmed with abhorrence for the religious status quo. The Separatists, as they became known, fled England, first for Protestant Holland and then for the New World.

BELOW: A replica of the Mayflower sets sail as part of ceremonies in Plymouth harbor in 1990. The original made the trip from England to America in 67 days, with fair winds at the start. Later storms cracked a cross beam and even made the pilgrims consider turning back. The voyage was completed with the loss of only two lives and the addition of one—Elizabeth Hopkins gave birth to a son. He was appropriately named Oceanus.

The English state church, closely linked to the king rather than Catholicism in the 17th century, was riddled with what Puritans considered to be the offensive excesses of "Popery." Others had emigrated for the infant settlements in America before seeking increased wealth and new opportunities as trail-blazing pioneers. The Separatists had a different impetus. Their aim was to establish a Utopian religious society on what was for them the acceptable lines of Puritanism.

Life was a pilgrimage for the Separatists and they consequently became known as the Pilgrim Fathers. The result was a blueprint colony whose beliefs would help to shape the nation and culture of the future United States. By definition they were disciplined, uncompromising, highly moral, courageous, and extremist. It was with these values that the new colony was governed.

The Pilgrim Fathers' story began in the village of Scrooby in Nottinghamshire, England, where a new church was established in 1606 by Puritans who felt that Reformation of the English Church had not gone far enough. By today's standards this seems innocent enough, but back then such

action was heresy and as such was punishable by imprisonment or death.

In 1609 they fled from persecution in England to religiously tolerant Holland. Even there, in the cloth-manufacturing city of Leiden, life was far from ideal. As immigrants, the Separatists were poor and had few prospects. Their children, growing up in Dutch society, seemed less likely to pursue Separatist principles and there were few new converts other than offspring. Making matters even more uncertain, war was looming between Holland and Spain.

The little community chose to move on again, less than a decade after relocating to Holland. South America was deemed too hot; England, France, and Spain too dangerous. Instead, they planned to sail to the new English colony of Virginia, with the aim of settling far away from other colonists to avoid persecution.

IMMIGRATION BUREAUCRACY

Preparations took some time. First they had to obtain a license for settlement in the colony, and the authorities forced them to wait. When they finally obtained the license, two community leaders, John Carver and Robert Cushman, went to London to negotiate for financial backing.

The Separatists left the Dutch port of Delftshaven aboard the *Speedwell* on July 22, 1620, heading for the English port of Southampton. There they were joined by other immigrants and the old wineship *Mayflower*. Two false starts hindered their progress—both times the *Speedwell* was found to be taking on water. Eventually the ship was judged unseaworthy and was left behind in Plymouth, the last European port of call. Some cargo and passengers from the *Speedwell* transferred to the *Mayflower* before it set sail on September 6, 1620.

On board were 41 families, including some non-Puritans. At first the weather was good and spirits remained high. Fall storms finally set in on the long journey, and these, together with the overcrowded conditions,

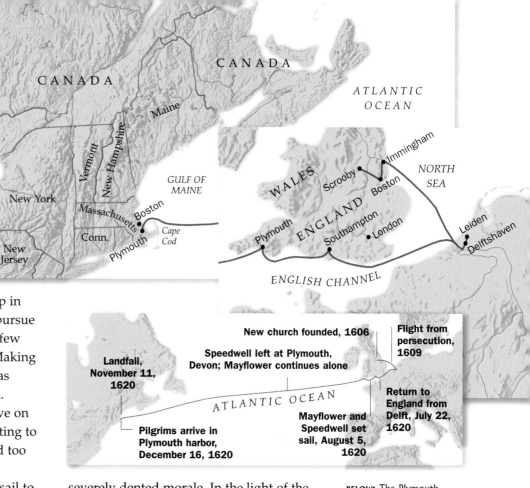

severely dented morale. In the light of the gathering unrest, community leaders called a meeting in the *Mayflower*'s main cabin on November 21. The purpose was to define a code of conduct to prevail for the rest of the voyage and in the new colony.

The Mayflower Compact was inspired by Biblical doctrine and its function was to promote justice and equality. The Compact was signed by the head of each family and became the basis of the legal code after the colonists landed at New Plymouth in what was to become the state of Massachusetts. Ultimately, the Mayflower Compact contributed in great measure to the establishment of American democracy.

BELOW: The Plymouth Plantation preserves the original Pilgrim settlement. Community leader John Carver became the first governor of the Plymouth colony in 1620. He was instrumental in negotiating a peace pact with Massasoit, chief of the Wampanoag Indians, a deed which stood the pilgrims in good stead when other tribes rose up against the colonists (see picture, page 57).

Mormonism—*a* New Mission

In New York the new faith of Mormonism claimed to be "the True Church," one that believed in the Second Coming of Christ and the ability of man to become god-like through spiritual evolution.

Throughout history new religions have been born after existing faiths were deemed to have turned away from God. So it was with the Mormon Church, also known as the Church of Jesus Christ of Latter-Day Saints. Founder Joseph Smith (1805–44) was told in a revelation that all existing Churches were abominations.

Casting around for a system of beliefs to invest in, Smith had a vision of the angel Moroni, who directed him to a set of golden tablets inscribed in obscure hieroglyphics hidden upon a hillside near New York. Once in possession of the tablets, Smith donned what he described as "sacred spectacles" in order to transcribe the mysterious writing.

The result was *The Book of Mormon*, published in 1830, revealing how a group of Hebrews had traveled to America shortly before the Exile of 597 BC and established a colony. Hard-working, devout settlers thrived but were eventually wiped out by non-believers. Now Smith sought to reintroduce "the True Church" to echo that of the ancients.

By 1831 the first Mormon temple was built in Kirtland, Ohio. But here, as in other areas, the arrival of the Mormons was accompanied by violence. Radical teachings, including that of polygamy, sparked unrest, further ignited by the obvious political ambitions harbored by Smith. Mormons were hounded out of Ohio, Missouri, and Illinois. Antipathy between Mormons and their neighbors became so bad that in 1844 Joseph Smith and his brother Hyrum were shot dead by a furious mob before they could stand trial on conspiracy charges. Controversy continued to surround Joseph Smith, including the accusation that he "borrowed" the notion of Hebrews emigrating to America from a book of fiction published in 1825. In the ensuing chaos the infant church fractured.

DIVINITY THROUGH PERFECTION

Smith's successor, Brigham Young (1801–77), led the faithful to Utah, where they founded Salt Lake City. In 1851 Young became governor of Utah, but attempts to have the territory incorporated into the United States was thwarted by his continued support for plural marriages. He admitted to having numerous wives. "I know of no one

who has more. But some of those sealed to me are old ladies, whom I regard rather as mothers than wives but whom I have taken home to cherish and support."

Mormons finally outlawed polygamy in 1890 and the way was clear for Utah to become a state. In 1916 the first non-Mormon governor was elected, flagging a general decline in the faith's political aspirations. Smith's son, also called Joseph, led an alternative ministry called the Reorganized Church of Jesus Christ of Latter Day Saints based in Illinois. Other splinter groups also existed.

All accept the Bible as a partial insight into the heavenly kingdom, alongside the *Book of Mormon* and other writings by Smith and Young. Both authorities assert that Jesus came to Earth to atone for human sins. His resurrection is an important theme. However, in other aspects Mormons diverge from orthodox Christianity.

According to the *Book of Mormon*: "As man is, God once was. As God is, man may become." They believe that God was once human and achieved divinity through perfection. Likewise, humans—whose souls lived with God before coming to Earth—can achieve the same lofty status. Devotion to the church is one way of securing heavenly rewards and the Mormon Church is famous for the obedience of its congregations. Services include the laying on of hands to transmit the Holy Spirit.

Great emphasis is placed upon personal conduct. Mormons do not smoke or drink, nor take tea or coffee. Family life is fundamental to the faith, although young people are encouraged to carry out missionary work away from home for a period of two years. Those entering the Mormon faith are immersed in water by way of baptism. Curiously, ancestors can be accepted into the religion. The practice met the fury of Jewish genealogists, when victims of the Holocaust were posthumously baptized. Mormons have developed superb genealogical records.

Jehovah's Witnesses

ABOVE: French Jehovah's Witnesses gather in an enormous congregation annually—more than enough to pack a large exhibition hall in Villepinte, Seine St-Denis.

Study of two of the Bible's more obscure texts has brought forth stark but significant religious groups. Adventists and Jehovah's Witnesses set great store by the Biblical books of Revelation and Daniel—particularly its prophetic visions.

The books of Daniel and Revelation elaborate on God's ultimate victory over evil and talk of symbols and secret codes. Each was written when the Jews were enduring great persecution, hence the nature of its content.

Charles Taze Russell (1852–1916), credited with founding the Jehovah's Witnesses, became disillusioned with Protestantism but inspired by the Adventists. As a haberdasher in Pittsburgh he spent his free time trawling Greek and Hebrew dictionaries in a bid to better understand the messages and

meanings of the Bible. At the age of 20 he devoted himself to his evolving faith full time and began hosting Bible classes. In 1879 Russell launched *The Watchtower*, a journal to accompany Bible study expounding his beliefs, and three years later he formed a society of believers.

It wasn't until 1931 that members of this society became known as Jehovah's Witnesses. By now Joseph Rutherford (1869–1942) was at the helm, who encouraged his flock with the words, "Millions now living will never die." Under his leadership the contentious suggestion that 144,000 "anointed ones" were assured of living in paradise, while the "other sheep" were subject to the Final Judgment, came under scrutiny.

Upon Rutherford's death, his successor Nathan Homer Knorr oversaw a colossal expansion in membership—coinciding with unprecedented international persecution of Witnesses. The world was at war but Witnesses refused to salute the flag of any one nation, believing nationalism to be a distraction from God, nor would they bear arms. Many found themselves in Nazi concentration camps, for years afterward remaining unrecognized victims of the Holocaust era. The idea of a theocracy, a kingdom of God on Earth, still earns them the enmity of some nations.

APOCALYPTIC VISION

Three groups now direct the work of the Witnesses. They are the Watchtower Bible and Tract Society of Pennsylvania, the Watchtower Bible and Tract Society Inc. of New York, and the International Bible Students Association. Despite a wholesale commitment to the Bible, Witnesses are not associated with any other religious group and have thus developed a somewhat insular approach.

Critics feel that some of the Biblical translations supported by the Witnesses are incorrect. They have plucked from its pages the following beliefs, among others: that Christ died on a stake, not a cross; that God's rightful name is Jehovah; that the wicked will be destroyed forever; that the earth is eternal; and that man was created and did not evolve. Witnesses have courted controversy with a refusal to accept blood transfusions, even to save a life, believing it is against God's law. They have repudiated Christmas and birthday celebrations because both are rooted in Pagan tradition. World leaders, corporations, and even other Churches are under Satan's control, according to established Witness belief, and only after the Battle of Armageddon will his evil hold be relinquished. Through the ransom sacrifice of Christ, the deserving will be resurrected for eternal life.

Witnesses are zealous missionaries, famous for knocking on doors to distribute literature. Their conviction in the word of God is so strong that they see this as an act of neighborly love. None are interested in holding public office and there is no priesthood or paid ministry. Witnesses meet in Kingdom Halls for prayer and debate. When they are baptized each is fully immersed in water.

Both Jehovah's Witnesses and Adventists have fallen foul of one of their favorite themes, the Second Coming of Christ. The announcement of the Second Coming invariably made an impact, and followers waited agog to watch events unfold. When the prescribed day passed inconsequentially, their faith was inevitably shaken.

ABOVE: Charles Taze Russell—or Pastor Russell, as he was known—is accredited with founding the Jehovah's Witness movement in and around Pittsburgh, Pennsylvania.

Out *of the* Dark – Spiritualism

BELOW: Seances became a favorite among the fashionable in the second half of the 19th century. People would meet in drawing rooms and communicate with "the other side" by means of holding hands, table turning, and object levitation.

Spiritualism, where a medium acts as a channel for information received from "across the veil," is an attractive form of faith for anyone who despairs of tradition and ritual or is bereaved of someone dear. It began following troubling incidents in a Methodist household in 1848.

The Fox family of Hydesville, New York was kept awake at night by apparently disembodied knocking. Sisters Margaret and Catherine discovered that they could interact with the mysterious presence in a

It was a sensation that took America by storm. Circus impresario Phineas T. Barnum signed up the girls. Tests carried out to prove they were frauds were inconclusive.

Mediumship was suddenly in vogue,

series of raps that corresponded to letters of the alphabet. They were supposedly in contact with Charles Rosa, a peddler whose throat had been cut by a previous occupant of the house. After digging in the cellar, the girls uncovered some teeth, hair, and bones.

with some convincing clairvoyants among many hoaxers. After hearing a paper on spiritualism read at the White House in 1861, Abraham Lincoln (1809–65) observed: "Well, for those who like that sort of thing, I should think it is just about the sort of thing they would like. Notwithstanding, his wife pursued the faith following Lincoln's untimely death. One estimate says that Spiritualism had attracted as many as 11 million adherents worldwide by 1870.

The phenomenon of spiritualism had fervent supporters and ardent detractors. In Britain, where the movement was slower to spread, its most vocal champion was author Sir Arthur Conan Doyle (1859–1930). The man who created the rational genius Sherlock Holmes devoted money and literary expertise to support spiritualism. His wife claimed to have medium powers. Like countless others, their conviction in life after death was considerably boosted after a son was killed during the World War I.

In opposition was escapologist Harry Houdini (1874–1926), who was convinced that all mediums were guilty of chicanery. He wrote extensively on the subject, revealing "tricks of the trade" used by "mystics."

THE ILLUSION CRUMBLES

Houdini attended a séance hosted by Lady Doyle. She claimed to be in touch with his mother, made the sign of the cross, and wrote a message purportedly from the dead woman. Houdini furiously debunked the spectacle, pointing out his mother was a Jewess so most unlikely to make the sign of the cross, and was unable to write in English anyway.

The waters were muddied by the shock confession of Margaret Fox, who claimed that she and her sister created the rapping sounds by toe cracking, initially to trick their mother. Catherine continued to work as a medium, however, and Margaret recanted the confession a year later.

In 1898 the Vatican condemned spiritualism, although it supported further investigation into its manifestations. By 1920 the heyday of Spiritualism was largely over. Its attraction had been the promise of contact with the spirit world with minimum personal effort by the believer and that was particularly potent immediately following the carnage of World War I.

Mediums have existed throughout history. In the Old Testament, Saul consulted the medium of Endor to discover supernatural information. The practice of mediumship sent numerous women to burn at the stake during the European witch hunts of medieval times—although most were not clairvoyants but "guilty" of having pet cats, using herbs for medicine, and being alone in old age.

Spiritualist churches still exist, more sought after today for healing rather than communication with the dead. A healer, who is generally trained and adheres to the rules of a national or international body, calls on a higher power (God) to cure

maladies. Skeptics believe there is ample opportunity for fraud. Today the spiritualist church aims to root its beliefs in science, as well as the worship of God. In doing so it has regard for the teachings of many other

Christian Science

When an American woman married her passions of Bible study and spiritual healing, the result was Christian Science. It mushroomed in the vibrancy of the United States, where people were hungry for hitherto-unrealized aspects of religion.

As a child in New Hampshire, Mary Baker Eddy (1821–1910) was dogged by ill health. Hours spent in bed, reflecting on this misfortune and the stern Calvinist views forcefully expounded by her father, gave Eddy opportunity to derive her own religious views.

Pivotal events in her life also fashioned her outlook, one of which was meeting the charismatic Phineas Parkhurst Quimby. A

BELOW: A photographic portrait of Christian Science founder Mary Baker Eddy taken during the late 1870s.

healer from Maine, Quimby practiced hypnosis, hydrotheraphy, and homeopathy. Eddy was inspired, believing Quimby cured in the same manner as Jesus, and she came to the conclusion that strength of mind was crucial for faith and health. They parted

company when she became convinced that God alone was responsible for healing.

The extent of Quimby's influence became apparent when Eddy sued a former student for plagiarism. In response, the student accused her of copying Quimby's work. Later scholars dismissed allegations that Eddy imitated Quimby.

In 1866 Eddy suffered a fall which exacerbated a serious spinal condition. Quimby had recently died and even Eddy thought the prognosis was hopeless. However, close Bible study and intense personal belief appeared to effect a cure. She had pondered at length the words of Jesus to a paralyzed man: "Take up your bed and go home." Afterward she set about defining her beliefs in earnest and sought to cure others.

In 1875 Eddy published *Science and Health*, which began to attract a body of followers. She organized the First Church of Christ Scientist in Boston in 1879, followed two years later by the Metaphysical College. She taught there until its closure a decade later. By 1883 the *Christian Science Journal* was in publication, eventually evolving into the influential *Christian Science Monitor*.

MIND OVER MATTER

Eddy was not the most likely candidate for a faith founder. She married three times, first in 1843 to George W. Glover, who did not live to see the birth of their son, also called George. Her persistent ill health meant she was unable to care properly for the child, who was brought up by others.

In 1853 she wed dentist Daniel Patterson, who shared her interest in alternative medicine; they divorced 20 years later. She married her third husband, Asa G. Eddy, in 1877 at the age of 56. He died within five years of the marriage—his wife believed he had been the victim of a psychic attack. In

In the first decades of the 20th century, Christian Science established 3,200 branches in 48 countries. In his *History of the American People* (1997) author Paul Johnson uses Christian Science as an example of a new American phenomenon: "Religious belief, often of a strange and (some would say) implausible character, produced hugely creative movements with a strong cultural and educational content."

Worship at Christian Science centers is led by readers rather than ordained clergy. The Mother Church in Boston still controls Christian Science activities, although boards of directors runs its branches. Christian Scientists still favor their own methods above those of modern medicine, although they do consult dentists, opticians, and midwives.

the last years of his life he became the first professional Christian Science practitioner.

Eddy often vacillated, constantly tweaking her written work. She became a pastor, then rejected the notion of ministry. In 1889 she dissolved the church, college, and everything she had worked for. Christian Science was in a state of flux until she re-organized it three years later. She was secretive, too, fearing Christian Scientists could use their influence for evil. Relations with the rival New Thought Movement, a system of mental healing, were acrimonious. She had to fend off accusations of witchcraft and occultism.

Eddy's aim was to establish "primitive Christianity and its lost element of healing." God is omnipotent, Jesus was a man rather than a deity, evil is an illusion, and spiritual salvation is the way forward. It is the "mind over matter" element of Christian Science that separates it from orthodox Christianity.

Scientology

Scientology is a system of beliefs that aims to alleviate the human condition. It remains closely associated with its founder, Lafayette Ron Hubbard, a former navy man and science fiction writer, who bequeathed recorded lectures in order to maintain a presence at Scientology meetings after his death.

The architect of the Scientology Church and its principles was L. Ron Hubbard (1911–86). The books he wrote on his philosophy for life are considered its scriptures. Born in Nebraska, Hubbard inherited a passion for travel from his father, a naval commander, and from his teacher mother he acquired a love of learning. Aged two he moved to Montana, where he developed an affinity for horses and enduring respect for Blackfoot Indians.

As a young man he traveled extensively in the Far East and the Pacific, a keen observer of different religious traditions. Hubbard returned home to undertake demanding academic courses at George Washington University but soon became disillusioned with college life. He embarked once more on an international trip, upon which he concentrated on the state of mankind, trying to define his philosophy and the reason for existence.

"I suddenly realized that survival was the pin on which you could hang the rest of this, with adequate and ample proof. It's a very simple problem. Idiotically simple! That's why it never got solved," Hubbard declared. He advocated that activities supporting survival are good, while the opposite pursuits are destructive.

During World War II he served in the navy and suffered injuries. Hubbard believed his cure came about thanks to the power of his positive thinking, at least in part. Brooding on all he had seen and understood, he formulated one of his first theories, Dianetics, assisted by science

BATTLEFIELD EARTH

L. Ron Hubbard is not only known for Dianetics and Scientology. During 1980 he wrote a mammoth science fiction novel with slight links to Scientology: *Battlefield Earth*. It was only the first, and a ten-part series titled *Mission Earth* followed. In 2000, Hollywood star and Scientology adherent John Travolta made a movie adaption of *Battlefield Earth*. Unlike the book, it was a flop.

ABOVE: The power and the glory—to skeptical European minds, Hubbard's theocracy seemed suspect, even dangerous. He appeared to be a part of the 1960–80s American mania for all things religious, from fundamentalist Bible-ism to West Coast hippie trancendalist madness.

fiction writer A.E. Van Vogt (1912–2000).

Dianetics explained that people were scarred by engrams, the residue of bad memories or experiences, which brought forth negative feelings later in life. He aimed to use counseling to eliminate engrams, which he measured using an electrically powered E-meter. He saw Dianetics as being key to mental health. Word about the book in which he expounded his theories quickly spread and during the 1950s hundreds of groups sprang up across the U.S. to put his theories into practice.

SALVATION IN SELF-AWARENESS

The psychotherapy continued to evolve and Hubbard realized the true spiritual self existed apart from the human body. This he identified as the "thetan," which had known previous existences. His postulations were not unlike those of eastern beliefs centered on reincarnation. He believed that self-awareness would provide for religious salvation and he called his developed system Scientology.

In 1959 Hubbard and his family moved across the Atlantic to Britain to establish the international headquarters of the Church of Scientology in East Grinstead. It enjoyed tremendous success, not least because Hubbard never once denied the existence of a supremely powerful God. "Men without a strong and lasting faith in a Supreme Being are less capable, less ethical, and less valuable to themselves and society." But his teachings concentrate on knowing the inner self.

Scientology has faced criticism. Professional therapists feared it was operating in a medical sphere without a license. For years its activities were probed by America's revenue service. In 1967 Britain's health minister Kenneth Robinson spoke against it in the House of Commons. "Its authoritarian principles and practices are a potential menace to the personality and well-being of those so deluded as to become its followers."

But British Scientologist Graeme Wilson observed: "All great movements that sought to bring man wisdom and greater freedom have faced often vicious and virulent attacks. But if even a fraction of what has been said about Scientology were true it would have ceased to exist." Today it operates in 120 countries and hostility to it has been tempered by the drug rehabilitation programs that it operates.

ABOVE LEFT: The brave and the beautiful—Hubbard's Scientology appealed to elements in Hollywood (see box). One of the best-known movie stars to espouse the benefits of Dianetics is Tom Cruise.

ABOVE RIGHT: Exterior of the Founding Church of Scientology in Washington, D.C.

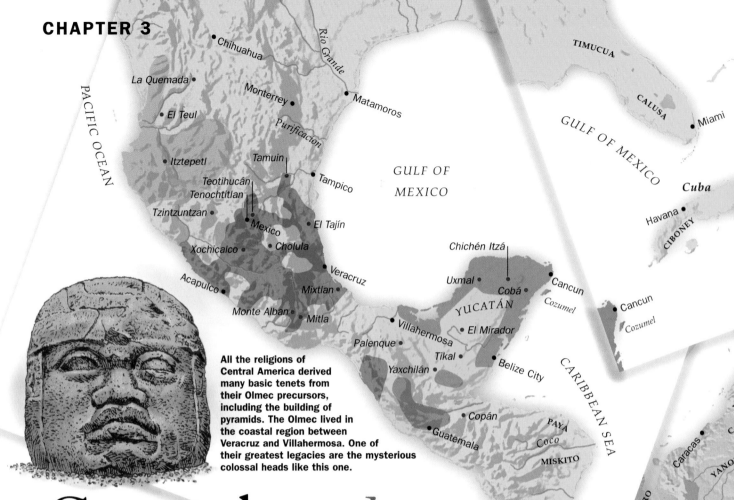

CHAPTER 3

All the religions of Central America derived many basic tenets from their Olmec precursors, including the building of pyramids. The Olmec lived in the coastal region between Veracruz and Villahermosa. One of their greatest legacies are the mysterious colossal heads like this one.

Central *and* South America

The great native religions of the Americas shared many threads. There was worship of natural phenomena such as the sun, moon, and stars, a belief that animals—sometimes even mountains and rivers—possessed spiritual force, and a conviction that the cosmos could be balanced and influenced through ritual and ceremony. Underpinning these foundations lay a powerful mythology, re-invented and re-told down the centuries, often using the equivalent and even the same deities.

For the leaders of civilizations such as the Toltec, Maya, Aztec, and Inca this was all colorful and mystical but not necessarily enough to maintain power. The crucial additional ingredient was to instill fear in enemies; fear of all-powerful militaristic regimes, fear of gods insufficiently

appeased, and, above all, fear of sacrifice at the hands of the high priests. The Aztecs' bloodthirsty excesses, such as the mass sacrifice of prisoners of war, made them many enemies. By contrast the Inca religion, which revolved around the divine authority of god-kings, was arguably undermined by its rigidity and obsession with divination.

The arrival of the conquistadors in the 16th century marked the speedy destruction of the Inca state. Fortunately, sufficient archaeology survived to provide an insight into the region's pre-Christian heritage, though this is sadly not the case elsewhere. The moundbuilders of North America, for instance, left behind hundreds of extravagant animal-shaped earth-structures, together with forts and flat-topped

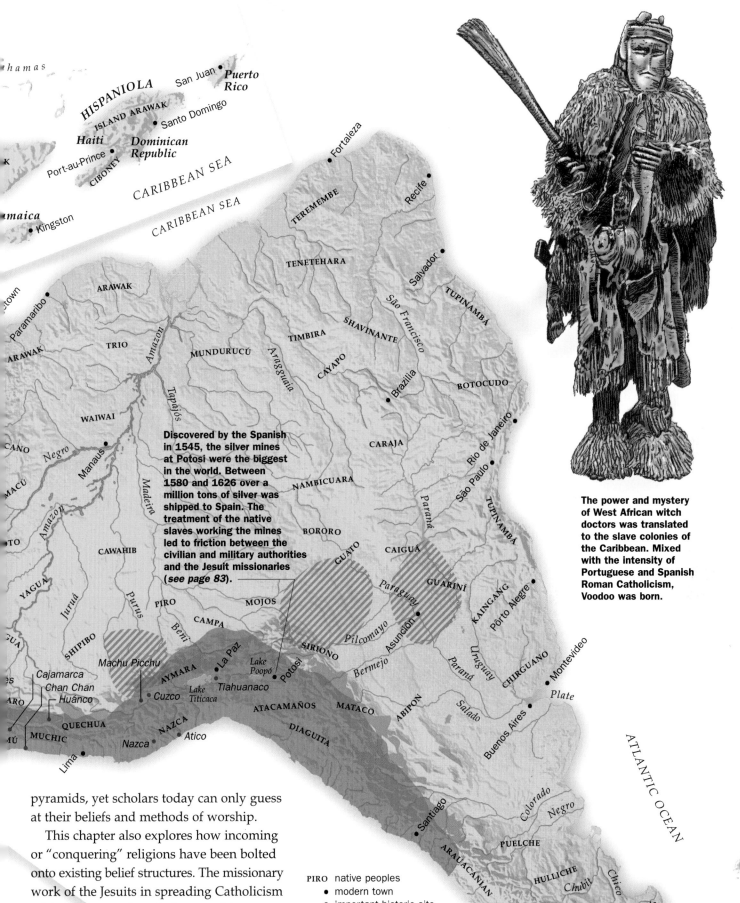

HISPANIOLA

San Juan • *Puerto Rico*

ISLAND ARAWAK
• Santo Domingo

Haiti • *Dominican Republic*

Port-au-Prince • CIBONEY

...hamas

CARIBBEAN SEA

CARIBBEAN SEA

...maica
• Kingston

...town

ARAWAK

• Paramaribo

...ARAWAK

TRIO

WAIWAI

...CANO

Negro

• Manaus

...MACÚ

Amazon

Amazon

...TO

YAGUA

Juruá

Purus

CAWAHIB

Madeira

Tapajós

MUNDURUCÚ

Araguaia

TIMBIRA

CAYAPO

SHAVINANTE

São Francisco

TENETEHARA

TEREMEMBE

• Fortaleza

• Recife

Salvador •

TUPINAMBÁ

Brazilia •

BOTOCUDO

Rio de Janeiro •

São Paulo •

TUPINAMBÁ

CARAJA

NAMBICUARA

BORORO

GUATO

CAIGUÁ

Paraguay

GUARINÍ

Paraná

KAINGANG

Pôrto Alegre •

...GUA

SHIPIBO

PIRO

Beni

CAMPA

MOJOS

SIRIONO

Pilcomayo

Asunción •

Bermejo

Paraná

Uruguay

CHIRGUANO

• Montevideo

Plate

Machu Picchu

AYMARA

La Paz

Lake Poopó

Potosi •

Tiahuanaco

Lake Titicaca

Cuzco •

ATACAMAÑOS

MATACO

ABIPON

Salado

Buenos Aires •

Cajamarca
Chan Chan
Huánco

...ARO

QUECHUA

...Ú

MUCHIC

• Lima

NAZCA

• Atico

Nazca

DIAGUITA

ATLANTIC OCEAN

Santiago •

Colorado

Negro

ARAUCANIAN

PUELCHE

HULLICHE

Chubut

Chico

Deseado

HULLICHE

ALACALUF

> Discovered by the Spanish in 1545, the silver mines at Potosi were the biggest in the world. Between 1580 and 1626 over a million tons of silver was shipped to Spain. The treatment of the native slaves working the mines led to friction between the civilian and military authorities and the Jesuit missionaries (*see page 83*).

The power and mystery of West African witch doctors was translated to the slave colonies of the Caribbean. Mixed with the intensity of Portuguese and Spanish Roman Catholicism, Voodoo was born.

PIRO native peoples
• modern town
• important historic site

Pre-Classic Mexican tomb culture, 300 BC–AD 300

Pre-Classic Maya, 300 BC–AD 800

Classic/Post-Classic Maya

Inca Empire at 1525

Jesuit Mission state to 1767

pyramids, yet scholars today can only guess at their beliefs and methods of worship.

This chapter also explores how incoming or "conquering" religions have been bolted onto existing belief structures. The missionary work of the Jesuits in spreading Catholicism achieved success largely by promising education and nursing care for all who converted. In this way, elements of Christianity permeated the ancient Voodoo religion, even though the two seem theologically incompatible.

The Maya – Order *from* Chaos

The Maya civilization in central America spanned at least 2,700 years and laid the cultural and religious foundations of the later Aztec state. Its ancestors, the Olmec, an identifiable entity c.1500 BC, evolved into a Classic Maya period by around AD 300, but decline gradually set in with the influx of the aggressive Toltec from the north.

Ancient Maya spirituality is a challenging and barely understood area, but its central themes lay in astrology and the tenet that people and buildings were symbolic incarnations of a wider universe. This was the reasoning behind the mysterious ball game, which represented the threshold between this world and the afterlife in Xibalba, the Underworld.

The game was partly a re-enactment of the myth in which the Hero Twins entered Xibalba, outwitted the lords of death, and returned unscathed to the realm of mortals. Played on a court with two parallel walls some 262 feet long and 120 feet apart, the aim was to send a ball through stone rings fixed 25 feet high on each wall. There was a major incentive for participants to win— losers were sometimes ritually sacrificed.

Human sacrifice was not uncommon, despite attempts to portray the Maya as somehow intellectually superior to their bloodthirsty Aztec successors. In spring, Mayan priests sacrificed young women to water gods by casting them into deep pools, to ensure the life-sustaining rains would come. Caves and other fissures in the earth were revered as portals to Xibalba and there is evidence that some human sacrifices— willing or otherwise—were buried alive.

One of the most fascinating examples of cave worship is at Naj Tunich in Petén province, Guatemala, which extends some $1^1/_4$ miles underground. This ritual center, with its stunning rock-art, was where Maya communicated with the spirit world and made private blood sacrifices to deities.

The religious mythology of the Maya

(and later the Aztec) rests on a conflict between light and darkness; the deities of the sun with their attributes of warmth, light, order, and joy, versus those of darkness, resembling night, fear, and chaos. The balance between the two—and in life itself—was personified by Itzamna, the creator god. He controlled decay and re-birth, upholding the Mayan belief that new life is possible only through sacrifice.

THE FEATHERED SERPENT RISES

Unlike the Aztec, there was no vast pantheon of gods; rather the various tribes worshipped similar deities under different

names. They accepted the supreme power of Hunab Ku, Itzamna's incarnation as creator of the Universe, and regarded the sun as the father of their culture. Chac, the rain god, had aspects linked to the four main compass directions and four winds, each of which had control over one quarter of the 260-day ritual calendar. Other important gods portrayed in Mayan records were the maize god, bat-god, and god of unlucky days.

The emergence of the Toltec state, centered on the city of Tula, brought with it a religion dominated by two deities co-existing in a constant state of rivalry. Quetzalcoatl, portrayed in art and sculpture as a feathered serpent, was the god of philosophy, learning, culture, and fertility. Tezcatlipoca, or Smoking Mirror, celebrated war and tyranny. Toltec legend has it that Tezcatlipoca's followers drove Ce Acatl Topiltzin, believed to have established Tula and who later took Quetzalcoatl's name, from his own city C.AD 1000. He and his followers moved south, defeating Mayan armies and seizing the city of Chichén Itzá.

Quetzalcoatl apparently vowed that he would one day return from the east to reclaim Tula and take vengeance on his enemies. This story survived long after the decline of the Toltec empire in the 12th century and was embraced by the Aztec. It is thought Aztec leader Moctezuma II initially believed that Hernán Cortés might be Quetzalcoatl's reincarnation, come to battle Moctezuma's patron deity, Huitzilopochtli, explaining the Aztec's weak response to the conquistadors' arrival.

Religious and ceremonial centers of the Maya
- major Pre-Classic site
- main regional center
- major Classic site
- other Classic site
- major Post-Classic site
- other Post-Classic site

The Aztec — Divine Fire of Sacrifice

Aztec life was ruled by ritual, a belief that interpretation of omens and tributes to deities could ensure balance and harmony. Here was a religion born of mythology, nourished by a warrior elite… and apparently emasculated by its own superstition.

FACING: A mask of Tezcatlipoca (Smoking Mirror) made from a human skull covered with a turquoise and lignite mosaic. Leather straps allowed the wearer to hinge the jaw. When the Aztec arrived in the Valley of Mexico, Tezcatlipoca and Quetzalcoatl were deities of the people living there. The Aztec fused the personality of Tezcatlipoca with Huitzilopochtli, their warrior god. Quetzalcoatl and Huitzilopochtli's opposition then expressed a duality that was fundamental to the Aztec view of life.

BELOW: Mictlantecuhtli, Lord of the Underworld, was another god the Aztec adopted on their arrival in the Valley of Mexico. He was variously depicted, but this skeletal version is unusually graphic.

Like the other principal Mesoamerican religions—Maya, Zapotec, and Mixtec—Aztec worship was bound up in sacrifice, divination, and the idea of a spiritual force that marked out living things from the inanimate. A cornerstone of the culture was a legend predicting that the Aztec would found a great and powerful civilization in a swampy area where an eagle—the symbol of Tezcatlipoca—perched on a cactus would be seen eating a snake.

In the 11th century waves of immigrants fleeing the collapse of the Toltec state began colonizing the central plains of what is now Mexico. Lake Texcoco was the focal point of these settlements, although by the time the Aztec arrived much of the best land had been claimed. They were driven away from their settlement, Chapultepec, by rival warriors from Culhuacán into marshes to the west of the lake. The Aztec culture was firmly established years later, when the eagle, snake, and cactus were spotted, as foretold. The city of Tenochtitlan (now Mexico City) was founded and a militaristic regime rose to establish unchallenged power from central Mexico to the Guatemalan border.

Aztecs believed in *teyolia*, a kind of energy or spiritual force that pervaded everything and inspired those who came into contact with it. It was released when the heart of a captive was given as an offering to the deities, but also when

a poet composed a fine verse or a *tlamatinime* priest made a profound speech or statement. Similar energies were supposed to emanate from sacred mountains and the temples on the summits of pyramids that echoed mountain shapes.

They also believed everything was a gift from the deities and made daily offerings and prayers to shrines in their homes. Each day and every activity had a patron deity, and important decisions were made only after temple priests consulted calendars and determined an auspicious date. The 18 months of the year, each of 20 days, were dedicated to different deities and festivals.

PANTHEON OF DEITIES

There were many Aztec deities, some with multiple identities. The most important god was Tezcatlipoca (Smoking Mirror), patron of sorcerers and the master of human destiny. In his guise as Huitzilopochtli he was both the god of war and the sun god, and thus the patron deity of the entire Aztec nation. In opposition to Tezcatlipoca was Quetzalcoatl (Feathered Serpent), who appears as both the evil Evening Star and benign Morning Star, as well as the god of the winds, Ehecatl.

Huitzilopochtli needed human blood for nourishment, a belief which also served as a convenient political tool. Prisoners of war were sought specifically to provide fresh blood; as part of treaties with neighboring states, mock battles known as the War of Flowers were held to provide victims. Beneath Huitzilopochtli's shrine in the Templo Mayor, the ritual temple at the heart of Tenochtitlan, is a stone wedge over which sacrificial victims would be stretched, face up, their chests arched ready for the removal of their hearts. Aztec warriors volunteered for sacrifice at major rituals, believing it was an honor matched only by death in battle.

Huitzilopochtli murdered his sister, the moon goddess Coyolxauhqui, when she led the stars against him, and the Aztec avenged her death by casting sacrificial victims down temple pyramids. This is reflected in a circular stone relief uncovered in the Templo Mayor which shows the naked Coyolxauhqui, limbs severed, with down-balls on her hair—a way of marking those chosen for sacrifice.

Below Tezcatlipoca and Quetzalcoatl were other important deities, such as the rain god Tlaloc, his sister/wife Chalchihuitlicue, goddess of fresh waters, and Coatlicue, mother of the gods. Centeotl and Xilonen presided over the growth and ripening of crops, and were often in alliance with Tlaloc and Chalchihuitlicue. They were also associated with Xipe Totec (Flayed God), who demanded sacrifice and whose priests wore the flayed skins of their victims.

The Inca — Time *and* Space

The breathtaking rise of the Inca Empire during the early 15th century is unparalleled. From a heartland around Cuzco, where its rule once extended no more than 25 miles in any direction, Inca armies conquered an area totaling 2,175 miles north to south and some 500 miles east to west within a century.

Inca power was built on rigid socialist lines, with a rigidly controlled system of agriculture and a culture of unquestioning obedience. At the head of this vast state apparatus was the Inca himself—an emperor revered as a living god—while deified features of the natural world included the sun, moon, stars, nature, and the seasons. There was also a strong cult of ancestor-worship.

Although the emperor, as son of the sun, was the earthly head of Inca spiritual life, he shared some power with the *hullac umac* or high priest. This man was chosen from the nobility and would oversee the duties of priests as they made sacrifices, prayed for the souls of believers, listened to confessions (a way of allaying private disasters), and divined omens.

The most important feast, IntipRaimi, was held in honor of Inti, the sun god, who nourished all life. This highly ritualistic festival required the emperor to make a drink-offering to the sun, after which the royal family would partake of *chicha* (an alcoholic drink made from cassava or maize), make further temple offerings, oversee the sacrifice of llamas, and listen to the latest omens.

Omens and divination formed a central part of the Inca religion. Oracles were consulted over everything from sickness to criminal investigations, suitable sites for agricultural or building, and, most important, the offering of the right sacrifice at the right time. Divination techniques included following the path of a spider in an upturned bowl, interpreting the position of coca leaves, drinking the hallucinogen *ayahuasca*, and interpreting the marks on lungs of sacrificed llamas.

SOULS OF BIRTH AND BODY

Daily offerings to Inca gods were commonplace, but animal or human sacrifices were reserved for special occasions or in times of disaster such as floods, disease, and famine. There is evidence that hundreds of children were killed to mark the crowning of an Inca king and individual children were sometimes selected to be messengers to the gods.

The body of one such messenger, sacrificed on Mount Aconcagua in the late 15th century, has been recovered intact, preserved in the permafrost at 17,550 feet. There was no sign of violence on the corpse and the cause of death is unclear. However, the boy had been well prepared for his supernatural journey; a red pigment was smeared on his face, he wore two embroidered tunics, a turquoise necklace, plumed headdress, and woven sandals.

Ornaments discovered beside him included gold and shell figurines of humans and animals (probably llamas or alpacas) and thorny oyster shells from the coast of Ecuador. Coca leaves, the source of cocaine, were packed into small bags attached to the figures, though chemical analysis of the child's body has proved that as he awaited death he was denied this palliative.

The Inca believed that after death two souls within each person took different paths. One would seek out its place of origin (depending on the virtue of the life it had led, its social standing, and the manner in which its mortal body had died); the other would remain in the body, which was mummified and interred with personal belongings.

This philosophy appears to conform to the Inca perception of time, space, and the Universe—the principles of Uku Pacha, the past and interior world, Kay Pacha, the present and visible world, and Hana Pacha, the future and the wider cosmos. Time was seen not as a linear structure, but multi-dimensional and accessible to human beings across all its manifestations.

FACING: The Inca left behind little in the way of religious monuments. For much of its life, the Inca state was small, confined to Cuzco, and the untimely arrival of the Spanish curtailed schemes there may have been. Most monuments, therefore, belong to earlier eras which influenced the Inca, such as these ceremonial structures at Tiahuanaco. Inca engineering was another matter, as the superb terraced remains, BELOW, of Huinay Huayna (Vilcabamba) near Cuzco demonstrate.

Jesuits—Missionaries Abroad

BELOW: After a spiritual conversion at the mature age of 33, Ignatius Loyola left Spain to attend university in Paris. Here, he conceived a new religious order based on "spiritual exercises" and teaching, to be run like an army. The Establishment tried to stop him, but in 1538 the pope finally put the visionary to work. His life inspired many paintings, such as this one of 1628 by Claude Vignon.

Just when it looked like Protestants were cornering all of Europe's religious impetus through the Reformation, the Roman Catholic Church staged a fight back. Their weapon was the Society of Jesus, whose members held missions in South America.

The Jesuits were a hard-working body of men concerned with education, missionary work, and other charitable exercises, all of which raised the profile of the pope and the Catholic Church. One of the most successful arenas of Jesuit activity was South America.

As he convalesced from a battle wound, Ignatius of Loyola (1491–1556) experienced a religious revelation that would alter the course of his existence. No longer was he the highborn adventurer making the most of Spanish hegemony in Europe. Now he sought to find new ways of serving God. Together with six students from the University of Paris, he set out the ground rules for his new organization, which received papal approval in 1540.

In effect Ignatius overhauled the practice of Catholicism, losing some of its more medieval aspects yet instilling ever-greater obedience to religious authority. In doing so the Society of Jesus developed a special relationship with the pope, which fueled envy among rivals. But it is in their work overseas that Jesuits are best remembered. Before his death, Ignatius personally directed a thousand missionaries to Asia, Africa, and the New World. By the middle of the 18th century the number of Jesuit missionaries had topped 22,500.

In South America they faced the hardships common to missionaries of the era—hostile natives, tough terrain, extreme weather conditions, and so forth. But fellow Europeans provided their greatest headache. The Spanish and Portuguese were intent on exploiting the continent for gold. To do so they needed numerous slaves, who were ruthlessly rounded up. The sight of nursing mothers in fetters and men being torn away from their families was more than the Jesuits could tolerate.

HOSTILITY ON ALL SIDES

At first Jesuits naïvely believed that natives would be safe from slave traders if they converted to Catholicism. Jesuits formed communities known as *reducciones*, the first of which was founded in 1608. Marked by a mission church, the natives within its boundaries cultivated crops and studied the scriptures.

In 1629 slave traders or *bandeirantes*

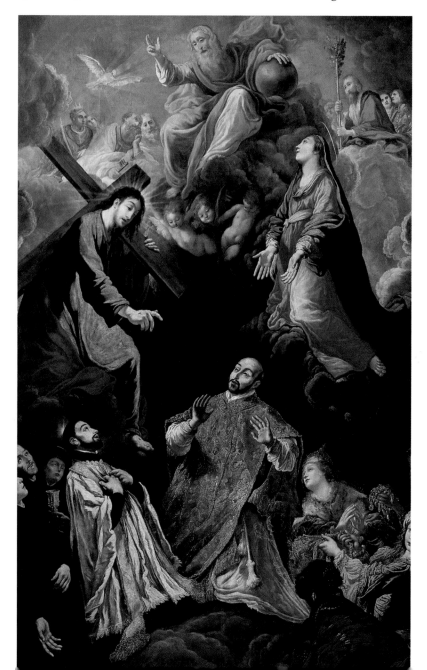

sacked five such communities, burning down the churches and forcing the residents into a treacherous march to the coast. Two Jesuits, Fathers Montoya and Macedo, responded by transporting 12,000 natives to a safe haven further inland. Another notable Jesuit triumph was the conversion of hostile natives in remote marshlands in 1658, who until then had rebuffed all attempts at communication.

Thus Jesuits were working contrary to the interests of colonialists, implying that, as papal appointees, they had righteousness on their side. Dutch theologian Cornelius Jansen (1585–1638) was critical of the Jesuits, believing a zealous response to Protestantism brought them into the realms of heresy.

Jesuits contributed to the earliest charts made of the region, many of which were surprisingly accurate. Jose de Acosta (1539–1600), who went to Peru in 1571 and traveled the region for the next 16 years, left books detailing South American life. A century later Father Samuel Fritz began his exploits, which included canoeing up the Amazon and falling dangerously ill during

a flood. His writings were re-discovered in 1902 and told how, as he lay prostrate with fever, he could hear "the grunting of the crocodiles that were roving around the village… rats so hungry that they gnawed even my spoon and my plate and the haft of my knife."

The influence and power built up by the Jesuits attracted both clerical and lay enemies. European heads of state put pressure on the pope to suppress Jesuit missionaries, who were interfering with colonial amibitions. Catholics pursuing a different theology felt the Jesuits were misguided, although envy was probably behind their enmity. Eventually papal opposition brought about the Jesuits' downfall. Portugal expelled the Jesuits from its territories in 1759, France followed suit five years later, while Spain made them illegal in 1767. Ultimately, Pope Clement XIV (1769–74) suppressed the Jesuits. Ironically they survived only in the Protestant and Orthodox countries of Prussia and Russia. In 1814 their status was restored, but their fall from grace had cost the Jesuits dearly.

ABOVE: Detail from a marquetry cabinet of the 17th century showing two Indios des Chacos (an area now belonging to Paraguay and Bolivia) preventing a Spanish officer from entering a Jesuit mission. Conflict between the Jesuits and Spanish colonists was sparked by the treatment of the native population, especially over the slaves who worked the massive silver mines at Potosi (see page 75). Inevitably, the Spanish army had to take action against the troublesome missionaries, until by the mid-18th century the Jesuits were granted several states of their own to adminster— well away from sensitive commercial ventures.

Voodoo – Africa *meets* America

Voodoo is a faith of both radiant and sinister aspects. Adherents worship a high god, Bon Dieu, and revere spirits called Ioa who are identified with Roman Catholic saints, deified ancestors, and African gods. Other aspects are uniquely controversial.

BELOW: Papa Doc, here photographed in 1959, was an ex-country doctor who became a repressive dictator through the use of voodoo terror tactics. By the mid-1960s he had driven his opponents into exile, asylums, or prison.

In the eyes of the faithful, Ioa spirits are usually protectors who guide mortals through life, though Haiti also has a harsh, malevolent faction. The faithful court an Ioa's favors with ritual service that has similarities with Roman Catholicism. Priests (*houngans*) and priestesses (*mambos*) use bells, candles, crosses, and prayers during worship. However, they also instigate drumming, dancing, and feasting to draw the congregation into ecstatic worship, while voodoo's shadowy side centers on witchcraft and warped minds.

In the past, the Vatican has denounced the followers of voodoo and even inspired persecution. These days the policy appears to be one of cautious co-existence.

Haiti is the home of voodoo, although the religion is also practiced in Brazil, Trinidad, Cuba, and the southern states of the U.S. It was in Haiti— then known as Hispaniola— that slaves imported to work on sugar plantations blended the Catholic faith of their Spanish masters with their own West African religion to create voodoo.

Voodoo provided comfort and support for the half-million slaves that lived in abject poverty in the 18th and 19th centuries under French rule, the island having been handed to the French as part of the seesaw power struggle in the Pacific and re-named Haiti. Errant slaves—especially runaways— were shown sadistic cruelty. Despite the threat of torture and execution, numerous escapees fled to the mountains to join a

RIGHT: A worshipper holds a large white fetish doll at a voodoo ceremony in Ouidah, Benin, West Africa. The advent of Western toys has given a new sinister aspect to the age-old "Ju Ju doll," which could be used for good purposes, such as healing, or evil.

resistance led by voodoo leaders. In that leafy seclusion they learnt the refined art of poisoning and visited it first upon livestock and then Europeans.

Before Haiti won its independence in 1804, voodoo was the savior of the people, as it was targeted at the oppressors. Afterward, its powers could be directed against anyone who challenged those in authority, namely the witch doctors. Accordingly the residents of Haiti were enslaved once more, this time by the cynical manipulation of their own religion.

ZOMBIE NATION

One of its most terrifying features was the zombie, half-conscious creatures allegedly raised from the dead, then kept in the thrall of voodoo masters. Alfred Metraux

(1902–63), the author of *Voodoo in Haiti* (1958), commented: "There are few, even among the educated, who do not give some credence to these macabre stories."

Sugar plantation workers fled screaming back to their home village after they were given a sweet biscuit at a church festival. The change of diet had altered their zombie state; neighbors testified that each one had died and been buried in the recent past.

Using the awesome threat of zombieism, Haiti's autocratic ruler Dr. François Duvalier (1907–71), known as Papa Doc, contrived an iron grip on the country. He scaled down the army and expanded the *Ton Ton Macoute* (bogeymen) to act as a personal bodyguard and security force, specializing in terror tactics. Duvalier enhanced his reputation by publicly cursing President John Kennedy after the latter withdrew aid. (Kennedy was assassinated the following year.) Acting as witchdoctor in chief, Duvalier developed a personality cult, which succeeded in keeping him in power, even though he had been excommunicated from the Roman Catholic faith by the pope and was in diplomatic isolation.

The reins of power were taken up by his son, Jean-Claude (Baby Doc), who at 19 was the world's youngest president. He tweaked the undemocratic system but failed to provide any meaningful changes. By 1986 he had been driven out of the country to make way for a six-man council.

Jean-Claude Duvalier's loss of power coincided with revelations about the nature of zombieism. In the 1980s researchers realized that witch doctors were in possession of a powerful drug which rendered the victim motionless, like a corpse. The drug comprised toxins from a plant called jimsonweed, the poisonous liver of a puffer fish, and a substance from the toad *Bufo marinus*. Witch doctors could administer an antidote, bringing the "corpse" back to life, then give other substances to keep the victim docile and compliant.

ABOVE: Onlookers beat out rhythms with sticks and their hands while chanting as a man dances during a trance ceremony at Gonaives, Haiti.

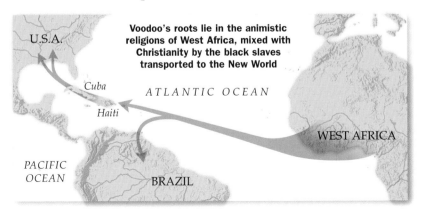

Voodoo's roots lie in the animistic religions of West Africa, mixed with Christianity by the black slaves transported to the New World

U.S.A.

Cuba

Haiti

ATLANTIC OCEAN

WEST AFRICA

PACIFIC OCEAN

BRAZIL

CHAPTER 4

Africa

Pygmy female fertility figure of the people of the Ituri Forest, Congo region. These people of the Bantu tribes share with the Dogon tribe of Mali a system of worship based on astral bodies. The Bantus' knowledge of the planet Saturn amazed early anthropologists who visited the region.

To generalize about the colorful, chaotic, beating heart of African religion is naïve and foolhardy. The continent is vast and the religious map was labyrinthine even before the arrival of modern, mainstream faiths.

An in-depth analysis of tribal faith has no space in this snapshot. However, one or two points bear scrutiny. Many tribes acknowledge a Supreme Being, in the same way Muslims have Allah and Christians know God. In the Congo he is known as Leza, in the Cameroons he is Nyambe, while tribes in East Africa identify him as Mulungu. In general terms, this powerful deity resides in the sky and the outbursts of nature, including thunder and rainfall, are his expressions of satisfaction or otherwise.

Using broad brush strokes, tribal religion is the third most popular pursued on the continent, with an estimated 95 million adherents. Within a century of Mohammed's revelations, Islam was firmly established across North Africa. Today the continent has some 310 million resident Muslims, the majority still living above the Sahara.

Most of the 351 million Christians are Roman Catholic, but there is also the Coptic Church, which claims descent from St. Mark

and was independently run in Egypt after AD 451. Christians who believed Christ had a single divine nature (Monophysites) were the founders; other branches of Christianity asserted that Christ had two natures, divine and human. The two trains of thought could not be reconciled. The Coptic Church survived the onslaught of Islam and was left largely untroubled by the ruling Caliphs.

Apart from the question of Christ's single or dual nature, Coptic theology resembles that of the Eastern Orthodox Church. Services are mostly heard in Arabic, and

Map labels: MEDITERRANEAN SEA · Tunis · Tripoli · SAHARA DESERT · TUAREG · AIR · MARRAKECH · MAURETANIA · MALI · Timbuktu · Bandiagara Escarpment · Gao · NIGER · BANU HASSAN ARABS · SONGHAI · Niamey · Sokoto · BERBER · Niger · DOGON · MOSSI · BURKINA · Ouagadougou · NIGER · BENIN · TOGO · ATLANTIC OCEAN · WALO · CAYOR · Bamako · GHANA · ASANTE · IVORY COAST · NIGER · BAOL · FULANI · West Indies & North America · MANDING · Sénégal · GUINEA · Sokoto · HAUSA · Kano · Dakar · Gambia · FULA · KEBBI · NUPE · IGALA · Banjul · SUSU · BURKINA · BENIN · Niger · NIGERIA · BORGU · OYO · Benue · Brazil · Freetown · TOGO · YORUBA · Ife · Brazil · DAHOMEY · Lagos · Calabar · CAMEROON · Port Harcourt · Brazil

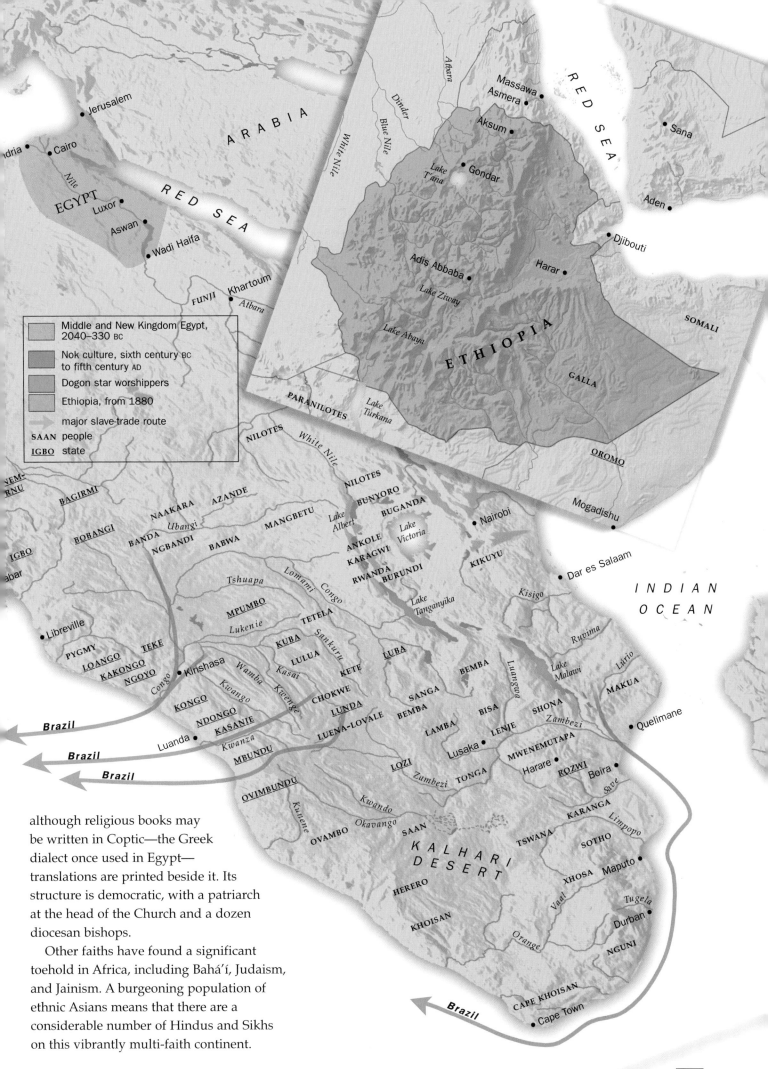

Legend

- Middle and New Kingdom Egypt, 2040–330 BC
- Nok culture, sixth century BC to fifth century AD
- Dogon star worshippers
- Ethiopia, from 1880
- major slave-trade route
- SAAN people
- IGBO state

although religious books may be written in Coptic—the Greek dialect once used in Egypt— translations are printed beside it. Its structure is democratic, with a patriarch at the head of the Church and a dozen diocesan bishops.

Other faiths have found a significant toehold in Africa, including Bahá'í, Judaism, and Jainism. A burgeoning population of ethnic Asians means that there are a considerable number of Hindus and Sikhs on this vibrantly multi-faith continent.

The Terracotta Gods

BELOW AND FACING: A Nok head, c.900 BC–AD 200, and head of a king from Ife, 12th–14th centuries.

Piecing together the religious traditions of Stone and Iron Age Africa is one of the most challenging tasks in archaeology. Limited fieldwork has held back discoveries of intact sites and—frustratingly for scholars—areas known to be rich in artifacts have often been damaged by treasure hunters.

Driven by an insatiable international art market, poverty-line farmers in Nigeria and West Africa have understandably supplemented their wages by digging for relics; a practice which began at the end of the 19th century and has subsequently destroyed the sources and context of thousands of pieces. Much archaeological investigation is now needed to build a clearer picture of early African spirituality and its influence on succeeding generations.

There have been glimpses of fabulously skilled and innovative cultures such as Nok, which flourished between the Jos Plateau of central Nigeria and along the Benue valley somewhere between the sixth century BC and AD 300. The existence of these people—perhaps the earliest ironworkers in West Africa—emerged in 1928, when tin miners at the village of Nok discovered a terracotta head in river gravel. Since then, many more animal and human terracotta figures, some life-size, have been unearthed.

Although we do not even know what this culture called itself, it is possible to glean something of its traditions and beliefs. Nok heads are disproportionately large and elongated—considered an indicator of intelligence in later African art—with elaborate hairstyles and ornate jewelry. Eyes are shown as triangles with a circular hole for pupils, while the Negroid features tend to be bold and abstract. These are not idealized images; on the contrary, some show evidence of gross enlargement, caused by elephantiasis, and facial paralysis. It is possible that the disfigured heads were produced as charms against sickness. Designs are too varied to have been molded and it is more likely that the clay was sculpted in the manner of a woodcarving.

NOK INFLUENCE

Some archaeologists believe the Nok figures may have been idols of an agricultural fertility cult. Recovered portions of fragmented limbs show that bodies were sculpted in genuflecting postures, as well as sitting and standing. Given what we know of first millennium BC religious tradition elsewhere in Africa, it is likely that ancestor-worship was widely practiced, suggesting that some of the heads were revered images of dead kings or tribal leaders.

The study of succeeding cultures in the region has provided further clues. The distinctive features of Nok terracotta emerge as influences in later artwork recovered from sites such as Igloo Ouch, Fe, Benin City, and Elsie.

At Igbo Ukwu, deep in the forests of southern Nigeria, the grave of what appears to be a priest-king has yielded crucial finds, including superb bronze and copper figures. This deep, wood-lined tomb dates to around AD 900, 600 years after the decline of Nok culture, but it is conceivable that the people who built it inherited some traditions from their Nok ancestors. Grave goods such as a bronze staff, a copper chest ornament, and over 100,000 glass and carnelian beads indicate a belief that worldly goods were valued in the afterlife.

The use of terracotta heads in religious practice is found again at Ife, center of an early second millennium AD kingdom in southwest Nigeria. Along with similar brass figures they were kept at shrines, altars, and houses and presumably worshipped as gods or ancestors

In South Africa evidence of an intriguing Iron Age ritual was discovered at Lydenburg, Eastern Transvaal province, in the early 1960s. Shards of terracotta were found to be elaborately decorated heads that had been hurled into deep pits, probably as part of an initiation rite. Similar finds have since turned up elsewhere in southern Africa, suggesting this practice was commonplace during the early and mid-first millennium AD.

Star Worshippers—*the* Dogon

FACING TOP: Dama dancers wearing traditional masks. The stick-figures with spread arms and legs on top of the Kananga masks represent the first human beings. Similar figures are painted on the walls of holy caves. The Dama dance generates a bridge so that the dead can cross over into the supernatural world.

FACING: A Binu ancestor figure (see box below).

In a remote corner of West Africa lives a people with a remarkable lifestyle. The Dogon tribe has attracted international publicity for their traditional religion, which centers on the worship of a little-known star called Sirius B.

Most people have seen Sirius, the brightest star in the sky, which is also known as the Dog Star. The worship of its night sky splendor is by no means surprising. However, few people gazing at Sirius, the sixth closest star to earth, would have been aware of a companion star in its vicinity. Invisible to the naked eye, *Sirius B* was first spotted by Westerners in 1862 with the use of a powerful telescope. It wasn't photographed until 1970. Yet the Dogon had been marking its passage for centuries.

The Dogon, numbering about 600,000, are farmers—no mean feat when their territory in the Bandiagara Escarpment in Mali is rocky, mountainous, and hard-baked by the sun. Some leather or metal craftsmen eke out an existence, too. They correctly revealed to astonished anthropologists that *Sirius B* has an elliptical orbit, rather than a circular one, and is a "heavy" star (it is a white dwarf, the classification given to dim, dense stars of planet size). The Dogon passed on this information by drawing pictures in the sand.

But how did these apparently primitive people avail themselves of such specific astronomical facts? According to the Dogon, it was thanks to fish-tailed aliens who visited the region 3,000 years ago. This amphibious race, the Nommos, hailed from the Sirius star system and imparted this information along with data about Jupiter and Saturn.

They told the Dogon that *Sirius B* took about 50 years to orbit its larger, brighter neighbor. Religious life among the Dogon is at its most vital when, about once every

DOGON WORSHIP

The Dogon are broadly split into three cults that still hold sway among them, in spite of the arrival of Islam and Christianity. Members of the Awa death cult dance with ornate masks at funerals and important death anniversaries to lead the deceased to their final resting place. The agricultural Lebe worship the Earth God. Their priests (*hogon*) are licked by the Serpent during sleep to purify. The Binu cult has associations with ancestor worship and their shrines house the spirits of mythic ancestors who lived before death came to the world.

RIGHT: A diviner prepares a Dogon star chart (*see also the picture on page 1*). Star charts answer questions and predict outcomes. The diviner draws a question in the sand as dusk approaches for the sacred fox to answer. The fox has supernatural powers and can see the future and into the hearts of men. In the morning, the diviner reads the footprints and interprets the answer.

50 years, the stars hover between two mountain peaks. In preparation for this event, called *sigui*, the tribe's young men disappear into seclusion for three months, during which they talk in a strange, apparently secret language.

THE MOONS OF SATURN

When the astonishing beliefs of the Dogon were revealed to the world by French scholars Marcel Griaule and Germaine Dieterien in 1950, the urge to believe that extra-terrestrials were the divine inspiration for a time-honored religious system was irresistible. Skeptics have since pointed out that Europeans were traveling to the region between the wars at a time when astronomy was as exhilarating as geographical exploration, and therefore apt to look favorably on the claims of star-worshipping natives. Further contentions made by the Dogon about another small star orbiting Sirius have yet to be proved by scientists.

Many of the Dogon have converted to Islam and a smaller number profess Christianity. Yet despite the arrival of other faiths, most see traditional religion as an integral part of daily life. Enormous respect is paid to the *hogon*, or spiritual leader, who heads each district, and the myths of creation remain important and well-loved.

It is usually possible to discern African religious beliefs by study of their arts. Sculpture, music, poetry, dance, costume, and even jewelry show a fundamental faith handed down from one generation to the next. Inevitably that faith is inspired by nature and all the natural forces outside the control of man. Despite major inroads made by Islam and Christianity, there remains widespread obedience to the superstitious laws of traditional religion.

The pygmies of the Ituri Forest in the Congo also divulged in-depth knowledge of astronomy. Anthropologist Jean Pierre Hallet was staggered to discover that they knew Saturn as "the star of the nine moons" (a tenth has recently been discovered). Of course, none of the moons is visible to the naked eye.

Although they spoke Bantu, the language of the region, the information about Saturn did not appear to be shared among Bantu-speakers. Hallet said: "I have never encountered a Bantu or Sudanese who credits Saturn with any moons, much less nine. Most Americans and Europeans are no better informed concerning the existence and number of Saturn's satellites."

Gods *of the* Nile—Ancient Egypt

Religion in Ancient Egypt was a potent mix of myth, magic, superstition, ancestor worship, animism, ritual, and deity cults. The array of gods and spirits is baffling, the result of an amalgamation of many local religions and millennia of development.

ABOVE: Painting inside the tomb of Horemheb in Thebes depicting the god Osiris with green skin—a symbol of his renewal of life in the spring. He is seen holding the crook and flail, symbols of divine royalty and dominion. On his head he wears the *Atef*, which is the *Hedjet* or white crown of Upper Egypt, combined with the red feathers associated with Busins, Osiris's cult center in the Nile delta.

Amun-Ra was the sun god and accordingly held immense power in Egypt. He was a hybrid of a local Memphis god, Amun, and the sun god Ra and is strongly associated with the temple at Karnak—the largest temple ever built—although he is found at numerous other religious sites.

The god Osiris, like Amun-Ra, was worshipped for scores of generations. According to Egyptian belief, Osiris ruled after Amun-Ra ascended to the heavens. He was the benevolent king who ruled on Earth with his sister/wife Isis until he was slain by his jealous brother Seth. Osiris went on to rule the Underworld. Commonly he is depicted with green skin, as a sign of his powers of rebirth and new growth. Isis reared their son Horus, who one day sought to avenge his father's death. In the process he lost an eye. That eye, redeemed and healed by Thoth, the god of wisdom, became an important symbol of healing and wholeness that has endured to the present day.

Other notable characters were Sekhmet, a lioness personifying the warmth of the sun; Khnum, a ram-headed god thought to be linked to the vital waters of the Nile; and Hathor, a goddess in cow form considered to be mother of the Pharaohs. Taweret, an oddly shaped figure with the body of a hippopotamus, tail of a crocodile, and mane and paws of a lion was the goddess of childbirth. Her mythical partner was Bes, a dwarf sticking out his tongue who served to keep demons away during labor.

PERILOUS JOURNEY TO THE UNDERWORLD

Pharaohs were considered gods on earth and so inspired worship from their people. As mediators between Earth and Heaven, it was the Pharaohs who communicated with the higher gods to ensure harmony in the two terrestrial kingdoms of Egypt. Scenes depicting the Pharaoh with gods are found on many Egyptian artifacts.

As a god, albeit a minor one, the Pharaoh commanded respect during life and in death, typified by the magnificent pyramids. Chambers within the pyramids were filled with earthly riches, mummified servants, food, and other goods to accompany the Pharaoh into the afterlife. Some were apparently left empty, although many were pillaged, even in antiquity, so we cannot be sure. The fundamental purpose of the pyramid was to enable the

Ra

Amun

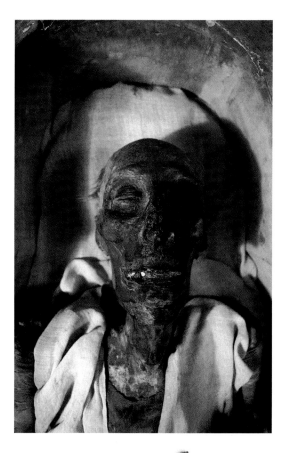

buried with the body of the deceased to assist in the traumatic journey to the underworld. One of the biggest hazards was the demon Apep, a giant snake who used his coils to trap the unwary.

Religion in Ancient Egypt was localized. Numerous temples were built and devoted to the deity that dominated in a particular region, and homes appear to have had shrines. The main temples were staffed by priests who were as much concerned with local government and administration as with spiritual matters. In these temples the priests were devout, celibate, shaven of all body hair, and manicured. However, outside the main religious centers local priests were permitted to marry and own a small business.

One of the most fascinating sidebars to religion in Ancient Egypt is the worship of animals. The sacred animal necropolis at Saqqara was excavated to reveal vast numbers of mummified hawks, baboons, cows, cats, dogs, hawks, and ibises, offered up by pilgrims in honor of various gods. The mummies of hard-to-trap hawks were often found to contain just a few bones, the bird being stuffed with twigs and detritus, while ibises—easier to catch and kill—had their skeletons intact.

LEFT: The mummified remains of Ramses II, Egyptian Museum, Cairo. To preserve the body, Egyptian funerary priests undertook many complex tasks. The viscera and soft organs were first removed and stored for the afterlife in canopic jars, while the corpse was immersed in natron (hydrated sodium carbonate). The body remained in this brine for up to 70 days, gradually drying and becoming solid. The mummy was then wrapped in bindings before entombment.

Isis

Toth

Horus

Pharaoh to be resurrected in the afterlife, but speculation about its precise role and meaning continues.

Another route by which people hoped to achieve an afterlife was through a collection of "Spells for Going Forth by Day," otherwise known as the Book of the Dead. It was written and drawn on papyrus or linen and

PHARAOHS AND EGYPT'S LIFEBLOOD

The very existence of Egypt was entirely dependent on the annual flooding of the Nile—the "innundation"—which was seen as a gift from the gods. As their representative on Earth, the pharaoh was responsible for controlling the flood, and many ceremonies were devoted to ensuring the regular occurrence of this phenomenon. If the flood failed, the Pharaoh's authority could be called into question, despite his (or her) divine descent.

Missionaries *in* Africa

When missionary David Livingstone died his heart was buried beneath a mulva tree on the banks of Lake Tanganyika—Livingstone's heart belonged to Africa. He was the most famous of a notable breed determined to spread the Christian message no matter what the personal cost.

BELOW: Livingstone worked relentlessly to end the traffic in slaves, what he referred to as "this open sore of the world." His activities jeopardized the income of Arab and Portuguese slave traders and his life became threatened. This illustration shows captive slaves being marched from the village of Mbame in the Zambezi area. Livingstone visited the village in 1860.

Missionaries like Livingstone (1813–73) were absorbed with the abolition of the slave trade and the mapping of uncharted territory. He lived in an imperial age in which white men were confident— no, certain—that their ways were superior and that the Christian faith was suitable for all. Livingstone was driven by the prospect of the conversion of tribesmen who could neither read the Bible nor comprehend the words of the Eucharist.

of 25 Livingstone was ordained by the London Missionary Society and three years later went to Africa to fulfill his dearest ambition. He worked in a mission run by fellow Scot Robert Moffat and ultimately married Moffat's daughter, Mary.

In seeking out new communities ripe for conversion, Livingstone, usually accompanied by his wife, notched up an impressive list of firsts. He traveled across the Kalahari Desert, saw Lake Ngami, and

FACING: A statue of David Livingstone stands above Victoria Falls on the Zambezi. Livingstone was the first European to set eyes on the mighty waterfall.

As a boy in Scotland, Livingstone lived with his parents and six siblings in a single room and from the age of ten worked a 14-hour day at the local mill. His parents were devout Christians and he was brought up in the discipline and piety of the Calvinist creed. His hard work and determination finally won him a place at medical school, where he also studied theology. At the age

encountered the great Zambezi river. He displayed a respect and care toward Africans that was wholly uncharacteristic in visiting Europeans of the time. It was the unquenchable desire to find new territories suitable for Christian missions that compelled Livingstone to undertake dangerous journeys, including one in which he was badly mauled by a lion.

AFRICAN HEART

Livingstone was a notoriously difficult companion and several of his expeditions fell apart. In 1866 he left London for the last time, charged with finding the source of the Nile, and disappeared into dense jungle. Journalist Henry Morton Stanley was given the task of locating Livingstone on behalf of the *New York Herald*. He discovered Livingstone, racked with illness and threatened by a shortage of supplies, at Ujiji by Lake Tanganyika in 1871. Famously, Stanley greeted the lost explorer with the words, "Dr. Livingstone, I presume." It is less commonly known that Stanley paid Livingstone this tribute: "I was converted by him, although he had not tried to do it."

Unwilling to leave with Stanley, Livingstone labored on in Africa until his death two years later. After burying his heart, Livingstone's African assistants embalmed his body and carried it to Zanzibar, despite being at risk from slave traders. Livingstone was sent to England, where he was buried in Westminster Abbey.

Livingstone had written extensively about his travels and his books propelled him to the forefront of missionary history. Inspired by his example and armed with his advice, others set off for missionary work in Africa for the purpose of religious conquest. Many perished, helpless in the face of the diseases that had beset white men and women since exploration of Africa began.

The barriers to missionaries remained constant. The Muslims in North Africa were resistant to Christian advances, although that did not stop Roman Catholic Archbishop Charles Lavigerie of Algiers in his enthusiastic efforts. In 1868 he launched the White Fathers, who lived largely in the same manner as local people but failed to make an impact. Extending the mission to East and West Africa was more successful.

However, the slave trade had made the people of West Africa supremely suspicious of white faces. Portuguese missionaries, active in the region long after other nations withdrew, made some headway on behalf of the Catholic Church, but progress was slow. White settlers in southern Africa helped to spread Christianity, largely the Protestant variety.

Despite the difficulties, missionaries were enormously successful. Africa has more than 350 million Christians within its shores out of a population of some 766.6 million.

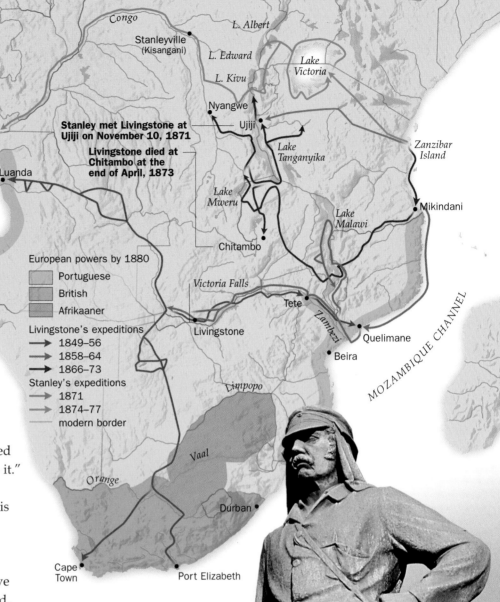

Stanley met Livingstone at Ujiji on November 10, 1871

Livingstone died at Chitambo at the end of April, 1873

European powers by 1880
- Portuguese
- British
- Afrikaaner

Livingstone's expeditions
- 1849–56
- 1858–64
- 1866–73

Stanley's expeditions
- 1871
- 1874–77
- modern border

Congo · Stanleyville (Kisangani) · L. Albert · L. Edward · L. Kivu · Lake Victoria · Nyangwe · Ujiji · Lake Tanganyika · Zanzibar Island · Mikindani · Lake Mweru · Lake Malawi · Chitambo · Luanda · Victoria Falls · Tete · Livingstone · Zambezi · Quelimane · Beira · MOZAMBIQUE CHANNEL · Limpopo · Vaal · Orange · Durban · Cape Town · Port Elizabeth

LIVINGSTONE 1873

Rastafarianism

Ethiopia's emperor, Haile Selassie, was a reluctant god to a foreign people. He was adopted as a divinity by the infant Rastafarian movement—even though he was a practicing Christian. Rastafarians, believing themselves to be the reincarnation of the Israelites, cherish his memory.

In 50 years of existence, Rastafarianism has defined itself as a low-key, largely contented religion, yet it has become associated with the appalling violence endemic in Jamaica and other black areas. The roots of Rastafarianism lay in the burgeoning Black Nationalist movement of the 1920s. One prominent campaigner is given credit for its inception.

Marcus Garvey (1887–1940) founded the

BELOW: Marcus Garvey, seen here riding in an open limousine during a Harlem parade, styled himself president of the Empire of Africa.

Universal Negro Improvement Association in his homeland of Jamaica, but failed to garner popular support. In 1916 he traveled to America, where blacks had long been oppressed. Support for the UNIA quickly escalated—membership topped the 2,000,000 mark within three years.

Garvey promoted the idea of a black-governed nation in Africa. This was in the age of imperialism, in which the continent had been divided between colonial European powers. Further, he hailed black heroes from the past, revered black culture that until then had been largely overlooked, and established a string of black-owned businesses, including hotels, shops, restaurants, and a printing press.

Two of Garvey's central themes proved controversial. He actively supported a policy of a return by blacks to Africa—no matter that black families had lived in America for several generations—and placed great emphasis on racial purity. He lent his support to the white supremacists of the Ku Klux Klan at a time when they were gaining in power and influence. Naturally, the flamboyant entrepreneur was opposed by other black leaders of the era.

His downfall finally came about when he was jailed for a mail fraud relating to one of his companies. In 1927 Garvey was released following a two-year spell behind bars and deported, dying in obscurity.

Garvey had, however, succeeded in giving black people in America and Jamaica a sense of empowerment. A young black king would one day take the throne in Africa and welcome exiles home, he declared. He perhaps had himself in mind, having declared that he was president of the Empire of Africa when he was riding high in Harlem.

THE RISE OF SELASSIE

To others it seemed Garvey's prophecy was fulfilled when Haile Selassie (1892–1974) became Emperor of Ethiopia in 1930. Born Tafari Makonnen, he was the son of a royal advisor and an able scholar who won the patronage of Emperor Menelik II. He eventually married one of Menelik's great granddaughters, Wayzaro Menen.

Menelik was succeeded by his grandson Lij Yasu, but the incoming emperor was a Muslim and remained unpopular among the largely Christian population. Within three years Makonnen staged a coup, Menelik's daughter was named empress, and Makonnen was her heir, Ras (prince) Tafari. In the years before he became emperor, Makonnen showed remarkable

diplomatic and political skills.

However, Makonnen largely dispensed with government when he achieved power. He took the name Haile Selassie, meaning "might of the trinity," but was also lauded with titles including Lord of Lords, King of

Kings, and the Lion of Judah. Black nationalists worldwide thought of him as Jah, a word derived from Jehovah or Jahweh. To them he was the Messiah who would redeem the black race through repatriation and create a heaven on Earth.

The Rastafarian agenda was first announced in 1953. Since then the importance of blacks returning to Africa has been played down and the Zion they frequently allude to is generally taken as a spiritual contentment. It remains a most relaxed religion with little by way of dogma. The most visible ritual is the smoking of cannabis, for which they have attracted constant trouble in countries where soft drug use is prohibited.

Rastafarians can be distinguished by their dreadlocks and often wear a hat in the colors of the Ethiopian flag—red, gold, and green, often with the addition of black. They express themselves and their aims musically through reggae, with the most renowned Rastafarians being Bob Marley and Peter Tosh.

ABOVE: A statue of reggae singer Bob Marley stands at the entrance to the museum named after him in Kingston, Jamaica. Marley became the iconic Rastafarian, sporting dreadlocks and woolen hats in the colors of the Ethiopian flag.

LEFT: Emperor of Ethiopia Haile Selassie attends a military parade in 1974. His 45-year rule was interrupted when he was exiled by the Italian occupation between 1936 and 1941.

CHAPTER 5

Europe

A map of Europe is alive with Christianity, yet the face of faith on the continent might have looked very different if rivals had flourished. One of the most likely candidates in the fourth century was the Manichaean Church. Its founder Mani (216–c.274), who lived in Persia, believed himself to be one in a long line of prophets that included Buddha, Zoroaster, and Jesus. He claimed his faith to be universal and that followers of other religions had lost their way. The Manichaean Church was exported across Asia and Africa and made significant inroads to Europe.

By the fourth century, with missionaries traveling from established bases in Spain and Gaul, the influence of Manichaeanism was at its height. But it could not withstand the combined opposition of the Christian Church and the Roman Empire. Within a century it had vanished from Europe, although it lived on in the Far East for some time.

Christian forces kept Europe closed to Muslims too, who earnestly spread the message of Mohammed after the seventh century. There has long been speculation that had it not been for the Frankish forces of Charles Martel driving back the Moors (Battle of Poitiers, 732), Europe would now be peppered with mosques rather than churches.

The 11th-century schism that split the Christian Church between east and west caused bad feeling that has taken centuries to repair. When Pope John Paul II visited Romania in 2000, it was the first time a pontiff had visited a predominantly Orthodox country since the schism.

Typically, the Christian Church of the Middle Ages would brook no opposition from without or within. When its promise of salvation was not enough to compel the faithful into unquestioning devotion, popes resorted to the use of force, hence the advent of the Inquisition in the 13th century.

The Reformation in England and Europe ultimately had a starburst effect on the continent's religions. Many new faiths were launched, some under the umbrella of established Churches and some in isolation. The success stories are those that have endured beside the ubiquity of Christianity.

The religions of medieval Europe c.1200

Roman Catholic Christians		†	archbishopric
Orthodox Christians		•	Cluniac/Benedictine monastery
Cathar heretics		•	Cistercian monastery
Bogomil (Manichaean) heretics		•	other monastery
Muslim lands			pagan
⊕	patriarchal see		border c.1200
†	Orthodox metropolitan see		

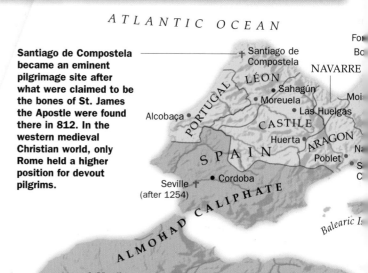

Santiago de Compostela became an eminent pilgrimage site after what were claimed to be the bones of St. James the Apostle were found there in 812. In the western medieval Christian world, only Rome held a higher position for devout pilgrims.

A Muslim army under the leadership of the Umayyad dynasty conquered most of Spain from the Christian Visigoths between AD 711 and 800. The Moors (from *Maurus*, people of Mauritania) were engaged by forces of the Holy Roman Empire between AD 1000 and 1250 in the *reconquista* of Spain, during which period the Umayyads were defeated by the Muslim Almoravid dynasty, and they in turn fell to the Almohads. The last Moorish bastion in Spain, Granada, fell in 1492 to Christian forces under the command of Ferdinand and Isabella, the monarchs who sponsored Christopher Columbus to cross the Atlantic in search of the Indies. Instead, he discovered the Americas, a vast new land ripe for the export of Christianity, Spanish style.

The Romans adopted the Greeks' chief god Zeus, but named him Jove or Jupiter. Unlike the capricious Zeus, Jove was a model of Roman rectitude, an image of Imperial tolerance.

Christian extremists: in the 14th century the terrible plague known as the Black Death swept across Europe, bringing in its wake a mixture of horror and fervor. No sect was more extreme than the Flagellants, who did penance for the sins of the world by beating themselves.

Iceland

Faroe Islands

Shetland Islands

Orkney Islands

NORWEGIAN SEA

FINNS

NORWAY

GULF OF BOTHNIA

FINNS

† Nidaros (Trondheim)

Hovedø

SWEDEN

FINNS

Lake Onega

Lake Lagoda

† Uppsala

Gulf of Finland

NOVGOROD

† Novgorod

Volga

SCOTLAND

• Dunfermline
• Fountains
• Lindisfarne
— Mount Grace
— Rievaulx
† York

ENGLAND

NORTH SEA

Borglum †

DENMARK

• Alvastra
• Nydala

ESTONIANS

Lake Peipus

† Riga

BALTIC SEA

POLOTSK

SMOLENSK

CHERNIGOV

Løgum †

Esrom •
Holm •

Lund †

LITHUANIANS

• Peterborough
• Bury St. Edmunds

Lübeck •

• Doberan

PRUS

TUROV-PINSK

KIEV

PEREYASLAV

• London
† Canterbury

Bremen •

Hamburg •
Hildesheim •

Bukowo •

Oliwa •
Pelplin •

Gniezno •

HOLY
Mountain

† Rouen
Premontré •
† Reims

Gembloux †

Corvey •

Cologne †

Magdeburg •

Chorin •

Lubiaz •

• Lad

Brogne —

Trier —

Fulda •

Pforta •

Mainz †

POLAND

† Wachock

Kiev †

Fleury

Gorze —

Bingen —

Prague †

Sulejów •

VOLHYNIA

to Kiev

Clairvaux
Vézelay

Ratisbon •

Sazawa •

Krakow •

GALICIA

CUMAN TURKS

Besançon †

St. Gall †

HOLY ROMAN

Szepes •

Volga

Lyon †

Salzburg †

EMPIRE

Borsmonostor •

† Milan

Grand Chartreuse

Venice †

Aquileia †

Esztergom •

Jak •

Zirc •

Kalosca †

SEA OF AZOV

CASPIAN SEA

• Reggio

Genoa †

Ravenna †

Tupuszco •

HUNGARY

Belákut •

Bosphorus •

Aix-en-Provence

Pisa †

Siena •

Camaldoli •

Split •

Danube

† Pliska

† Cherson

Corsica

Farfa •

Rome ⊕

Subiaco •

Ragusa †

Sardica •

† Mesembria

BLACK SEA

† Alania

Fossanova •

Benevento •

Monte Casino †

† Bari

† Dyrrhacium

Philippopolis †

Neocaesarea †

† Coloneia

GEORGIA

Naples †

Taranto †

Prespa •

Adrianople •

Salerno

Rossano •

Thessalonica †

ANATOLIA

Palermo •

Cosenza †

Mt. Athos †

⊕ Constantinople

Claudiopolis †

Ankara †

Messina •

Reggio †

BYZANTINE EMPIRE

SELJUK TURKS

Sardinia

Brindisi †

Sicily

Syracuse •

Patras †

Lucas •

Daphne †

Chios •

† Mytilene

Smyrna •

† Cotyaeum

Laodicea †

Malta

Ephesus †

† Rhodes

Crete

† Candia

Cyprus

M E D I T E R R A N E A N   S E A

The three Crusader States, founded after the First Crusade of 1097–99, had survived for less than two centuries when Acre finally fell to Muslim forces in 1291.

⊕ Antioch

PRINCIPALITY OF ANTIOCH

MESOPOTAMIA

Euphrates

Tigris

Constantia †

COUNTY OF TYRE

Tyre †

One of the earliest of Christian monasteries, St. Catherine's was founded in the fourth century AD on the reputed site of the Burning Bush and under Mount Moses (Sinai), where the prophet received the Ten Commandments. A community of 12 Greek Orthodox monks still resides there.

Caesarea †

Jerusalem ⊕

KINGDOM OF JERUSALEM

Alexandria ⊕

A Y Y U B I D   S U L T A N T A T E

• Cairo

Nile

EGYPT

St. Catherine's (Mount Sinai) ⊕

RED SEA

The Dawn of Man

Defining the period when our ancestors first began to hold religious beliefs is one of the most controversial and fascinating areas of modern archaeology. With Europe, we can't even be sure of religious practice 5,000 years ago, let alone rituals dating from the dawn of humanity.

This jaw bone and teeth of a pre-Neanderthal Man date from some point between 200,000 and 300,000 years ago. The jaw is part of the massive collection of Paleolithic era bones found in a pit near Atapuerca, Spain. The good condition of the remaining teeth suggests that the jaw bone is that of an adolescent.

There is no doubt that early prehistoric rituals did occur and that they represented a rudimentary form of religion. At Atapuerca in northern Spain more than 1,600 bones have been recovered, the remains of between 32 and 50 individuals. They were mostly adolescents and young adults from a transitional period in human evolution between *Homo erectus* and Neanderthal Man, making them at least 200,000 years old.

The bodies had been thrown down a 40-foot pit known locally as Sima de los Huesos, or Pit of Bones. Other than a ritual burial, there is no obvious explanation for this site. It was never occupied for any length of time and the bones were not brought there by carnivorous animals.

By the Ice Age (c.12,000 years ago) our true ancestor, *Homo sapiens*, was delving into more complex supernatural ideas. The evidence comes from some extraordinary European cave art, most notably at Lascaux, Dordogne, the Chauvet cavern in Ardeche, and Altamira, northern Spain—all finds that have contributed toward a major re-think on the motives of Stone Age artists.

Archaeologists now believe the pictures represent far more than random images of hunting and that they were drawn and re-touched during spurts of creative genius at various times throughout the last Ice Age. Interpretation is complex but most experts agree that the images are linked to a religious belief or mythology. Certainly the use of caves as places of worship was relatively common in the ancient world.

STANDING STONES—AND WOOD

By late Neolithic times (c.3000 BC) a new religious trend was firmly established in Western Europe: the raising of standing stones, stone circles, and huge burial chambers. The stone rows at Carnac, northwest France consist of thousands of

RIGHT: Stonehenge in the south of England is probably the best-known of the prehistoric stone rings, or henges. Their use as a seasonal calendar is now widely accepted, but evidence of ritual sacrifice has been discovered at many other British henge sites, including the skulls of women and children.

megalithic monuments arranged in three distinct groups. Their original purpose will probably never be known, although local legend links them to fire or sun worship (supported by the recovery of charred material at the bases of many). Though some stones might have been set for astronomical observations, the rows are too imprecise in their arrangement to be of value. More likely, Carnac was an important burial site and center of ancestor worship.

At Stonehenge in southern England, the greatest of Europe's prehistoric structures, the case for astronomical use is much stronger. Stonehenge would have allowed the prediction of eclipses, summer and winter solstices, and changes in the seasons—effectively serving as a giant calendar. To a primitive farming society, such knowledge would have been akin to direct communication with the gods, elevating priests to an extremely powerful position. The circular nature of the structure perhaps also reflected the cycle of birth and death, or the passing of the seasons. Given the huge quantity of labor required to build it, its importance as a religious and ceremonial center cannot be understated.

The first blocks were erected at Stonehenge around 4,800 years ago, although the main building phase began 700 years later with the man-hauling of 82 "bluestones" from the Preseli hills, 130 miles away in southwest Wales. At some point the Celtic Druids used the circle. They may

have been the incumbents when Roman invaders pulled down some blocks, possibly to destroy a symbol of British resistance.

At about the time the bluestones were being erected, an even more mysterious structure was taking shape off the Norfolk coast in eastern England. This recently discovered site, known as Seahenge, was then on dry land. It comprises 55 wooden posts surrounding an upturned oak tree and was built by the Saami people from Finland. They apparently believed in a parallel, upside-down universe—one more lost religion from a European landscape rich with belief.

ABOVE: Cave painting of a bull, horse, and other animals from Lascaux, France. Whatever interpretation is placed on the proliferation of paintings like these, there is no denying the skill of the Paleolithic artists who created these images. Sadly, in order to preserve the caves and images, visitors may now only view replica paintings.

Stonehenge is only one of over a hundred large stone circles in the British Isles. Several in the vicinity of the famous monument include Avebury Ring and Nine Stones. The northwest and northeast of England also have many prehistoric sites.

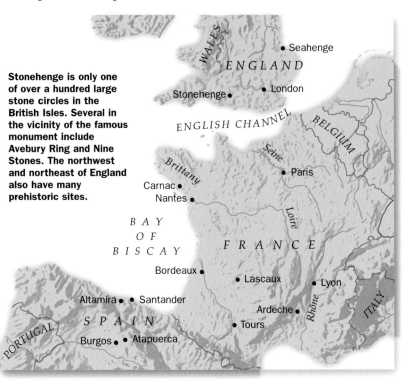

Gods *of the* Greeks

The Greek gods were as familiar as family to the Athenians of centuries ago. People were in awe of their adventures, comforted by their compassion, and smiled at their humor. They built extravagant treasures like the Parthenon to honor the gods.

Although the rational nature of Greek philosophy after the fifth century BC put the old religion in jeopardy, it was revived by the Romans and thus survived. Zeus was the god-father, by turns kindly, kingly, benevolent, and fierce. Armed with a thunderbolt and accompanied by an eagle, he was associated with the weather. Zeus was not perceived as a perfect being— indeed, he was well known for philandering with both mortal and immortal women. Hera was his partner: jealous, vindictive, and the goddess of marriage.

There were 12 leading deities— Zeus, Hera, Poseidon, Demeter, Aphrodite, Artemis, Athena, Apollo, Ares, Helios, Hermes, and Dionysus—and others who achieved a lesser ranking in the celestial hierarchy. All were subject to human emotions and dilemmas but dealt with them using supernatural powers. Poseidon, brother of Zeus, was god of the sea, Ares was god of war, Demeter goddess of agriculture, and Apollo the god of the sun. They resided on Mount Olympus, highest of the Greek mountains, along with the other deities, who were typically associated with realms of nature or extreme emotion.

People of Ancient Greece paid homage to the gods by way of sacrifice and ritual to secure benefits in this life, not the next. Those who did not deliver due respect could expect retribution both from the gods and fellow humans. The Olympic Games, first recorded in the eighth century BC, were initially held at Olympia to honor Zeus.

To determine the will of the gods it was necessary to visit an oracle, the most famous being at Delphi on the slopes of Mount Parnassus, devoted to Apollo. A medium resided at the Oracle, known as the Pythia, who indulged in strict ritual and imparted her prophecies while perched on a sacred tripod, chewing the leaves of a special laurel tree. At the peak of her fame in the seventh and sixth centuries BC she was consulted by lawmakers, military men, and civic leaders to divine the most auspicious course of action. At Dodona an oracle devoted to Zeus discerned heavenly messages by listening to the whispering of the leaves upon a sacred oak tree.

FAITH VERSUS PHILOSOPHY

The antics and adventures of the gods were extensive and these myths became a central part of Greek life. Greece went on to develop a literary tradition that was years ahead of its time. Doubtless it was the re-telling of the Olympus myths that contributed with this phenomenal growth of epic poems, plays, and stories.

A strong and significant school of philosophy emerged after the fifth century BC, which wielded influence in the West for generations. The influence of the Olympian gods diminished amid discussion of ideas like democracy, justice, life, and death.

Eminent philosopher Socrates (469–399 BC) was sentenced to death for, among other charges, "neglect of the gods." Such was the superstitious nature of Greek religion, his execution, by the intake of paralyzing hemlock, was delayed until a sacred ship arrived at the port of Athens. Socrates apparently believed in an all-powerful God through personal revelation and the everyday miracles of nature. He was convinced that out of his earthly body he would "receive the joys of the blessed" and become immortal. However, even the firmly rooted Socrates was moved to pray to the gods before his death, "that my departure hence be a fortunate one."

The Greeks' religion, as well as their literature and philosophy, was taken abroad by the roving marauder, Alexander the Great (356–23 BC). He first toppled the Persians, time-honored enemies of the Greeks, and ended up undertaking one of the most extensive campaigns ever, taking in vast tracts of Asia and Africa. Addled by drink, Alexander declared himself a god in his final years and ordered his subjects to worship him.

Greek religious sites, 1100–500 BC

Argos (**Hera**)	religious site and associated deity

The Roman Empire

Religion in the Roman Empire had as many different identities as the races conquered by foot-weary legionnaires. Rome began with its own faith, mythology, and superstitions and adopted many more as its territories grew.

BELOW: Mythology says that the world and all its wonders came into being after Mithras reluctantly slaughtered a white bull, thus he is perceived as the creator. Images of Mithras abound in later Roman periods, especially wherever concentrations of legionaries were housed. This second-century AD statue was found near Budapest.

FACING: The Pantheon was begun in 27 BC and rebuilt some 130 years later by the emperor Hadrian. Its perfectly hemispherical dome is constructed from concrete.

The Romans manifested their respect for deities in monuments. From the ruins in the Forum evident today, we know they worshipped, among others, Castor and Pollux, Mars, Minerva, Saturn, and Vesta. Alongside the buildings devoted to gods were equally great edifices honoring Roman emperors. Rulers were keen to pave their way to celestial greatness and prepared the ground for the deification that generally followed their deaths.

But the true religion of the early Romans is difficult to distil. After the empire took in Greece there was a wide-ranging embrace of Hellenistic culture, which included gods and rituals. The chief god known to the Greeks as Zeus became Jupiter, or Jove. Hera became Juno, while Diana usurped the Grecian Artemis. It is at this time that most of the fabulous commemorative buildings appeared.

What occurred prior to the Imperial age, before the spread of Greek culture, has largely been lost in the passage of time. It seems likely that the early Romans venerated nature and objects that were considered to possess supernatural powers. Their word for the sacred was *numen* and bloody sacrifice was almost certainly part of ritual worship. Etruscans, who dominated before the Romans came to power, were unusually devoted to religious rites.

The Roman citizen sought a peaceful, productive relationship with the gods. Therefore, there was due reverence paid to those on high, in order to establish mutual trust. People lived by a code of rules that delineated good practice from bad. But gods were kept at a distance and did not appear to play a significant part in everyday life. There was no powerful body of priests to browbeat ordinary people into prayer.

Those who sought a more meaningful relationship with the deities turned to the numerous Eastern cults of the era, including the Egyptian goddess Isis, Cybele from Anatolia, and Atargatis, a fertility goddess of Syria. One of the most enduring was Mithraism, popular among Roman soldiers. This faith had been imported from Persia and dates back to a time before the Roman Empire was established. However, it was overhauled and updated when it emerged in Roman culture.

TOLERANT RULE

Before he converted to Christianity, the emperor Constantine worshipped the Sun God, in common with many Romans. The Romans were surprisingly tolerant of different religions. Given the years of Roman mastery (some 800) and the extent of the empire, this was perhaps a matter of necessity. Judaism was tolerated and so, as a sect, was Christianity. There are no recorded examples of fundamentalist centurions compelling conquered peoples to worship in the Roman way.

This laxity permitted certain emperors to capitalize on religion. Augustus brought it to the fore in his reign to shore up his power base. People were quickly convinced that their neglect of the old religion had brought about years of civil strife. Worshipping gods—and the implication was that Augustus himself was a deity—would right wrongs, and indeed this newfound fervor did induce a period of peace. However, despite a centuries-old heritage, Roman religion failed to endure.

In Rome the fate of the Pantheon was symptomatic of the fate of the pagan faith. As a "shrine to the gods" it was a magnificent example of marbled classical architecture. No one knows how it was constructed but it boasted a dome 144 feet in diameter and walls 19 feet thick. A circular hole at its pinnacle, the *oculus*, illuminated statues of the gods standing in niches around the walls. However, in 609 it was dedicated as the Church of the Sancta Maria ad Martyres.

Old Norse Religion

Until missionaries began targeting Scandinavia in the early tenth century, the Vikings rejoiced in a faith that catered to their whims, promised hedonistic rewards in the afterlife, and explained everything from the dawn of creation to the end of the world.

The Norse had gods for every trade, pastime, and profession—gods for war and pillage, for kings and the wise, for blacksmiths, brewers, cattle breeders and brides, for poets and traders, soldiers and sailors, executed prisoners, and even "men on skis." All these deities had specific powers, yet these seemed to overlap to the point that Odin's man, Thor's man, Frey's man *et al* could be assured of all-embracing supernatural care.

The religion had little formal organization and no vocational priesthood. There appears to have been a heavy emphasis on myth (as opposed to natural phenomena, such as heavenly bodies and nature), although our knowledge is limited and therefore questionable. Much of what is known comes from two famous works: the poem *Völuspá*, composed early in the 11th century, and the *Edda*, dating from around AD 1220. Along with later associated volumes, these tell of a great void called Ginnungagap that divided the shadowy, sinister realm of death (Niflheim) from the fiery kingdom of Muspell, governed by the giant Surt.

When the 11 rivers of Niflheim froze, the explosive combination of fire and ice created the giant Ymir, whose sweating left armpit produced offspring. Ymir survived by drinking the milk of his cow Audumbla, while she produced the first human, Buri, by literally licking him into shape from the

VALHALLA AND THE KINGDOM OF GOD IN CO-EXISTENCE

Having been the scourge of Christianity for 200 years after 795, the Viking homelands of Sweden, Norway, and Denmark became a target for Christian missionaries. In the mid-tenth century the Danish king Harald Bluetooth finally adopted Christianity on behalf of his people, as a result of observing a miracle. The new religion was firmly established by the start of the 11th century. The Vikings probably accepted the Christian faith because their own pagan beliefs were so loose—Christ was just another useful ally in the daily struggle.

Archaeological evidence backs up this somewhat cavalier approach to the new faith. An enterprising mid-tenth-century artisan from Trendgården in Denmark's Jutland peninsula left behind a soapstone mold (right) that had allowed him to produce two religious emblems at the same time: a small Christian crucifix and a model of Thor's hammer. This archaeological testimony shows that the two religions existed side by side for some considerable time before Denmark officially became a Christian kingdom late in the tenth century. Thor's hammer, Mjöllnir, which returned to the god's hand whenever he threw it, was a popular Viking charm that meant much the same to Vikings as the cross does to Christians.

ice. Buri's son Bor married a giantess and fathered three sons by her: Odin, Vili, and Ve.

Later the brothers killed Ymir and made the earth from his flesh; lakes, rivers, and sea from his blood; mountains from his skeleton; boulders from his teeth; the sky from his skull; and clouds from his brain. They created the stars, sun, and moon from sparks and arranged for wolves to chase the sun across the sky, so producing night and day.

HEAVENS AND HEL

There were three principal kingdoms of the living. Midgard, where the first man and woman, Ask and Embla, procreated the human race; Jotunheim, land of the giants, which lay across a vast ocean; and above the clouds Asgard, home of the gods, with its feasting hall Valhalla (Hall of the Slain).

It was to Valhalla that maidens known as Valkyries brought the spirits of the bravest mortal warriors from the battlefield. Every day, these men would fight on meadows outside the hall and every evening the slain would rise again to feast with the victors on sumptuous pork and mead courtesy of Odin, leader of the Norse gods. Those not worthy went down to Hel, where monsters lurked. This is a wonderfully colorful picture of the afterlife, but Norse beliefs on this—as on other aspects of religion—varied enormously.

Linking the realms of men, giants, and the dead were the roots and branches of the great tree Yggdrasil—the World Tree—destined to survive until the world's end. Scandinavian mythology is very clear on doomsday, foretelling the rise of the fire giants and their allies; and the death of Odin in the jaws of the wolf Fenrir, Frey by the dazzling sword of Surt, and Thor by the fangs of a snake. Yet out of this chaos would emerge a new order, led by surviving sons of the gods.

Norse worship was originally convened in the open, beside sacred trees or wells or within standing stones. Later, wooden temples were built, complete with carved statues of the gods, and family or communal ceremonies and feasts were held. The greatest of these, at Old Uppsala, Sweden, has yielded traces of both animal and human sacrifice.

Christianity *in the* Middle Ages

"My feet are as toads, for I stood in sin: a serpent creepeth forth by the lowers parts of my stomach unto the higher parts, for my lust was inordinate…. My breast is open and gnawed with worms for I loved foul and rotten things more than God."

Hell loomed large for people of the medieval era. Fervid imaginations were fed with horrors like the scene of torment above, provided by the fifth-century St. Bridget who was supposedly illuminated on the sufferings in Hell by a vision of one of the damned. There was complete certainty about the existence of Hell and its function as the destination of wrong-doers by the God-fearing folk of the Middle Ages, who were haunted by images of the Devil and his henchmen. Humans were most vulnerable to these lurking evil spirits when they lay on their death beds, as art of the era reveals.

Some chose to display their piety and penance in extended prayer. The other option was a pilgrimage, a trek to sites made famous by the lives—and deaths—

of an ever-growing number of saints. Frequently the aim was to pay homage to a relic, a body part of a saint, which were highly valued artifacts thought to deliver cures, as well as forgiveness.

For all the goodness these relics inspired, there was a grim reality behind their very existence. The corpses of saints were chopped to pieces to provide enough to go around. This was done soon after the death of a Godly man or woman—or their bodies were later exhumed for the purpose.

Given that the presence of a relic was sufficient to revive the economy of a small town, the scope for forgery was immense. During the Middle Ages some of the most venerated objects included the Holy Tunic, which the Virgin Mary allegedly wore while giving birth; tears, blood, and even the

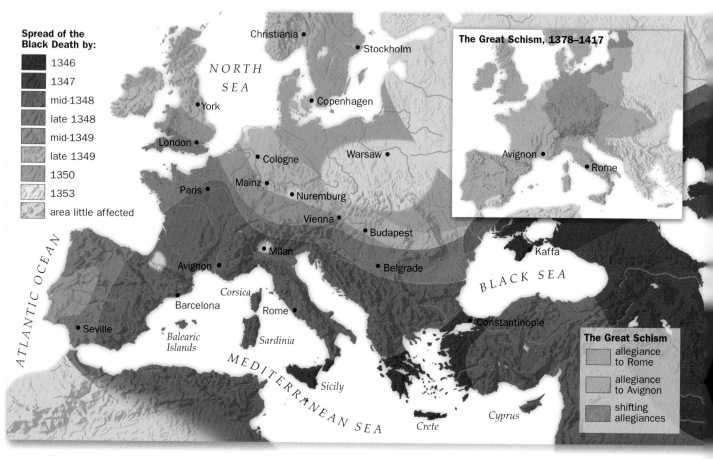

Spread of the Black Death by:

- 1346
- 1347
- mid-1348
- late 1348
- mid-1349
- late 1349
- 1350
- 1353
- area little affected

The Great Schism, 1378–1417

The Great Schism
- allegiance to Rome
- allegiance to Avignon
- shifting allegiances

circumcised foreskin of Jesus; hands, nails, nipples, whole skeletons, and fragments of bones from the saints. All were revered by the faithful across Europe in large numbers. In retrospect this seems grisly and naïve, yet so real did the threats of disease, death, and Hell appear according to beliefs of the time that people were desperate to find any link with Godliness that could offer salvation.

PAPAL CONFLICT

The Black Death reached Europe in 1347 from the East, probably transmitted through fleas traveling on rats. Estimates that between a third and a half of Europe's population died are not exaggerated. Gruesome scenes of bodies piling up in the streets, houses boarded up, and villages left deserted as all its inhabitants succumbed or fled were reported throughout the continent.

Traumatized by the desolation, fearful survivors believed the dreadful scourge was sent as punishment by God. A consequence was the emergence of flagellants, who walked the towns bare-chested and whipped themselves in the hope of appeasing the wrath of God.

The Church, meanwhile, had problems of its own. Civil unrest in Italy had persuaded successive Catholic popes to reside at Avignon in France instead of Rome. The move also reflected the ascendancy of France and so was politically unpopular abroad. Between 1309 and 1377 all elected popes were French and chose to remain in France where the lifestyle was opulent. Worse was to follow. After Urban VI (p.1378–89) was chosen as pope in Rome, the cardinals grew concerned for his mental fitness for the post. His election was declared invalid and Clement VII (p.1378–94) was picked as his successor. However, Urban refused to go quietly. He excommunicated his rival and established a ring of cardinals of his own so there were two elected popes. Attempts to resolve the crisis in 1409 only led to the election of a third pope.

Christianity was in chaos, with numerous allegiances being formed and broken. Only after the Council of Constance (1414–18) was a solution agreed when compromise candidate Martin V (p.1417–31) took office.

The Crusades *and* Papal Control

Muslims in Jerusalem had generally lived peaceably with Christian and Jewish populations since the seventh century. The Seljuk Turks who invaded in the late 11th century, however, attacked Christian sites and people at a time when Westerners were looking for an excuse to conquer new lands.

The Byzantine Empire, battered by the advances of the Seljuk Turks since a disastrous defeat at Manzikert, Armenia in 1071, appealed to the papacy for help in 1095. This was an opportunity for the fragmenting Church to unite under a common cause and reassert papal control across Europe. The same year, Pope Urban II (p.1088–99) held an address in Clermont, France, calling kings, princes, knights, and noblemen to "exterminate this vile race from the lands of your eastern brethren." Those who fought for the Holy Land were assured of forgiveness of their sins.

The crusaders achieved significant victories, taking Nicaea, Dorylaeum, and Antioch from the Turks before arriving at Jerusalem in 1099. They laid siege on June 8; 38 days later they overran the city and slaughtered every Muslim they found. Subsequent expeditions were equally ruthless, but greed began to replace the high ideals. The noblemen used the Crusades to increase their assets and territory as they drove Muslims from these lands and the Crusader States were established, led by a king of Jerusalem.

Christianity became more pro-active with the formation of the Military Orders, Knights of St. John of Jerusalem (the Hospitallers) in 1113 and the Knights Templar in 1119. Faced with such a sustained onslaught, Muslim armies unified and won decisive battles, and took back land wrested from them in the First Crusade. The Second Crusade, launched in 1146, was singularly unsuccessful in its aims to retake these territories.

By the time the Third Crusade was initiated in 1187 by Pope Gregory VIII, the Muslims were fighting under the inspired leadership of Saladin and had regained control of Jerusalem. Despite the efforts of Philip II of France, Holy Roman Emperor Frederick I, and King Richard I, the Lionheart, the venture failed to liberate Jerusalem,

although Richard agreed a three-year truce with Saladin.

In 1204 the influential trading center of Venice and the Holy Roman Empire redirected the Fourth Crusade from Alexandria to sack the city of Constantinople, seat of the eastern branch of Christianity. Pope Innocent III (p.1198–1216) was horrified. The initial Christian cause had become hopelessly lost in an orgy of violence and greed. Crusades continued for another two centuries but made pitifully few gains, although new trade routes were created and previously unknown lands were explored with ultimately far-reaching consequences for Western expansion.

DEALING WITH HERESY

Between the 13th and 16th centuries successive popes used the Inquisition to quell dissension toward the Church. Otherwise known as the Holy Office, it was the brainchild of Pope Gregory IX, who announced its inception in 1231 to deal with the increasing numbers of heretics. These people were at odds with the Catholic interpretation of God's message and challenged papal supremacy.

The job of rooting out heretics was at first a secular post but was ultimately awarded to friars, who tackled it with zeal. By 1256 they were permitted by the pope to use torture to uncover the truth. Traveling from town to town the friars investigated heresy claims and presented their findings to juries of priests. It took the word of two witnesses to establish guilt. Those who confessed were allowed to live after making amends with a fine or extended prayer. Victims who maintained their innocence were handed over to local authorities to be burned at the stake. Through the Inquisition, vendettas were settled as neighbor turned on neighbor.

So blinkered was the Church that scientist Galileo Galilei was twice hauled before the Inquisition for his belief that the earth moved around the sun when the papacy had clearly stated that it was the other way around. In a bizarre act of censorship, Galileo was banned from discussing planetary movements.

Much of the north and east of Antioch was lost to the Seljuk Turks after the fall of Edessa, and the western was lost to the Byzantine Lesser Armenia after 1198.

King Richard the Lionheart captured Cyprus from the Christian Byzantines.

Castles of the Assassins. Although Muslims, the Shi'ite-Ismaili Assassins aided with the Christians against the Sunni Seljuk Turks.

The last crusader bastion, Acre, fell to the Muslims in May 1291.

Crusader castles between Kerak and Taba were sited to interfere with Muslim pilgrimage routes to Mecca. These were among the first to fall to the disciplined armies of Saladin in 1187 as he began to recover Palestine.

Mara • • Edessa •
• Turbessel
• Adana
Tarsus •
Mersin •
• Aleppo   *Euphrates*
St. Simeon • • Antioch
• Seleucia
• Marra
Latakia • • Saône
Margat •   • Hamah
• Famagusta   Tortosa •   • Homs
CYPRUS   Tripoli •
• Akrotiri
Beirut •
• Damascus
Sidon •
Tyre •
Acre •
Caiphas •   *Sea of Galilee*
Tiberias
• Asur
Nablus •
• Jaffa   • Ahamant
Jerusalem •
• Bethlehem
Ascalon •   *Dead Sea*
Gaza •
• Kerak
• Damietta

GREAT SELJUK SULTANATE

Principality of Antioch, 1098–1268
County of Edessa, 1098–1144
County of Tripoli, 1109–1289
Kingdom of Jerusalem, 1099–1187
Kingdom of Jerusalem after the Treaty of Jaffa, 1229
Kingdom of Lesser Armenia, 1198–1375

FATIMID CALIPHATE
Ayyubid dynasty after 1171 and the rise of Saladin

EGYPT   SINAI

• Aqaba
Taba •

The Reformation *in* England

In England the break with Catholicism was the product of Henry VIII's irascible nature. In the king's eyes papal power and Church doctrines amounted to corrupt interference, and he set about changing the religious face of the nation to suit his own needs.

When Henry VIII (r.1509-47) acceded to the throne he was 18 years old and, for the sake of expediency, agreed to marry his brother Arthur's widow, Catherine of Aragon, winning special papal dispensation to do so. She bore him five children but only one, Mary, survived. Henry was keen to sire a male heir so he began to search for a new wife and a convenient way of divorcing Catherine.

In Henry's eyes the matter could be simply resolved. It was against ecclesiastical law to marry the spouse of a sibling, thus the marriage should be annulled. But the pope refused to agree and, to Henry's wrath, he was trapped in wedlock. Henry exercised his able mind and realized his escape route lay in legislation. In a series of bold new laws, Henry and his subservient Parliament took the power of the Church away from Rome and home to England. The Act of Supremacy in 1534 made him head of the Church of England, establishing the notion of the Anglican Church.

Henry's subsequent excommunication from the Church of Rome had little effect, serving only to validate his increasingly vindictive attitude toward Catholicism. During the ensuing Reformation, Henry suppressed the monasteries so that wealth which would otherwise have gone to Rome came his way. With this new-found injection of money he lined his own pockets and bought the allegiance of the nobility, who might otherwise have challenged him.

The dissolution of the monasteries undoubtedly swept away corrupt practices, but with them went shelter, food, education, and care for the poor. Some of England's finest Gothic buildings were razed by royal decree. Destroyed with them were religious treasures and libraries.

Henry married Anne Boleyn but she too bore a daughter, Elizabeth. Boleyn was duly beheaded and replaced by Jane Seymour. This third queen died giving birth to a son.

REVERSALS OF ROYAL FAITH

Opposition against Rome had been voiced by others in Britain. Dutchman Desiderius Erasmus (1466–1536), the leading humanist of the day, who valued reason alongside Biblical piety, paid several visits to England during the Reformation era and created his own version of the New Testament in Cambridge. Catherine Parr, Henry's sixth and final wife, became a keen student of Erasmusian thought, but the majority of the public in England had yet to confront the issues that were already dividing the faithful across Europe.

There were numerous anomalies in England following the Reformation. While Henry believed wholeheartedly in his right to oppose Rome on matters directly affecting his rule, he was less persuaded about the merits of the new wave of Protestantism above the established Catholic Church. As a consequence Lutherans in England were burned as heretics under Henry's rule, while Catholics were beheaded if they failed to recognize his supremacy.

Issues became more clear-cut when his son Edward VI (r.1547–53) came to the throne. Although only ten, he was a committed Protestant, not least because his closest advisors were Protestant. The infant Anglican Church absorbed Protestant principles. Significantly, two Books of Common Prayer were published in 1549 and 1552, endorsing the new creed.

These developments were temporarily reversed when the sickly Edward died and his sister Mary (r.1553–58) came to the throne. Unlucky in love and fertility, with plain features and a personal bitterness about the way she and her mother had been treated, Mary was a dour monarch determined to re-establish pure Catholicism as the state religion. To this end, at least 287 Protestants were burned at the stake. Others were jailed or fled the country.

Mary's sister Elizabeth was persuaded of the legitimacy of the Protestant cause, and on becoming monarch she ruled with a degree of religious tolerance, although there remained a bias against Catholicism.

BELOW: Mary I of England earned her epithet of Bloody Mary. Her determined campaign to reinstate Catholicism led to many outspoken Protestants being burned at the stake. This portrait by Antonis Mor of 1554 shows her holding the red Tudor rose, a flower whose petals were said to have been stained by the blood of martyrs.

The Reformation *in* Europe

In the Middle Ages the Catholic Church enjoyed an unrivaled position of authority that touched on every area of life. But with power came corruption. The credibility gap between the ideals of the Bible and the reality of the Church slowly led to dissent.

BELOW: Four men whose vision threw Europe into a religious ferment: Martin Luther, John Wycliffe, John Calvin, and Jan Huss. Luther and Calvin capitalized on earlier work done by Wycliffe and Huss, who was burned as a heretic in 1416. His followers held out against the Catholics in Bohemia for 20 years.
FACING: In Switzerland, Zwingli led a war against Catholicism in which he was slain during the Battle of Kappel.

Above and beyond its spiritual duties, the Church levied taxes, owned as much as 40 percent of Europe's fertile lands, persecuted and punished the errant, and dictated moral standards. One of the first critics to question the dominion of the Church was John Wycliffe (c.1330–84) in England, whose followers were known as Lollards. The doubts he voiced about the standards of behavior among priests were embraced by religious reformer John Huss of Bohemia (1372–1415), who was eventually executed as a heretic.

A century later Martin Luther (1483–1546) laid down the most radical challenge against the Church to date. Like Wycliffe, he was disturbed by the practice of selling indulgences, by which people were forgiven sins for a forfeit of money that went into priests' coffers. His objections were set out in the 95 Theses which he dramatically nailed to the door of a church in Wittenburg, Germany in 1517 for all to see. Pressure exerted by the papacy to have him recant failed. Indeed, his opposition to the Church became increasingly focused and vocal. He was excommunicated and declared an outlaw following the Diet (assembly) of Worms.

While Luther was provoking outrage among Germany's princes and priests, the peasants were seized by the idea and the issue led to an uprising. Luther found himself unable to wholeheartedly support the peasants who, he felt, were misinterpreting his message. However, the resulting Lutheranism soon found a secure foothold in the north of Germany. A compromise was reached in 1526 which permitted German princes to follow this new theology. When the agreement was overturned three years later, the Lutherans protested—and were consequently given the title of Protestants.

The bitter gulf between Catholics and Protestants in Germany existed until the Peace of Augsburg was drawn up in 1555, which allowed rulers of the country's 300 or so principalities to choose which faith their subjects would follow. The result was effectively an equal split between Catholic and Protestant regions.

TECHNOLOGY SPEEDS REFORM
Luther succeeded where Wycliffe had failed, not least because the advent of printing had ensured a wider distribution of information. Society was also changing. The Renaissance was spreading from Italy across Europe and with it came new philosophies, such as humanism, which emphasized the worth of individuality. A revolution in science also gathered momentum. Fresh attitudes and new ways of thinking were welcomed.

Lutheranism did not stay within the borders of Germany but spread to Scandinavia, Holland, and Switzerland, where pastor Huldreich Zwingli galvanized the people against Catholicism. After Zwingli was slain in a religious war, French-born John Calvin (1509–64) stepped forward to lead reform. However, his Protestantism turned out to be equally as tyrannical as the Catholic Church had been. Calvin was instrumental in establishing Geneva as a Protestant state where standards of dress and behavior were strictly governed by the Church. Those who objected were punished and even put to death. John Knox (1513–72), the founder of Scottish Presbyterianism, encountered Calvin in Geneva and adopted many of his ideas.

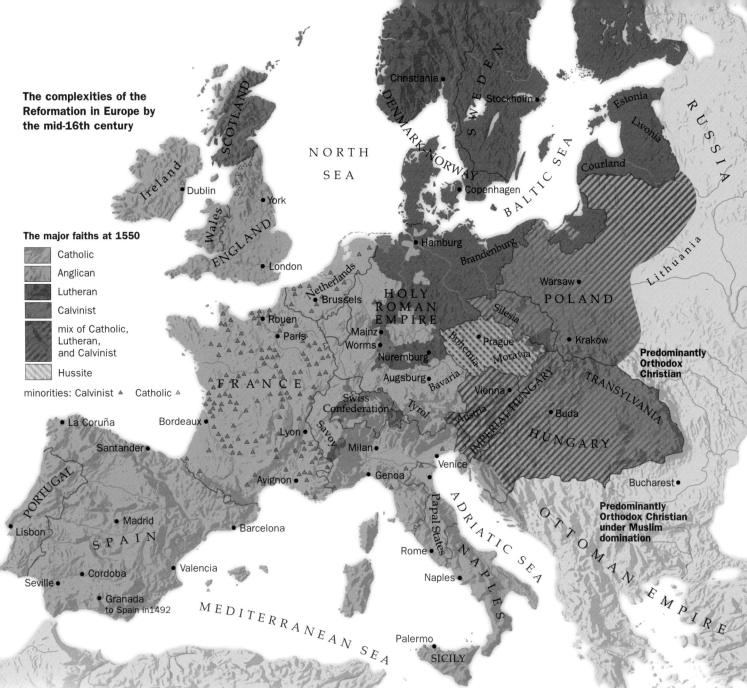

The complexities of the Reformation in Europe by the mid-16th century

The major faiths at 1550

- Catholic
- Anglican
- Lutheran
- Calvinist
- mix of Catholic, Lutheran, and Calvinist
- Hussite

minorities: Calvinist ▲   Catholic △

NORTH SEA

SCOTLAND

Ireland • Dublin

Wales • York

ENGLAND • London

Christiania •

SWEDEN • Stockholm

DENMARK-NORWAY

Estonia

Livonia

BALTIC SEA

Courland

RUSSIA

• Copenhagen

• Hamburg

Brandenburg

Lithuania

Netherlands

• Brussels

• Rouen

• Paris

Mainz •

Worms •

HOLY ROMAN EMPIRE

• Nuremburg

Bohemia • Prague

Moravia

Silesia

Warsaw •

POLAND

• Krakow

Predominantly Orthodox Christian

F R A N C E

Augsburg •

Bavaria

Vienna •

Swiss Confederation

Tyrol

Austria

IMPERIAL HUNGARY

TRANSYLVANIA

Bordeaux •

Lyon •

Savoy

Milan •

• Buda

HUNGARY

La Coruña •

Santander •

• Buda

Avignon •

Genoa •

Venice •

Papal States

ADRIATIC SEA

OTTOMAN EMPIRE

• Bucharest

Predominantly Orthodox Christian under Muslim domination

PORTUGAL

Lisbon •

• Madrid

SPAIN

• Barcelona

NAPLES

Rome •

Seville •

• Cordoba

• Valencia

• Granada
to Spain in 1492

Naples •

MEDITERRANEAN SEA

Palermo •

SICILY

In France the process of Reformation was slower and altogether less successful. Opponents of the Catholic Church, like Calvin, were driven from the country. The Protestant cause did not get a large audience until the mid-16th century, when 120 pastors who had trained in Calvin's University of Geneva came to France. In 1559 members of the 66 Protestant churches in existence met and were thereafter known as Huguenots.

They enjoyed mixed fortunes, with the French monarchy occasionally siding with them but more often lining up against them with the country's Catholic majority. There were skirmishes and considerable loss of life throughout the remainder of the 16th century. Protestant sympathizer King Henry IV attempted to ensure religious tolerance in 1598 by issuing the Edict of Nantes, legislating for Huguenot freedom. The edict

was revoked in 1685 and Protestants were once again forced out of France.

To Reach God—Cathedrals

For some it is a sanctuary of peace; others see it as a place for solemn worship. Some cathedrals are adorned with works of art; a few are stripped of embellishment. Just about all cathedrals tower toward Heaven to symbolize the greatness of God.

BELOW: The crowning glory of St. Peter's Basilica is the dome. Originally conceived as lower and more spherical by the first architect, Boromini, Michelangelo's radical design broke with many established High Renaissance tenets. In this view, the Vatican gardens rising uphill hide the lower bulk of the basilica.

Undoubtedly, a cathedral represents the religious heart of a community. Despite the fading relevance of religion today, a cathedral often becomes the symbol by which a city is known. In New York on December 6, 1941 the world's largest cathedral, St. John the Divine, officially opened. Any fanfare of welcome was drowned out by the Japanese attack on Pearl Harbor the following day. Indeed, the cathedral project had been dogged by ill fortune since its foundation stone was laid in 1892.

It took two years and vast quantities of money to locate the bedrock beneath the site off Fifth Avenue in order that building work could begin. The first architect of the Romanesque design died as the choir was completed and his successor sought to instill a Gothic flavor. His grand plans were stalled by World War I and then the Great Depression. In fact the very final stage of construction did not get underway until 1979.

But with a nave measuring 601 feet and a floor area of 121,000 square feet, the cathedral is the epitome of a Christian cathedral: palatial and grand. The name cathedral comes from the Latin word meaning "bishop's seat," thus cathedrals tend to be found in administrative centers.

Christianity has divided into Protestantism, Catholicism, and Orthodoxy and each section has further branched down different roads. But all express themselves in terms of immense and impressive buildings, with towers, spires, and domes. A few are modern but most are Saxon, Norman, Romanesque, Gothic, Baroque, or Orthodox in style, built at a time when religion was considered more vital and worthy of physical expression than it is today.

Some features, like sculptures and stained glass, are now commonplace in cathedrals. Yet when stained glass windows were introduced into British churches during the reign of Charles I, they were seen as concessions to Catholicism and became a major contributory factor to the start of the English Civil War.

DOMES OF FAITH

St. Peter's Basilica in Rome, built on the supposed site of Peter's tomb, lies at the very heart of the Catholic faith. It took several architects more than a century to construct this architectural gem, completed with the help of Michelangelo (1475–1564), Raphael (1483–1520), and 11 other designers. Perhaps the most striking element of the Basilica is its dome, some 435 feet high, largely the work of Michelangelo. In common with other major cathedrals, it contains many significant works of art.

Like other important Christian monuments, Notre Dame cathedral in Paris was built upon land held sacred by pagan tribes, including the Celts and Romans.

Construction of the present building on the Île de la Cite began in 1163 and replaced two previous churches. When it was completed in 1345 it was considered the finest Gothic cathedral ever built; it remains one of the most striking religious buildings in the world. Notre Dame survived the French Revolution and was refurbished first by Napoleon and later by the architect Eugene Viollet-le-Duc (1814–79).

In London the familiar lines of St. Paul's Cathedral are the work of Sir Christopher Wren (1632–1723). He set to work following the Great Fire of London in 1666 that destroyed the wooden building previously on the site. Completed within 23 years, Wren lived to see his dream become a reality and his body lies buried in the crypt of the building. The cathedral cross stands 365 feet high—a foot for each day of the year.

The most famous Russian Orthodox cathedrals lie within the Kremlin in Moscow: the Cathedral of the Assumption, completed in 1479, and the Cathedral of the Annunciation, finished a decade later. The Kremlin also includes the seat of Russian government, former royal palaces, and a museum. The multi-domes of the buildings are fabulously embellished and attract tourists from across the globe.

ABOVE: The Gothic style of church architecture, which first emerged in the medieval era, was an expression of a new religious spirit. The powerful horizontal and vertical dynamics of the nave directed worshippers to the altar and to Heaven above, exemplified here by Amiens Cathedral, France, contemporary of other glories like Beauvais and Chartres cathedrals.

Greek *Orthodox* Church

The Orthodox Church of Greece sees itself as a direct descendant of the first missions by St. Paul. It is supported by a strong monastic tradition, but the history that bridges the Church of modern Greece with the New Testament has been troubled.

The early Christian communities established in Thessalonica, Philippi, Corinth, and Athens gave Greece an early investment in the new Church, but an

ABOVE: The greatest Christian church in the East was Hagia Sophia. Built by the emperor Justinian I (r.527–565) over a fourth-century basilica, the minarets and further extensions were added after the Ottoman conquest in 1453, when the church became a mosque. Its glorious Byzantine mosaics were overpainted but restored in 1847 under Sultan Abdul Mecit. Now a museum, it is also a mosque and church.

independent church tradition was a long time evolving. The Church claimed autonomy from the Patriarch of Constantinople as recently as 1833 when Greece was liberated from the Turkish Empire. It is one in a fellowship of Churches that is autocephalous—that is, governed by its own head bishop. Previously it was part of the Eastern Orthodox Church, which was embroiled in a thousand-year feud with Rome over doctrinal matters.

Acrimony between the Orthodox and Roman Churches runs so deep that when Pope John Paul II visited Athens during 2001 there were no church representatives at the airport to meet him and curious onlookers were kept away from the papal cortege as it motored into the city. Some Greek Orthodox radicals had held all-night vigils in an

attempt to have the trip canceled.

One archbishop said: "The second devil is coming. He wants to turn us Greeks into heretics, but we will sacrifice even our lives to oppose him." There are fears that the Vatican is prepared to wield influence in areas of Eastern Europe that have recently shrugged off communism, areas in the Orthodox Church's backyard.

Protected by thousands of riot police, Pope John Paul II asked forgiveness for sins "by action and omission" visited on the Orthodox Church by Catholics. His apology embraced the sacking of Constantinople by crusaders in 1204, an event which still causes anguish among devout Orthodox worshippers. The response to his humility among Greeks—many of whom were acutely embarrassed by what they saw as overreaction by the Orthodox Church—remains to be seen.

FLEEING THE PAPISTS

Since the schism, nominally dated at 1054, and the attack on Constantinople, which was followed by a period of Latin rule, there have been efforts to unify the Christian Churches of East and West. Before the Ottomans moved into Constantinople in 1453, the reconciliation bids were inspired politically from the East as rulers cast around for support against the aspirant Turks. Church leaders were reluctantly dragged along in the wake of such efforts, all of which ended in failure.

The most promising was the Council of Ferrara-Florence (1438–45). Eastern delegates caved in to the majority of papal demands, only to recant in the face of a domestic backlash from a population still

repelled by Rome. The prevailing attitude was summed up by Orthodox Saint Mark Eugenicus who urged: "Flee from the papists as you would from a snake and the flames of a fire."

After the Turks took power, in principle the Eastern Orthodox Church was allowed to continue, for the Muslim leaders took the faith to be incomplete rather than heretical. In practice Christians were relegated to a ghetto. Their focal point of worship, the Hagia Sophia, was turned into a mosque and dissension between Turks and Christians began to escalate.

Greeks rose to positions of power in the Church and found themselves in the front line when revolution brewed in the early 19th century. Patriarch Gregory V was hanged from the city gates in Constantinople on Easter Day 1821 by ruling Turks. The barbarous act merely consolidated support for the uprising, which by 1830 was successful.

The Greek Orthodox Church enjoyed a revival in fortunes with World War I, when membership trebled. Reflecting the surge in support, a group known as Zoe or the Brotherhood of Theologians was formed in 1907 by Eusebius Matthopoulos. It comprised more than one hundred unmarried members who spent a month each year in retreat and then worked in the community, teaching and preaching. Its influence has waned in the face of opposition for a rival group, Sotor, and support of the military junta who took over Greece in a coup in 1967 and ruled until 1974.

ABOVE: Greek Orthodox Patriarch Athenagoras gives Mass at the Church of the Nativity in Bethlehem, Israel, during the visit of Pope Paul VI in 1964. Under the autocephalous structure of Greek Orthodoxy, there are also Patriarchs of Constantinople and of Alexandria And All Africa, among other communities.

Russian *Orthodox* Church

The Russian Orthodox Church has the unenviable accolade of being one of the most repressed in history. It is a tribute to its potency that despite every effort to dismantle the Church, it maintained the faith of its people.

Prince Vladimir, the master of Kiev and Novogorod, introduced the Orthodox Church to Russia. At the time he did not have the highest motives, but for his devotion and faith he was later made a saint. In the eyes of Vladimir, the liturgies of the Eastern Orthodox Church were more perfect and beautiful than anything that the German Church, Judaism, or Islam could offer—or so the story goes.

The Orthodox Church is indeed famous for the ornate glory of its icons and the affecting qualities of its worship. However, Vladimir converted to Christianity largely for the sake of political expediency, as part of a pact with Byzantine Emperor Basil II in about 987. Basil received Vladimir's military help to suppress internal rivals. In exchange Vladimir was given Basil's sister Anne in marriage. If Vladimir fostered the belief that Orthodoxy was an aesthetic choice, it was because he felt it underlined his independence of thought.

Christianity had already reached Kiev—indeed, Vladimir's grandfather had been baptized—but until the agreement with Basil II this saint was a pagan rumored to have indulged in human sacrifice. Upon his baptism, all the idols in Kiev and the surrounding area were tossed into the River Dneiper and the population forced to become Christian. The Kievan era ended in the 13th century with the arrival of the Mongols. The Church was not unduly harassed and even secured tax-free status. There was also a rise in the monastic tradition at this time.

In 1448 the Russian Church elected its own patriarch, signifying a break with Constantinople. The Muscovite princes dominated now, establishing an independent state with the backing of the Church. However, harmony between Church and State ended with the arrival of the czars, who ruled first Moscow and then the Russian Empire.

BOOSTED BY STALIN

The ambitions of Peter I, the Great (r.1682–1725) were entirely secular and he foresaw only a limited role for the Church in his sleek empire. In 1721 he replaced the post of patriarch with a Holy Synod, a bureaucracy to control the activities of the Church. The priesthood was reduced to a minor rank of the civil service, ultimately represented in government by a minister. Church institutions were paralyzed and isolated. Peter undermined the Russian Orthodox Church in a bid to modernize a critically outdated country, but instead alienated many of his subjects, who looked to the Church for guidance and inspiration.

With the coming of the Russian Revolution in 1917, the Church seized the opportunity to re-establish a patriarch and resume a position of influence. The renaissance was short-lived for the ascendant Bolsheviks who, in common with the czars, had little use for a strong Church.

Soon Church lands were nationalized and clerics were persecuted. Orthodoxy was further endangered when a breakaway movement, the Renovated Church, was launched with government approval.

The advent of Stalin promised little until the outbreak of World War II. Traditionally, conflict reinvigorates religion like nothing else. After Hitler's treacherous attack on Russia, Stalin elevated the Orthodox Church to be a rallying point for the nation.

In September 1943 Stalin met with three metropolitans and permitted the election of a Patriarch of Moscow. There was to be a Holy Synod and a new theological institution. In return the bishops pronounced "A Condemnation of Traitors to the Faith and to the Motherland," which threatened to excommunicate anyone who consorted with the Germans. With the constraints of the communist Church, communities in America, Canada, and Japan linked with the Russian Orthodox Church had to go it alone. They have since become autonomous.

In the Ukraine there was a brief spell of independence for the Ukrainian Autocephalous Orthodox Church, until it was forcibly united with the mainstream Russian Orthodox Church. In protest some clergy formed an underground movement to offer freedom of worship, finally emerging in 1991 as the Ukrainian Orthodox Church. Other Orthodox Churches exist in Romania, Georgia, Cyprus, Albania, Bulgaria, and the Czech and Slovak republics.

Methodism — *a* Precise Approach

In the 18th century, the Anglican Church was subject to dissension and division. One of the factions that came to the fore was Methodism, born out of the dynamism of its founder, John Wesley.

BELOW: Palmer's Chapel Methodist Church, Cataloochee, North Carolina, U.S.A. For Methodists, the local church means both the congregation and the building. Those wishing to become a Methodist must undergo a period of training. Only when the local church council is sure of the applicant's sincerity can they be confirmed into the congregation.

John Wesley (1703–91) was a radical preacher for whom the shortcomings of the established Anglican Church loomed large. He remained true to his convictions and in his wake a new faith was formed. Wesley lived a remarkable life. The son of a Non-conformist minister, he grew up in a rectory in Epworth, Lincolnshire, which was haunted by a knocking ghost nicknamed Old Jeffrey.

After an academic career that took him to Oxford University, Wesley was ordained a minister on September 28, 1728. He returned to Oxford the following year to join his brother Charles (1707–88) and two others in a religious study group known as the Holy Club. So precise was its approach, its members were dubbed Methodists. They busied themselves with welfare work among the poor and needy, in addition to spiritual pursuits. "O Lord, let us not live to be useless, for Christ's sake," wrote John Wesley, and it was by this tenet that he lived and worked.

In 1735 the Wesleys left Oxford and the Holy Club folded. Still casting around for a rewarding religious endeavor, John and Charles Wesley embarked on a mission to the American colonies. Charles was ordained for the purpose. But high ideals about converting Indian savages and enlightening settlers proved abortive. The pair made little impact on a frontier society pre-occupied with expansion. There was unpleasantness when John was accused of exacting revenge from the pulpit by refusing to give Holy Communion to a woman who would not wed him.

Returning in morose mood, John Wesley encountered a group of Moravians during the passage home and was struck by their tranquility. Moravians originated in Germany, seeking sanctuary from religious upheaval on the Saxony estate of Count Nikolaus Ludwig von Zinzendorf. Worshipping mostly in a Lutheran tradition, the Moravians had a simple evangelical message of strength of faith, and traveled the world to spread the gospel following their diaspora.

SELF-ORDAINED MISSIONARIES

On May 24, 1738 at a meeting largely composed of Moravians, Wesley was overwhelmed by a sense of enlightenment while listening to Luther's words about the letter St. Paul sent to the Galatians. Full of religious fervor, Wesley traveled across the country urging people to find salvation through faith. His ardor antagonized the Anglican Church, which began to close its doors to him. Consequently Wesley tried preaching in the open air to those who were not part of regular church congregations. He founded the first Methodist chapel in Bristol in 1739, and then the Foundry at Moorfields in London, which became the group's headquarters.

So successful were his efforts that societies were formed across the country for which he wrote rules, published in 1743. Wesley was outraged when the Church of England refused to ordain his missionaries, who were bound for the American colonies.

In 1784 he decided to do the job himself, coming into conflict with his brother Charles. The two were also estranged over Charles' perceived interference in John's betrothal. Charles is best remembered as a writer of popular hymns, including *Hark the Herald Angels Sing, Love Divine, All Loves Excelling,* and *Jesus, Lover of My Soul.* Music remains an important part of Methodist worship.

Methodists in America quickly established a church organization of their own. John continued an itinerant lifestyle into old age, writing and preaching wherever he went. Before his death he was seen as something of a celebrity.

Methodism was set apart from the existing Church of England in the eyes of both Wesley and the Church elders. Yet it was not officially seen as a separate body until 1795, four years after Wesley's death. Only after that could Methodist ministers perform the sacraments and conduct marriages.

Historically, Methodists have earned a reputation as campaigners against social injustice. They are enthusiastic advocates of greater ecumenical co-operation. Methodism fractured into several strands but was largely reunited by the start of the 21st century.

ABOVE: John Wesley, seen here in a portrait of 1788 by William Hamilton, followed in the footsteps of earlier reformers like John Wycliffe and Martin Luther (see pages 114–115), except that in 18th-century England it was the Established Anglican Church that was under attack for its spiritual and ecclesiastical failings.

Quakers—*The* Society *of* Friends

The Quakers were another splinter group from the Anglican Church, born at a time when Puritanism was in the ascendancy in England. They hold a traditionally mild, marginal faith, yet in history Quakers had great influence on Western society.

RIGHT: George Fox, credited with founding the Society of Friends, clashed with the Anglican clergy at almost every step of his mission through the counties of England. Fox was imprisoned at least ten times for periods of between one and six years for preaching his beliefs. On one occasion, it was the Lord Protector, Oliver Cromwell, who had him set at liberty. Cromwell would have liked to dine with Fox, but the Quaker preacher refused his "meat and drink."

George Fox (1624–91) is credited with being the founder of the Quakers, or Society of Friends, as it was then known. There were already a number of Separatists, unhappy with the established Protestant faith, and Seekers, dissenters hoping for divine interaction. In 1652 Fox won the support of a Lancashire magistrate and his wife and their home, Swarthmore Hall, England, became headquarters for a growing group who became known as Quakers, with Fox's assertion that they would "quake at the word of the Lord."

The U.S. state of Pennsylvania was founded as a Quaker colony in 1682 by William Penn, who determined it should be run on appropriate religious lines. Consequently there was religious toleration, even though the Quakers risked being subsumed by other faiths. It was pacifist by inclination, reaching peaceful agreements with Native Americans in the vicinity. Although it had numerous shortcomings and the Quaker administration did not endure, by any standards Pennsylvania had a noble birth.

Quakers are concerned with a personal relationship with God and this is achieved through the Inward Light (*i.e.* God is within us all). Communication occurs at quiet, unstructured gatherings at Meeting Houses. Worshippers do not meditate in the manner of Buddhists but await divine inspiration before making a contribution. Accordingly, Quakers were creedless, churchless, and declined to employ ministers. Quakers insisted they had found God's light while others were in darkness. By contrast, the powerful Puritans appeared archly orthodox and displayed little tolerance to rivals.

A stream of measures was taken against Quakers in England during those early days. They were penalized for refusing to swear

oaths, for refraining from attending Church of England services, and for professing Quakerism. Thousands were jailed as they stoutly refused to take their faith underground. The grim experience of incarceration caused the death of hundreds. Fox himself was jailed for blasphemy. In America four Quakers were put to death as heretics prior to 1661. In 1689 the Toleration Act was passed, relieving pressure on religious groups on both sides of the Atlantic.

THE PRICE OF PACIFICSM

Quakers have divided and adapted down the centuries. One group led by Elias Hicks (1748–1830), an eminent opponent of the slave trade in the U.S., fell out with mainstream Quakers over issues of evangelism and formed his own group. Other splits ensued, which remained for decades but have been healed.

At first there were strict dress codes, rules of abstinence, and no one married outside the faith. These obligations are largely obsolete. Some elements of the Quakers embraced hymns during services. One message that has stayed the same is that of simplicity—Quakers are still urged to avoid ostentation and extravagance.

Quaker capitalists were faced with dilemmas that loom large even today. Barclays Bank supported breweries at a time when Quakers believed alcohol was evil. Those with interests in iron-makers were confronted with the activities of gun-manufacturers. Some Quakers traded in tobacco that had been produced on slave plantations. But Quakers are best remembered for reform rather than reluctant hypocrisy. Elizabeth Fry made wide-ranging changes in the British prison system. Others tackled the slave trade, urban poverty, and the like.

The 20th century brought some of the most challenging personal dilemmas for pacifist Quakers. They found immense difficulty in persuading recruitment boards of their sincere beliefs during the man-hungry World War I. In response, the Quakers formed the Friends Ambulance Unit, working under the direction of the military but as non-combatants. Its members faced as much misery and horror as the servicemen.

The Friends Ambulance Unit was at work again in World War II, along with a highly effective war victims relief committee. In 1947 the Friends Service Council and the American Friends Service Committee were together awarded the Nobel Peace Prize.

BELOW: A devout Quaker, William Penn (1644–1718) is best known for founding the state of Pennsylvania, although he remained there for only two short periods in 1682–83 and 1699–1701. After the second spell, he returned to England and never returned to his colony.

The Salvation Army

Some Christians believe they are engaged in spiritual warfare against Satan and sin and must battle to save people's souls. This militant evangelism is accommodated by the Salvation Army, whose charitable works among the poor are central to its existence.

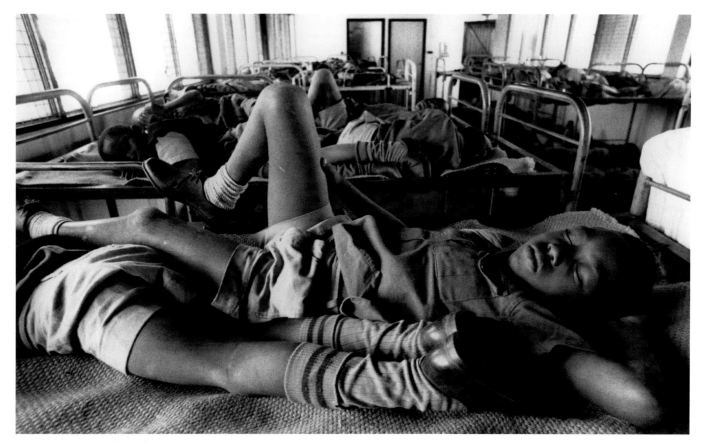

ABOVE: Homeless boys sleeping in the Salvation Army's shelter in Nairobi, Kenya. The Salvation Army operates in 98 countries acrosss the globe, providing food and accommodation to the needy. The modern organization, while remaining true to its founder's dictats, is less likely to ply the poor with religious instruction than it did in the late 19th and early 20th centuries while feeding and caring for them.

The founder and first general of the Salvation Army was William Booth (1829–1912), an apprentice pawnbroker turned preacher. At first he embraced Methodism but within a decade he sheered away from the established faith and worked alone. Appalled by the poverty and vice of London's East End, Booth felt drawn to work in the city and resolved to find new ways of connecting with its people. He decided upon processions with brass bands and hymn singing, cheap food for the hungry, and tent shelters for the homeless. Although his mission was popular with the people who stood to benefit, it inspired hostility among some conservative elements of the Anglican Church.

Opponents were scarcely mollified when in 1878 Booth decided to organize his supporters along military lines. Using a similar format to the British Army—a model of success at the time—Booth made soldiers of his supporters with uniforms and rank, with himself an all-powerful general who demanded mute obedience. Salvation Army members were arrested and fined for public order offenses or even attacked by their enemies. Undaunted, Booth continued to speak and preach in public and lived by these words: "Your days at the most cannot be very long, so use them to the best of your ability for the glory of God and the benefit of your generation."

At his side was his faithful wife Catherine (1829–90), who was herself a powerful orator. Remarkably for the era, she was convinced women had equal rights in law and in the pulpit. She was equally at home with the poorest hovel dweller in London's most deprived areas and the wealthiest patron, persuaded by her passionate words to give extra cash to the cause. She authored hymns and mothered eight children; it was probably her influence, rather than that of fiery disciplinarian Booth, that kept the children loyal to the Salvation Army.

Convinced by the sincerity of the Booths,

to extend the army's work there. After a falling out with Booth senior in 1896, the pair established the Volunteers of America, an enduring and sympathetic organization with similar aims to the Salvation Army. Administration of the Salvation Army in America was taken over by the popular and efficient Evangeline Cory Booth, a daughter

polite society gradually changed its opinion and began to salute their efforts. They were further endorsed by the public support of King Edward VII, whose coronation in 1902 Booth attended. Two years later the king invited Booth to sign an autograph book. Booth wrote, "Some men's ambition is art. Some men's ambition is fame. Some men's ambition is gold. My ambition is the souls of men."

GLOBAL SALVATION

William and Catherine's eldest son, William Bramwell Booth, took over as general on the death of his father, having been a trusted lieutenant since his teenage years. One of his achievements was to expose the extent of the white slave-trade in Britain.

Another son, Ballington Booth and his wife Maud, had traveled to America in 1887

of William and Catherine. Between 1934–39 she was the fourth general, the last member of the Booth family to hold the post.

The principle that social and spiritual labors go hand-in-hand still holds good. The Salvation Army remains best known for its work among the urban needy and operates in 98 countries worldwide. In modern Russia it has been suspected of having paramilitary connections. Officials in Moscow have refused to give it charitable status, making its mission in the city impossible to undertake. Difficulties like this have prompted the Salvation Army to review its commitment to uniforms. Rather than abolish it entirely there has been a move to update appearances and shake off a quaint or austere Victorian image, but members still pledge obedience, abstain from alcohol, and distribute *War Cry*, the Salvation Army literature.

ABOVE: An enthusiastic crowd greets the man who styled himself General William Bramwell Booth, International Commander of the Salvation Army, on his arrival in Tokyo. Booth was on a tour of Japan, Korea, and China, where he officiated at many Salvation Army meetings.

Theosophy

A faith to unite the beliefs of East and West, Theosophy hinges on internal examination and finding a personal route to God. There are identifiable elements of Hinduism, Buddhism, Christianity, and Islam, in addition to a goodly amount of spiritualism.

RIGHT: In her childhood Helena Blavatsky attracted attention with her psychic powers, it was said. Later, she impressed Henry Steel Olcott, BELOW, who became the first president of the Theosophical Society. But Blavatsky's skeptical critics remained unconvinced of her occult powers, particularly after the publication of her two major books: Isis Unveiled and The Secret Doctrine.

Theosophy is derived from two Greek words, *theos* meaning god and *sophia* meaning wisdom. Another commonly held translation is "divine knowledge." In essence, theosophy aims to bring together numerous strands of religious conviction that have unraveled throughout history. The contention is that all major faiths and many myths and symbols are esoterically inter-linked and that there are sacred texts to prove this. Suspicions of manipulation and duplicity on the part of its leading lights led to its decline, although there are still hundreds of theosophists in America today.

The woman behind the theosophy movement was Helena Petrovna Blavatsky (1831–91), a Russian born mystic and traveler. Known as HPB, she developed an abiding interest in the occult, blending it with the work of classical writers, Gnostic teachers, and eminent mystics. She claimed to have entered Tibet and studied with a group of "Masters," whose identities were never explicitly revealed.

In 1873, HPB emigrated to New York, where she developed a following after revealing allegedly impressive psychic powers. Five years later she met Colonel Henry Steel Olcott, a lawyer with an abiding interest in the world of spiritualism. Within two years they had founded the

Theosophical Society, with Olcott as president. Together they embarked for a life-changing trip to India, gathering further supporters while overseas.

Among them was journalist A.P. Sinnett, who helped facilitate introductions between the visitors and eminent high-caste Indians and English colonialists. There followed one of the most controversial series of incidents that dogged the progress of theosophy.

HPB encouraged her new associates to write to the enlightened Masters she had allegedly consorted with in Tibet. They received replies from Masters Koot Hoomi and Morya, allegedly delivered by paranormal means. But cynics declared she was the author of the letters and the believers were victims of an elaborate hoax.

REJECTING THE MASTERS

In 1885 a researcher from the Society of Psychical Research affirmed that HPB was a fraud. A century later the society decided the investigation had been flawed but this partial retraction was, of course, too late to prevent allegations shadowing the theosophy movement. Though her contribution to 19th century theology was received with skepticism in the West, HPB is still revered in India, where her death is commemorated with White Lotus Day.

HPB was the author of four books, outlining her theories of evolution and cosmology. One of her readers, Annie Wood Besant, became a convert to theosophy and was a major figure in the movement after HPB's death. Another important figure was William Q. Judge.

Following HPB's death, the Theosophical Society divided into groups, with Besant the head of the European section. She was also the first woman to be elected president of the Indian National Congress, freedom fighters against British colonialists.

Besant's colleague Charles W. Leadbeater identified Jiddu Krishnamurti (1895–1986), a young Indian, as the New World Teacher, in the manner of a *bodhisattva*. He was installed as the head of the Order of the Star of the East in 1911, a theosophical group set up by Besant and Leadbeater. Besant eventually financed his move to the U.S. and the

Krishnamurti Foundation was established in California. Krishnamurti ultimately rejected the Masters, apparently after he begged in vain for his brother to be spared death from a serious illness. He urged his followers to find spiritual liberation through personal discovery and gave specific orders that he was not to be deified.

Although theosophy in isolation only had marginal significance, it was a contributory factor in the revival in the West of Buddhism, Hinduism, and other ancient beliefs, as well as an inspiration for modern philosophies.

ABOVE: Annie Besant and Jiddu Krishnamurti arrive in Chicago, August 30, 1926. At this time, Besant was recognized as the leader of the Theosophists; she had also become the young Indian's foster mother.

Religious Conflicts *in* Europe

While Europe has been dominated by Christianity, its single-faith focus has not prevented violence and bloodshed. The reverberations caused by the Reformation, when the unity of the Christian Church shattered beyond repair, were felt across the continent for centuries afterward.

For years Europe was the bastion of Christianity. Islam found tremendous success in its campaigns across Asia and Africa but was unable to penetrate Europe to any great degree. At first, incursions into Europe boded well. In 711 the Arab commander Tariq landed by the great rock he named *Jebel Tariq* (Mount Tariq, which gives its name to Gibraltar) and, in a sweeping campaign, defeated the Visigoths who had been the significant power on the Iberian peninsula. The Islamic army, mostly fierce Berbers, even got a foothold across the Pyrenees in Gaul.

However, an attempt made in 732 by Abd ar-Rahman, governor of Cordoba, to extend the Islamic empire ended in a rout for Muslims at the Battle of Poitiers. At the head of the Frankish victors was Charles Martel (688–741), grandfather of the powerful emperor Charlemagne. Muslims remained in Spain until 1492, when they were finally ousted by Christian forces loyal to Isabella and Ferdinand. The unification of Spain followed soon afterward.

But Europe's preoccupation with Christianity was both a strength and a terrible weakness. When the established Church split between Catholicism and Protestantism a vicious and unforgiving campaign evolved on both sides.

The Thirty Years War (1618–48) began when the King of Bohemia tried to force the Catholic faith upon his subjects, many of whom preferred to support Protestantism. His actions sucked in neighboring powers. This vastly over-simplifies a political situation beset with rivalries among nations and regions, commercial considerations, and longstanding territorial feuds. Nevertheless, religion was at the root of the conflict.

Soldiers of both sides, many of whom were mercenaries, plundered and pillaged their way through the war, with the result that the principalities of Germany were laid to waste. The carnage ended at the signing of the Treaty of Westphalia, when the map of Europe was decisively redrawn.

Britain avoided involvement, probably because it was embroiled in a religious battle of its own. Puritans were becoming increasingly concerned at what they saw as the Catholic bias of King Charles I. The result was the English Civil War, played out in Scotland and Ireland. The killings in Ireland created enmities that prevail today.

UNREST IN THE BALKANS

In shorthand form, problems began in Ireland during the rule of Queen Elizabeth I, although these early rebellions were put down. Protestant settlers exploited the land at the expense of Catholics. Retaliation by the Catholics ultimately attracted the attention of Oliver Cromwell, who waged a ruthless campaign in Ireland in 1649. Catholic aspirations were severely damaged by the victory of the Protestant William III over the Catholic James II at the Battle of the Boyne in 1690. The chasm that opened up between the two faiths has never been bridged.

Traditional Christian concepts were challenged during the Age of Enlightenment in the 18th century and suddenly religion did not command the same urgency. In the 19th century, following the French Revolution, kings, governments, and the people were more concerned with matters of politics than faith.

But religious feuds were by no means consigned to the scrap heap of history, as the wars of the late 20th century in Serbia, Bosnia, and Croatia proved. All were once part of Yugoslavia, held together by dictator

Europe at the time of the Thirty Years War, 1600–48

Between 1630 and 1635, Swedish Protestant armies ravaged the heart of Catholic Germany, attacking as far south as Frankfurt and Munich.

The Protestant Dutch threw off the Catholic yoke of Spain in 1609.

Protestant England avoided conflict in Europe, embroiled as it was in a civil war against a Catholic king, Charles I. Charles was executed in 1649 and a republic was declared under the control of Oliver Cromwell. Cromwell's subjugation of all Ireland left behind a Catholic-Protestant sore that festers to this day.

The mixture of Catholic and Orthodox Christians with the Muslim Ottoman Turks in the Adriatic Balkans during the 17th and 18th centuries left a legacy of conflict.

European conflict, 1620

- Austrian Habsburg
- Spanish Habsburg
- France
- German Protestants
- United Provinces
- Sweden
- Habsburg allies
- Habsburg enemies

English Civil War, advance of Parliament forces by:
- August 1642
- 1644
- 1649

Tito's iron hand. But as different regions sought independence, war broke out. First Muslims fought with Croats (Catholic), then trouble flared between Serbs (Orthodox) and Croats. Ultimately there was war between Serbs and Muslims. Slavic Muslims had been targeted in Bosnia before communism collapsed, by enemies who believed Islam to be a dangerous influence.

When war broke out the actions of Serb nationalists were brutal. By the beginning of 1993 a thousand mosques had been attacked. Graveyards were ploughed up and there were systematic killings in concentration camps. Ultimately, NATO in concert with the United Nations intervened. After a cease-fire in 1995, international peacekeeping forces stayed in place and the situation remained volatile.

CHAPTER 6

Asia

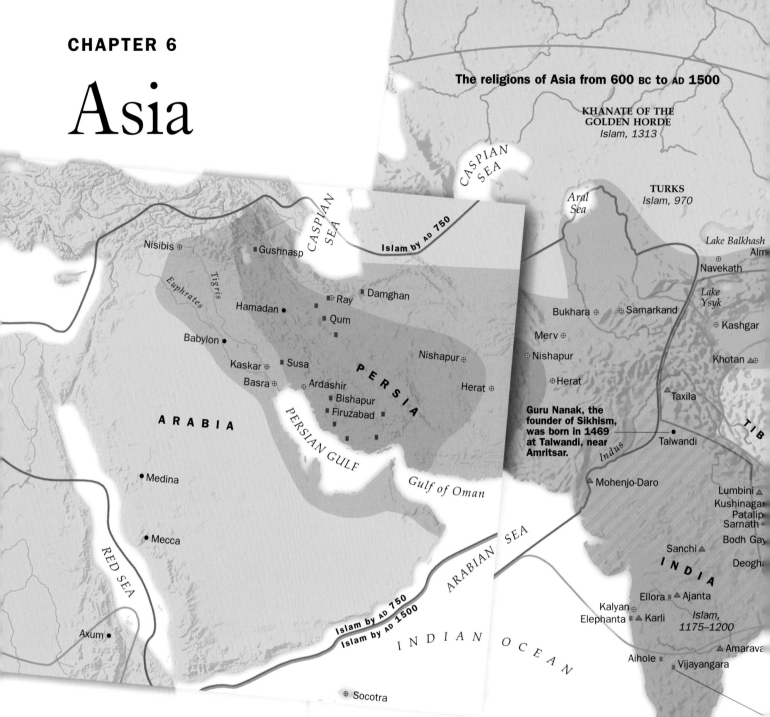

The religions of Asia from 600 BC to AD 1500

KHANATE OF THE GOLDEN HORDE
Islam, 1313

TURKS
Islam, 970

CASPIAN SEA

CASPIAN SEA

Aral Sea

Lake Balkhash
Alm

Nisibis ⊕

• Gushnasp

Islam by AD 750

⊕ Navekath

Euphrates

Tigris

Hamadan •

⊞ Ray • Damghan

• Qum

Bukhara ⊕   ⊕ Samarkand

Lake Ysyk

⊕ Kashgar

Babylon •

Merv ⊕

⊕ Nishapur

Khotan ⚊⊕

Kaskar ⊕   ■ Susa

Nishapur ⊕

P E R S I A

Basra ⊕   ⊕ Ardashir

■ Bishapur

■ Firuzabad   ■

Herat ⊕

⊕ Herat

Taxila

TIB

A R A B I A

PERSIAN GULF

Guru Nanak, the founder of Sikhism, was born in 1469 at Talwandi, near Amritsar.

• Talwandi

Indus

Gulf of Oman

• Medina

⊕ Mohenjo-Daro

Lumbini ⚊
Kushinaga
Pataliṕ
Sarnath ⚊

Sanchi ⚊

Bodh Gay

• Mecca

RED SEA

ARABIAN SEA

Islam by AD 750
Islam by AD 1500

I N D I A

Deogha

Ellora ⊕   ⚊ Ajanta

Kalyan ⊕
Elephanta ■ ⚊ Karli

Islam, 1175–1200

I N D I A N   O C E A N

Aihole ■   • Vijayangara

⚊ Amarava

Axum •

⊕ Socotra

Cochin ⊕

⚊ Anuradha
⚊ Kandy
⊕
*Ceylon
(Sri La*

T he world's most populous continent, Asia occupies about one third of the planet's land. It possesses the globe's highest point and some of its most arid regions. There is jungle and tundra, industrial muscle and rank rural poverty, modern economies existing alongside countries yoked to the Stone Age. Its enormous diversity also stretches to faith. Nowhere in the world is the religious map more complex or fascinating.

A large number of Asians worship in the same manner as ancestors from the distant past. Hindus have populated the mighty sub-continent of India for some three-and-a-half millennia and still base their religious practices on the texts used long before Christianity and Islam were conceived. Yet some have eschewed the ancient or traditional faiths for the modern, like those who follow the Unification Church, which began in Korea.

All the major faiths have enjoyed longevity in Asia, but endurance has not always been coupled with success. There has been buoyancy and repression in similar measure. Buddhism triumphed as a missionary religion but failed to keep a significant foothold in India, the country where it began. Confucianism gave China polite society and a valuable social order for its mushrooming population.

132

In doing so it shackled millions
to a shallow existence.

Swathes of people converted
to Islam when the faith was still
young, assuring it of a healthy
future. Yet it is here that the
ugly face of fundamentalism
has blighted lives. Hinduism
also has a dual face,
encouraging kindly acts in
order to gain good karma but
designating millions to misery
through its misguided caste system.

In Asia religious adherents have
become entrenched and increasingly
recalcitrant. Nevertheless, the progress of
religion around the region makes for
compelling reading and gives insight into
the emergence of religious conflicts.

Islam by AD 1500

UIGHURS
Manichaean,
762–1300

GATAI
NGOLS
, 1250

Hami ⊕

MONGOLS
Buddhism, 1200–1600

Qian △

⊕ Liaoyang

Yamato △

SEA OF
JAPAN

JAPAN

M o n g o l i a

TANGUTS
Buddhism,
1100–1200

Datong
Yungang △ ⊕

△ Kaesong

Kyongju △

⊕ Beijing

△ Wu-t'ai Shan

△ Jiuquan

Dunhuang

⊕ Tangut

Lake
Qinghai

Wangwu △

△ Sung
△ Longmen
Chang'an △ △ Hua
Zhongnan △
△ Wudang

YELLOW
SEA

△ Mao

Putuo Shan

K'uai Chi △ △ Tiantai
△ Kuocang

Lu △ △ Xi

Y
e
l
l
o
w

ddhism,
50

C H I N A

△ Heng

Yangtze

Hinduism,
1300

AL

DHA

Buddhism declined
in its original
center of Magadha
to be replaced by
Hinduism and Islam
by the 13th
century.

Taiwan

Pagan △

Irrawaddy

Red

Hainan

Lingjiu △ ⊕ Luofou

SOUTH
CHINA
SEA

▨	Zoroastrian, 500 BC–AD 600
▨	Sassanian Zoroastrianism after AD 226
■	major Zoroastrian temple
▨	Hindu, 500 BC–AD 600
▨	Hindu influence by AD 600
—	Hindu influence by 1500
■	major Hindu site, AD 600–1500
▨	Buddhist by third century BC
▨	Buddhist by AD 600
—	Buddhist influence by AD 1500
△	major Buddhist site, 300 BC–1500
▢	Taoism and Confucianism, 300 BC–AD 1500
△	Taoist mountain site
⊕	Nestorian Christian community by AD 1500

△ Pagan
Prome
PYU

△ Sukhothai

CHAMPA

Angkor △

Pegu
⊕ Rangoon △

FUNAN

Islam by AD 1500

CELEBES SEA

Islam,
1500

Borneo

Celebes

Gulf of
Thailand

Andaman
Sea

Malaya

Islam,
1414

Islam,
1290

Islam,
1400

JAVA SEA

Pura Besakih

Flores

Sumbawa

Sumba

Hinduism,
860

Sumatra

Srivijaya ●

Borobudur △ Java

Bali

Lombok

INDIAN OCEAN

133

The Story *of* Hinduism

BELOW RIGHT: Realistic Hindu gods and goddesses look down from a pediment on the Sri Murugan Temple, near Hampi, in southern India. Hampi is the site of the once-mighty capital of Vijayangara, cultural and religious center of a medieval-period Hindu empire that rivalled anything in China or Europe. Finds show that the sculptures of that period were also brightly colored, like these more modern counterparts.

The pursuit of spiritual liberty is nowhere more colorful, chaotic, and cryptic as among the world's Hindus. Their God, Brahman, has millions of aspects—even sharing gods from other religions—that are devoted to different traits and parts of life.

Scholars have long tried to neatly parcel up Hinduism into a straightforward, consumer-friendly soundbite of a definition. But as soon as it is boxed in, a thread unravels and it begins to buckle under pressure from mythology, magic, interpretation, and diversification. Hinduism refuses to be pinned down.

While there have been notable Hindus through the ages, there is no single founder to venerate. Hinduism aims to free the soul and it is teachers in the here-and-now who help the devout in this monumental task, not long-dead masters. There is no hierarchy equivalent to priests and bishops, and there is no central ecclesiastic authority.

The history of Hinduism extends back to early civilizations. It seems that charioteering Aryans who invaded India from the north in about 1500 BC brought their own faith, which fused with the religion of the region to lay the foundations of the faith we recognize today.

Hinduism is remarkable for its sponge-like quality that has allowed it to absorb aspects of other religions without being consumed by them. This astonishing degree of doctrinal flexibility means that some Hindus can adhere to other defined beliefs—while remaining true to Hinduism.

There are an estimated 330 million gods in the Hindu pantheon yet followers are not polytheists: There is only one God, Brahman, but He is represented in numerous ways. According to Hindu religious texts, "Verily, in the beginning this world was Brahman.

It knew only itself: 'I am Brahman.' Therefore it became the All." Brahman is timeless, faceless, and the creator of everything. His qualities are so immense that they are hard for the human mind to comprehend. Thus came the creation of the other gods, who are far more accessible.

MULTI-FACETED GODS

The triumvirate of Brahma, Vishnu, and Shiva are acknowledged as the key gods. Brahma is the quiet one of the three, in meditation following his exertions during the creation of the universe. He is partner to Saraswati, the goddess of wisdom. Vishnu is a favorite god, perceived as a preserver and both right-minded and benevolent. His partner is Lakshmi, the goddess of wealth.

Aryans from central Asia mid-second millennium

Indus

Indus valley civilization, c.2600–1700 BC

Harappa ■ *Sutlej*

Indus

■ Mohenjo-Daro

Atranjikhera •
Mathura • *Yamuna* *Ganges* • Kusingara

Kausambi • Pataliputra •

Narmada

high density of Painted Gray ware pottery, 1000–500 BC

The Aryans first settled between the Indus and Sutlej rivers, but began to move east into the Ganges plain some time after 11 BC. Their arrival and spread is associated with finds of pottery of the Painted Gray ware style.

Goa • •
Hampi (Vijayangara)

The great city of Vijayangara remained an important center of Hinduism despite the continuing invasions from the north of the Muslim Sultans of Delhi.

Shiva is fierce and disturbing in comparison. He is frequently associated with phallic imagery, and also linked to yoga, asceticism, and wisdom. A faithful and protective partner to Parvati, Shiva is often thought to exhibit the desirable qualities in a husband.

Each of the trio, along with their respective partners, has numerous embodiments with various names, essentially focusing on a different aspect of their nature. Vishnu, for example, has 22 different forms, including the popular Krishna and Buddha. Parvati is also Kali, a dark, menacing goddess who revels in blood sacrifices, and Durga, the object of a cult popular in Bengal.

Lesser gods that attract attention include Ganesh, god of good fortune and patron of scribes, depicted as a man with an elephant's head. In a case of mistaken identity, Ganesh was beheaded by his father, Shiva. Grief-stricken, Shiva vowed to make his son whole again with the head of the first live creature he came across—that happened to be an elephant. Murugan, god of war, is brother to Shiva.

Hindu worship is held at temples and within the home. A temple may be devoted to one or more deities who are daily treated with utmost reverence. They are symbolically fed and bathed, woken up and put to bed. To see a sacred form of god is enough to deliver blessings and purification.

Cows represent fertility and nurturing and as such have been worshipped since ancient times. Bulls are accorded a similar respect, since the influential Shiva rides a bull. Surprisingly, there is also a sacred dimension to snakes, because they are symbols of fertility and welfare.

ABOVE: Brahma, the first member of the Hindu triad of deities, is rarely portrayed in sculptural temple adornment. In this 13th-century example, the god is shown classically seated with his left foot raised. He has four faces (only three are shown) and is usually identified as holding a rosary (or scepter), an alms bowl, a bow, and the ancient Rig Veda (see next page). Traces of pigment indicate this sculpture was once as brightly colored as the modern equivalents on the left, which can sometimes resemble the cast of a Bollywood movie.

Sacred Texts—*the* Vedas

Hinduism's sacred texts are the world's oldest literature. The first of the Vedas (meaning "sacred knowledge") was committed to Sanskrit in about 1400 BC and was an oral tradition for many years earlier.

FACING: Hindu deities exist in many forms. This 12th-century bronze depicts Shiva as Nataraja, the lord of the dance, performing the dance of creation, from Chola, southeastern India.

The Vedas were originally divided into four books. First among them was the *Rig Veda*, comprising hymns of praise for a series of gods, most of which are obsolete in Hinduism today. Agni was the god of fire, Varuna the god of water, and Soma was identified with a hallucinogenic plant taken during religious ceremonies. Indra, the god of storm and war, survived in the guise of a weather god. Rudra evolved into Shiva, while Vishnu was a minor part of the *Rig Veda* before emerging as a major part of Hinduism.

Even in these early times there was a suggestion of a ceaseless creator behind the other gods. "For an awakened soul Indra, Agni, Yama, Aditya, Chandra—all these names represent only one basic power and spiritual reality."

The content of the other three Vedas—the *Sama Veda*, the *Yajar Veda*, and the *Athara Veda*—centered on the mystical rites of sacrifice, which still feature in the Hindu faith. Later came the *Upanishads* and the *Aranyakas*, by way of epilogue. The *Upanishads* were written no later than 400 BC, yet they were penned a staggering 1,100 years after the first Vedas. The *Brahamanas* were added through time as definition and debate of priestly rites.

Hindus acknowledge the Vedas as the eternal truth, transmitted through inspired seers who transcribed the words in Sanskrit. Together they are known as *sruti*, meaning "heard," while other doctrines are *smrti*—*remembered*. *Sruti* texts, ancient and more modern, have absolute authority.

There is an important philosophical element to the scriptures: "Those who do not know the field walk time and again over the treasure hidden beneath their feet and do not find it: in the same way all creatures pass through the world of Brahman day by day but do not find it for they are carried

away by unreality."

Revered though they are, the texts are not widely read or learned by most Hindus. Fortunately there are far more user-friendly religious works that use mythology and genealogy to illuminate themes and elaborate divine messages.

EPIC POEMS OF GUIDANCE

The *Puranas*, meaning "ancient lore," tell stories of creation, family lineage of gods and the royal dynasties, as well as general history. In doing so they encompass all aspects of worship and religious life. Written between about 400 and 1000 AD, 18 remain in existence, the most popular of which is the *Bhagavata-purana*, about the early life of Krishna, extending to 18,000 stanzas spread among 12 books. As a child the charming Krishna was amorous and mischievous. He was nevertheless still endowed with wisdom, with which he enlightens other characters.

Two epic poems are cherished by Hindus, for their language and passion. At the heart of both is the classic clash of good and evil. The *Mahabarata* and the *Ramayana* give historians an insight into the world of Hinduism between about 1000 BC and AD 200, during which time the poems evolved, first in oral then in written form. The stories have become imprinted on the consciousness of the Hindu people.

At almost 100,000 couplets, the *Mahabarata* is the world's longest poem. (It is eight times longer than the Greek epics *Iliad* and *Odyssey* combined.) The sage Vyasa is credited with authorship but it is likely that he orchestrated work that already existed. Every Hindu must live by *dhamma*, a code of conduct, and this poem elaborates on matters of duty and devotion, giving guidelines for a model existence.

At 24,000 couplets the *Ramayana* is shorter and concentrates on the trials and torments of the divine Rama. The villain of the piece is Ravana, demon king of Lanka, who kidnaps Rama's wife, Sita. Among the heroes are Laksmana, Rama's half brother, and Hanuman, a mystical monkey general. The written version is thought to be the work of a man called Valmiki. There is enormous religious merit attached to reading and performing the poems. Much Indian art is devoted to scenes from them.

Hindu Tradition

Naked sadhu holy men bathe alongside London waiters; housewives in saris take the plunge with Hollywood celebrities. This is the festival of Kumbh Mela, dubbed "the greatest show on Earth" by some.

Some Western observers of the Kumbh Mela focus on the minority of ascetics prone to undertaking bizarre penance in order to achieve unity with God. Some of these hermits haul trucks tied to their penises, others lie upon beds of nails or meditate within pyramids of cow dung. The sight of withered arms becomes relatively commonplace among those who determine to keep a limb above head height for years, until the skin shrivels around the bone and the fingernails plough into the palm. The less extreme refuse sex or will not cut their hair. The aim is to illustrate a psychically powered self-will but it gives this holy festival a reputation as a freak show.

In fact, the vast majority of those who attend are little interested in the eye-catching exertions of the few. They are there to bathe in holy waters that will, according to religious texts, mean salvation. No more will they be subject to reincarnation; they

will have attained *moksha*. For them, it is a lifetime's ambition.

The Kumbh Mela is held four times every 12 years, each time at a different riverside site. Its roots are based in mythology. Hindu gods and demons were at war over a pitcher of nectar, said to be the elixir of life. The jug was carried by Gardua, the flying steed of Lord Vishnu, who stopped four times and spilled a drop of juice on each occasion. Those sites—Haridwar on the Ganges, Ujjain on the Sipru, Nasik on the Godavari, and Allahabad at the confluence of the Ganges and Yamuna—are now the venues of the Mela.

In 2001 the Kumbh Mela held at Allahabad attracted an estimated 30 million people. Pilgrims mingled easily with the *sadhus*, naked holy men who cover their bodies with ash as a sign of renunciation and death in the material world. Hermits, saints, and frauds were there in numbers,

RIGHT: At Haridwar, north of Delhi, pilgrims bathe in the holy water of the Yamuna during the festival of Kumbh Mela.

as the riverbanks and beyond become a sprawling tent city. The records of the Buddhist monk Hsuan-tsang reveal the festival occurred as long ago as the seventh century. In the past it has acted as a kind of Hindu parliament. Kumbh Mela is holy to all Hindu sects.

HINDU SITES AND RIVERS

Among other notable Hindu traditions is Diwali, the festival of light, which occurs in late October. It is strongly associated with Laksmi, goddess of wealth, who is said to visit homes at this time to bring prosperity. Sometimes the birth of the goddess Kali is celebrated. Others hold that the festival is linked to the *Ramayana* and marks the return of Rama to his birthplace of Ayodhya after years in exile. It might yet be the anniversary of the victory of Vishnu over King Bali.

Whatever the reason, Diwali is a delightful festival—shared with Sikhs—in which temples, homes, and entire streets are festooned with lights. Four months later comes Holi, a riotous occasion during which people are pelted with colored powders and waters. It is the favorite festival of devotees to Krishna, who tend to imitate his ribald behavior on this occasion. There are numerous other Hindu festivals, some specific to certain sects or cults.

Tradition pinpoints seven sites of special religious significance to Hindus. These are Varanasi, associated with Shiva, Kanchipuram, the site of a temple devoted to Shiva, Haridwar, Ujjain, Ayodhya, and Mathura and Dwarka, both linked to Krishna. There are seven sacred rivers: the Ganges, Saraswati, Yamuna, Indus, Narmada, Godavari, and Cauvery. The Ganges (Ganga), said to have come down from the stars, is the most important. Thousands take a daily dip in its waters, fulfilling the ritual purification that is vital in Hinduism. Known as the Great Mother, it has become highly polluted. Along one 5-mile stretch of the 1,560 mile-long river, some 60,000 people take a daily ablution—in the vicinity of 30 sewers.

Centers of the Hindu religion after 1200

PUNJAB
Chenab
Sutlej
Indus
HIMALAYAS
Haridwar ■
Delhi •
NEPAL
Thar Desert
Mathura ■
Ganges
Yamuna
Ayodhya ■
Kanpur •
Gagahara
SIND
Pushkar ■
Chambal
Saraswati
Allahabad ■
Varanasi ■
• Pataliputra (Patna)
Dwarka ■
Ujjain ■
Sipra
Gondal •
GUJARAT
Narmada

After 1206, the Islamic faith swept through India under the sultans of Delhi. Only a region in the Thar Desert remained independent, and the Hindu state of Vijayangara fought a successful campaign against Muhammad ibn Tughluk in the mid-14th century. Thereafter, the Muslim power declined, although the northern areas of India remained Islamic.

Somnath •
• Calcutta
Nasik ■
Ellora ■
Mahanadi
Mouths of the Ganges
Bombay •
DECCAN
Godavari
Bhubaneshwar ■
• Konarak
Bidar •
Bijapur •
Krishna
EASTERN GHATS

■ Kumbh Mela site
■ site of special Hindu significance
■ other important Hindu site

▨ Islamic Delhi sultanate, 1325–51

▨ extent of Vijayangara, 1480

WESTERN GHATS
Penner
Vijayangara ■
Chandragiri •
Madras •
Vellore •
Kanchipuram ■
Seringapatam ■
Kumbakonam ■
Cauvery
Thanjavur ■
Madurai •
Korkai •

RIGHT: An Indian sadhu (holy man) decorated in colored powders during Holi. Also called the Festival of Color, Holi celebrates the start of spring, which adds further joy to the celebrants, who cover themselves—and others—in dyed water and colored powder called gullal. Their activities recall the impish behavior of Krishna.

Reincarnation *and the* Caste System

Their gods are various and their doctrines free-flowing, but one tenet held dear by all Hindus is reincarnation. In the past the caste system has restrained both life and aspirations of afterlife for Hindus in lower social groups.

BELOW: The Cholas were a naval people whose state dominated southern India between 1000 and 1279. Dating from the late Chola period, this relief sculpture from the palace foundations of Rajaraja II shows two men holding the Wheel of Time. The wheel is symbolic of the cosmos and the endless cycle of death and rebirth, or reincarnation.

Being born again isn't a joyful bodily return to home and hearth. Hindus aspire to an ideal far greater than life on Earth. They seek the revelation that exposes the *atman*—an inner flame, true nature, or eternal soul. It is this that departs a dead body and is reborn with a new baby. Ultimately, the ambition is to leave the wheel of life—*Samsara* in Sanskrit—to achieve union with God.

Key to liberation is the law of karma. This dictates that every daily action bears consequences affecting what occurs after death. Bad karma clings to the *atman*, making release from the misery of mankind impossible, while good karma assists in the journey to ultimate freedom or *moksha*. In this way Hinduism provides a moral

structure for society. Wrongdoers are deterred by the prospect of coming back to life as a human with a menial job or as an animal. The reward for doing good deeds is a more fortunate passage through the next life and getting one step closer to divine unity.

Yet this system also provided society with a rigid subtext that has wrought terrible suffering. After the Aryan invasion (c.1500 BC) people were divided into five groups, known as *varnas* or castes, reflecting their role and place in the world. The Brahmins were the priests, the Kashtriyas the warriors, the Vaishyas were merchants, and Shudras born to serve. Each group was associated with parts of God, the Brahmin being His mouth, the Kashtriyas His arms, the Vaishyas His thighs, and the Shudras

His feet. Beyond these were the Dalit (downtrodden), condemned to undertake the worst jobs at the lowest wages.

Each group was further divided into sub-castes or *jatis*, putting further constraints on the social hierarchy. Some of the sub-castes associated with the Dalit were deemed so unclean to other Hindus that they were compelled to keep out of sight and do their work at night.

LIFE OF THE TWICE-BORN

Caste was inherited and marriage between castes unheard of, therefore it was impossible to escape the condition into which one was born. The result was an underclass known as the untouchables whose members were deprived of the opportunity to climb the social ladder, regardless of their talents.

British rule began to dismantle the caste system. The occupying power's legal system would not allow lower castes to be punished more greatly than those in a higher caste accused of the same crime. There was aid for lower castes from the government. But it was the words and actions of Mohandas Gandhi (1869–1948), freedom fighter and social equalizer, which most profoundly advanced the cause of the lower castes.

By 1950 a law was passed that effectively scrapped the caste system. Alas, it has taken years for old prejudices to be forgotten. Steps to install positive discrimination—the allocation of government jobs for lower caste people, for example—have sparked violent protests. Gandhi's dream of a fair society remains just that.

Hindu boys (traditionally from the first three castes) undergo a ritual to become "twice born." This has nothing to do with reincarnation but is a coming of age celebration. Those who have been subject to it are distinguished by a thread worn around the waist. From then their lives are technically mapped out into four phases. The first is that of student. It is common for a boy to live with his teacher or guru to learn Hindu tradition. The second stage is that of householder, a time when he takes a wife and rears children. Then comes the phase of the forest dweller, when he renounces worldly goods and retires to live like a hermit. The fourth and final stage is lived as a wandering ascetic, considered dead by his family and relieved of all earthly duties. The aim is meditation and union with Brahman.

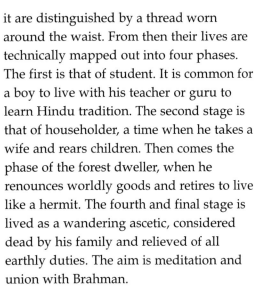

ABOVE: A member of the Harijan, or untouchable caste, attends the 1987 Communist Party protest march in New Delhi. Although of low status, the Urdhvapundra—pundra (religious mark), urdhva (upright)—on his forehead marks him as a Vaishnavite—a follower of the high-caste religion of Brahmanism introduced to India by the Aryans.

The Story *of* Buddhism

Born into great riches; a palace and its servants, fine horses, and splendid clothes at his disposal; a beautiful bride and a baby boy, Siddharta Gautama still was not satisfied. His search for fulfillment eventually ended with his rebirth as the Buddha.

Siddharta Gautama was unhappy with life because he saw the luxuries freely available to him as nothing more than worthless window dressing. His quest was to know the true meaning of his existence. It began in the sumptuous surroundings of his childhood home and ended when he became the Buddha.

As "the enlightened one" he founded what some brand a religion, while others insist is a philosophy. He taught Buddhism to willing followers for 45 years before his death. Statues across Asia, many on a grand scale, appear to confer deity status on the Buddha. Yet he is not a god, nor is he the object of worship. He is held in high esteem as a teacher and it is his ideas and words that are vital.

Stories of the Buddha's birth and early life have been fantastically embellished over the years. It is known that Siddharta Gautama was born into a warrior caste, the Sakya clan, in what was then their capital—now known as the town of Lumbini—some 2,500 years ago. Born a Hindu, it is not entirely unexpected to see the circumstances of his birth now suffused by mythology.

His mother, Queen Maya, is said to have dreamt of a white elephant with six tusks entering her side as her pregnancy began. Disembodied voices told her that the unborn son would be a great world leader. Gautama was born into a net of gold held by four gods and laid on a lotus blossom. Almost immediately he walked, claiming: "I am the chief in the world. This is my last birth. There is now no existence again."

MEDITATION

It seems his mother died soon afterward and Gautama was brought up by her sister, Maharprajapati, who later married his father, Suddhodana. A loving and cautious parent, Suddhodana was

told early on by a seer that the boy would abandon his princely world after seeing four signs.

Suddhodana vowed to protect his son in order that the royal line would continue and kept him in seclusion at the royal court, where he was surely bombarded by classical Hinduism. At the age of 29 Gautama slipped away from the confines of the palace on four occasions, witnessing for the first time an old man, a sick man, a corpse, and a holy man—the four signs. He was distressed by the suffering of the first three men and intrigued by the manifest contentment of the fourth.

Soon after, he left home, his wife, and their child to adopt the lifestyle of a wandering ascetic. "It is difficult to live a spiritual life completely perfect and pure in all its parts while cabinned inside," Gautama decided. At first he consulted the Brahmins, the wise priests that dominated Hindu society. Along with five others he began a fast, believing that disciplined self-denial

was a route to God. Only when he was skeletal did he reject this method, with the conviction that such privations were far removed from spiritual awareness.

Gautama's search continued until one day he settled beneath a bo (Indian fig) tree on the banks of the River Gaya at a place known today as Bodh Gaya and concentrated on overcoming the dilemma. He was tempted by an army of demons but remained strong-willed. After four weeks (some accounts put this period of deep meditation at seven weeks), Gautama at last realized the truth about the human condition. He was elated by the discovery and is identified after this event as the Buddha—the Enlightened One.

ABOVE: Monks walk around walls and stupas at Lumbini, Nepal, the birthplace of the Buddha.

LEFT: A 65-foot high stone statue of the Buddha, built in 1989, dominates a park near Bodh Gaya, where the Buddha first received enlightenment.

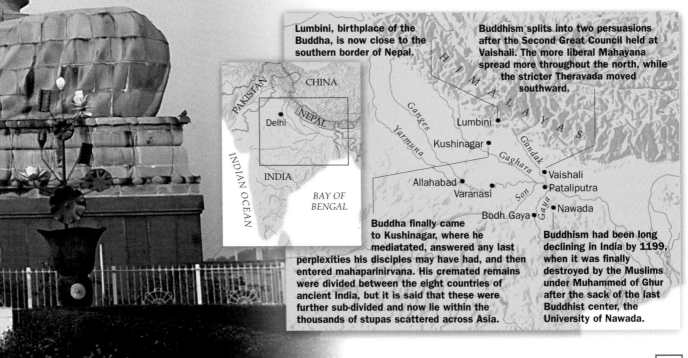

Lumbini, birthplace of the Buddha, is now close to the southern border of Nepal.

Buddhism splits into two persuasions after the Second Great Council held at Vaishali. The more liberal Mahayana spread more throughout the north, while the stricter Theravada moved southward.

Buddha finally came to Kushinagar, where he mediatated, answered any last perplexities his disciples may have had, and then entered mahaparinirvana. His cremated remains were divided between the eight countries of ancient India, but it is said that these were further sub-divided and now lie within the thousands of stupas scattered across Asia.

Buddhism had been long declining in India by 1199, when it was finally destroyed by the Muslims under Muhammed of Ghur after the sack of the last Buddhist center, the University of Nawada.

Buddhist Belief

"Go ye forth, O Bhikkhus, for the gain of the many, for the welfare of the many, in compassion for the world. Proclaim the Doctrine glorious, preach ye a life of holiness, perfect and pure." With these words, the charismatic Buddha dispatched his missionaries to spread the new belief.

The Buddha gave his first sermon at the Deer Park near Varanasi. His messages were committed to oral tradition, only written down centuries later. They must have sounded exciting and radical to those Indians used to Hindu elitism. He was evidently a gifted orator—his crystal-clear vision about life and the way it should be lived won immediate favor with his audience. The Buddha's teachings can be distilled into a series of maxims. First come the Four Noble Truths revealed to him as he meditated beneath the bo tree:

1. Life is full of suffering and disappointment (*dukka*).
2. The cause of suffering is pursuit of worldly pleasures or power (*samodaya*).
3. To end suffering people must abandon their material hopes and dreams (*nirodha*).
4. The Eightfold Path (*magga*) is the route to liberation from suffering.

The Eightfold Path is a charter intended to lead the adherent to nirvana (bliss):

i. Right Views: knowing and understanding the Four Noble Truths.
ii. Right Thoughts: release from desire, acting with kindness.
iii. Right Speech: telling the truth and avoiding causing hurt.
iv. Right Action: never stealing or cheating.
v. Right Livelihood: earning wages in a job that doesn't harm others.
vi. Right Effort: fostering positive attitudes.
vii. Right Mindfulness: being aware of the effect of thoughts and deeds.
viii. Right Concentration: finding tranquility through the Eightfold Path.

As further guidance, the Buddha imparted the Five Precepts, a reflection of the

Eightfold Path but not a copy of it. Keywords here are sympathy and empathy:

a. Be compassionate. Do not harm people or animals.
b. Do not steal or take what has not been given. Be generous to those in need.
c. Avoid drugs and alcohol because they inhibit meditation.
d. Do not bad-mouth other people.
e. Respect others and avoid sexual immorality.

There are a further three Precepts but only the most devout choose to abide by them. They involve not eating after midday, no dancing or singing, and no garlands or makeup. Together the Noble Truths, Eightfold Path, and Precepts combined to be the Middle Path (or Way) by which the Buddha hoped to lead people to enlightenment. The extremes of Hindu asceticism were abandoned in favor of a highly manageable life plan.

A group of people called the Kalamans sought an answer from the Buddha about a pressing problem. His reply is often quoted as an illustration of how Buddhism works from within: "When you know for yourselves that this is unskillful and that skilful, this blameworthy and that blameless, this deprecated by the wise because it conduces to suffering and ill and that praised because it conduces to well-being and happiness… when you know this for yourselves, Kalamans, you will reject the one and make a practice of the other."

The Buddha saw his mission as bringing light to the world's darkness. He veered away from dogma, choosing instead a highly moral approach involving self-analysis and appraisal. Apparently capable of performing miracles, he decided not to

FACING: A Vaishnavite Hindu ascetic, a devotee of Vishnu (see also picture, page 141), prays with prayer beads beneath a Bodhi (Bo) tree in the Sarnath Deer Park near Varanasi, where the Buddha gave his first sermon after receiving enlightenment under a bo tree at Bodh Gaya. Buddhism may no longer be a force in India, but Buddhist sacred sites still exert an influence on Hindu holy men and ascetics and especially appeals to those of the lower castes (see reference on page 151).

exhibit supernatural powers. He believed the route to enlightenment was the greatest miracle of all.

In old age he still traveled the land, including a spell on the shore of Lake Amritsar (*see page 171*), living frugally and preaching to his supporters. His death came in about 483 BC at Kushinagar in Uttar Pradesh, surrounded by disciples. Before passing away he lapsed into deep meditation; it is this state that statues of reclining Buddhas are mimicking (*see picture, pages 6–7*). The Buddha's final words were: "The doctrine and discipline which I have imparted to you will be your leader when I am gone. Try hard to reach the goal."

The Buddhist Lifestyle

To understand Buddhist doctrine involves more than scanning the pages of a book. Far better to live it, as Buddha himself pointed out. After his death, however, there was disagreement over how it should be done.

BELOW: A woman gives rice to three monks in the village of Wat Po, Cambodia. The nearest monk is only a teenager, and it is common in Buddhist communities for boys as young as eight or nine to become novices.

Millions have lived Buddhism since the time of its founder, joining the Sangha or "community of believers" to follow his path. Thus imprints of the Buddha's footsteps have enormous symbolic meaning. An early convert to the principles of sex equality, the "sage of the Sakyas" permitted both men and women in the Sangha; the Buddha's stepmother

circumstances is highly meritorious. The teaching of the Buddha's truth is known as the *dharma* in Sanskrit or *dhamma* in Pali, the Indian language probably used by him. The Sangha, the Buddha, and the *dhamma* comprise the Three Jewels, a fundamental Buddhist creed. "If you think of Buddha, of the dharma, and of the Sangha, fear, trembling, and terror will cease to exist," the

became an early devotee. Laymen and laywomen are also traditionally considered part of it.

In countries where Buddhism proliferates, the sight of a saffron-robed, shaven-headed Buddhist monk or *bhikku* clutching a food bowl is a common one. People living nearby willingly fill it. To give freely in such

Buddha pledged.

Like Hindus, Buddhists believe in reincarnation and karma, the law of cause and effect. Early on in his mission, the Buddha put forward the theory of "no self" or obliteration of the ego to vault ahead in the journey toward enlightenment.

Once a convert has comprehended the

reality of the Three Jewels, he is thought as a "once returner," with just one more life on Earth to endure. The next stage is a "non-returner," someone born into a higher heaven. Subsequently he is an *arhat*— "one who is worthy." He has achieved the perfection of nirvana and will not be born again. One school of Buddhism insists the higher state of attainment is that of a *bodhisattva*, one who chooses rebirth above nirvana in order to work for the benefit of others.

MAHAYANA AND THERAVADA SCHOOLS

Buddha and his disciples attracted the enmity of rival teachers and sects. There were allegedly three attempts on his life. The Buddha refused to name a successor, insisting instead that his teachings would remain as a universal guide. A few generations after his death, Buddhism fragmented into at least 18 and perhaps as many as 30 different schools of thought.

After the Second Great Buddhist Council, held at Vaishali, the world's Buddhist community polarized between two persuasions. The first school was called Mahayana (large vehicle) and embraced a liberal approach over interpretation of Buddhist scriptures. Offering more freedom to its followers, Mahayana was then subject to local variations, according to custom and belief. Tibetan Buddhism, with its figurehead of the Dalai Lama, became markedly different from Zen Buddhism, which flourished in China. Mahayana is associated with China, Japan, Korea, Nepal, and Tibet.

The second school was staunchly conservative, accepting only the word of the Buddha. This was called the Theravada or Hinayana (small vehicle) and is the form of Buddhism popular today in Sri Lanka, Burma, Thailand, Laos, and Cambodia.

One man did more to spread Theravada Buddhism around Asia than any other. Asoka, an emperor in the Mauryan dynasty in the middle of the third century BC, began his rule with a bloodthirsty campaign of conquest down the east coast of India. The devastation wrought by his forces was shocking, even to him. As Asoka toured the

newly defeated provinces, he encountered Buddhism and became an earnest believer. Not only did he choose to live by the tenets of Buddhism, he ensured his family, ministers, and other branches of government did so too.

Although other faiths were tolerated, Buddhism was actively encouraged. If the wealth of inscriptions from the era are to be believed, Asoka was just, sincere, zealous, rational, and community-minded. He was the patron of numerous missionaries who spread the Buddhist word beyond the extensive boundaries of his empire.

Asoka explained his philosophy like this: "All men are my children. As for my own children, I desire that they may be provided with all the welfare and happiness of this world and of the next, so do I desire for all men as well."

ABOVE: The Dhamekh Stupa was constructed by Asoka, the great Buddhist emperor, in the Deer Park at Sarnath, amid many other, lesser stupas. It is said that Dhamekh stands on the exact site of the Buddha's first sermon. Asoka erected numerous monuments to Buddhist beliefs the length and breadth of India, many of them embellished with detailed reliefs showing the life of his people, from the highest to the lowest stratas of society.

Buddhist Texts

"I, Buddha, who wept with all my brothers' tears, whose heart was broken by a whole world's woe, laugh and am happy, for there is liberty! Ye who suffer! Know ye suffer from yourself." These words refer to the second Noble Truth, but were written centuries after the Buddha's death.

D isagreement over which parts of Buddhist texts were spoken by its founder and which are the work of devout members of the Sangha has inevitably occurred between the two major schools of Buddhist thought. Western scholars have added their doubts, rooted in the time lapse between the Buddha's lifetime and the production of a written version of his teachings.

Confusion has further arisen because his sermons were delivered across a broad area where there were many different dialects. The Buddha himself was happy for his words to be translated so that his message could be understood. But the result was that numerous traditions sprang up, all of which could be traced back to the Buddha.

Nevertheless, there is a scripture that can confidently portray itself as representative of the oral history associated through religious communities with the Buddha. The Pali Canon was apparently compiled in Sri Lanka on palm leaves in the first century BC. It was in the northern Indian tongue similar to or the same as the Buddha's.

The stories and sayings in this scripture were recited by Ananda, Buddha's trusted companion, at the First Council, held at Rajagrha in the first rainy season after the Buddha's death. Some 500 members of the Sangha worked hard to memorize what Ananda said and that is the content of the first and largest book of the Pali Canon, the *Sutra Pitaka*. It has five collections or *nikayas* of the Buddha's discourses in prose and verse, each beginning with the phrase, "Thus I have heard."

The rules of the faith laid down

by the Buddha were quoted by another disciple, Upali, and likewise committed to memory. These became the second and smallest book, the *Vinaya Pitaka*. It is this that in theory governs monastic life for Buddhists today, although in reality large sections are disregarded.

THE ELUSIVE NIRVANA

The third tome is the Abhidhamma, which translates to "higher doctrine." In essence it is an analysis of the first two, evolving later in time. Together the three are also called the Tripitaka—the three baskets.

In Mahayana Buddhism the scriptures are in Sanskrit, although most of the originals have now been lost. Many exist only in their Tibetan or Chinese forms. There were additional texts disputed by the rival Theravada Buddhists. Mahayana texts also contain more commentary written by scholars and sages. Yet broadly both Theravada and Mahayana scriptures are comparable in content and can claim spiritual authority.

The words of the Tripitaka, spoken some 500 years before the Christian era, remain relevant even in a modern world: "Just as a mother would protect her only child even at risk of her own life, even so let one cultivate a boundless heart toward all beings."

Yet the mightiest challenge remains—to explain in words the concept of nirvana, the central message bequeathed by the Buddha. To firstly comprehend and secondly lucidly verbalize this positive, liberating notion is not easy. In essence, everyone burns with rapture and desire, but it is these that bring about misery. The aim is to put out the fire that burns to the detriment of all humans, to achieve a passionless state. Sometimes the condition is alluded to as "the far shore" or "the cool cave."

One reading from a Theravada text puts it like this:

As a blazing spark struck from the iron
Gradually fades to an unknown course,
So the one who has truly won release,
Crossed the floods of sensuality's bonds
And reached immovable peace,
Goes to a course that transcends definition.

FACING AND BELOW: Rows of small pagodas hold the 729 stone tablets which together contain the entire text of the Buddhist canon, the Tripitaka, in the Pali script. Each tablet is housed in a separate miniature pagoda. This complex sits at the foot of Mandalay Hill, Mandalay, Myanmar (Burma).

Buddhist Sects: Zen, Rinzai, Soto, *and* Tantric

BELOW: Rocks and raked sand in a Zen garden create a contemplative mood in Kyoto, Japan.

Buddhism and dogma are words that do not sit together easily. The free-flowing nature of the faith assisted its export around Asia and its character varies from region to region, from the meditative Zen Buddhism of China to India's marginalized Tantric sect.

BELOW: Rocks and raked sand in a Zen garden create a contemplative mood in Kyoto, Japan.

In China and Japan, Zen Buddhism emphasizes the importance of self-knowledge. Through this adherents will be able to achieve enlightenment in the same way as the Buddha, it is claimed. The key aspects of Zen Buddhism are wisdom, knowledge, and experience. Blind faith has no place in this style of Buddhism.

"Listen to the sound of one hand clapping." This is an example of an enigmatic *koan*, derived to exhaust the conscious mind, rendering it open to enlightenment. Sometimes the *koan* is a question. The answer to "What is Buddha?" is "Three pounds of flax." Bizarre they might seem, but *koans* are designed to make Zen meditation so easy it can be done while walking or working.

The 1,700 *koans* were derived from the sayings of ancient Chinese masters. The classic collections in use today are *Blue Cliff Records*, with commentaries by Chinese priest Yuan-wu, compiled in 1125, and another gathered a hundred years later by Hui-k'ai.

Buddhism reached the Far East at about the same time that Christianity was setting down roots around the Mediterranean. Buddhist ideas were initially expressed in the terms of Tao (*see page 158–159*). The Chinese readily embraced Buddhism for its similarities to Taoism—indeed, some believed that Lao Tzu had been reborn as the Buddha. Two monks are attributed with translating Buddhist scriptures into Chinese. Kumarajiva (AD 344–413) and his pupil Seng Chao (383–414), both talented philosophers, were influenced by Confucianism and Taoism. Another important figure, the Indian monk Bodhidharma (460–534), taught that "Nature, Mind, Buddha, Path, and Zen" were connected. Bodhidharma won fame—or notoriety—for meditating facing a wall for nine years, until his legs withered.

Buddhism in all its forms flourished until a state-sponsored suppression in 845 in which some 45,000 temples and shrines were destroyed and a quarter of a million Buddhist monks and nuns were forced into lay life. Afterward Zen Buddhism made the best recovery. One Chinese scholar described Zen Buddhism as "a reformation or revolution in Buddhism."

BUDDHISM REACHES THE KHANATE

Buddhism arrived in Japan via Korea and was often received with hostility as a rival to the existing Shinto religion (*see pages 162–163*). It wasn't until the 12th century and an overhaul in the governmental system that Buddhism stood on solid ground. A monk called Eisai (1141–1215) founded the Rinzai sect in 1191, which set great store in *koans*. The Soto sect emerged soon after, fashioned by another monk, Dogen (1200–53), lauding the virtues of silent meditation and a more gradual journey to enlightenment.

Buddhism was established in Tibet in the eighth century largely by one monk, who "tamed" the spirits and demons of the indigenous Tibetan religion to the satisfaction of the populace.

In 1578 the Tibetan Buddhist Sonam Gyatso converted Altan Khan, the chief of the Mongols, and was made Dalai Lama, translating to "ocean of wisdom." It was a post of political and spiritual significance. Tibet became a country of fortified monasteries and powerful *lamas* (religious leaders) and developed distinctive traditions, including the use of prayer wheels and flags.

Tantric Buddhism, which blends ritual, magic, and meditation, emerged as the face of the faith in seventh century India. Yet after that Buddhism waned in India, until it was almost non-existent in the land in which it was born. This was partly due to the robust counterattack staged by Hindus after seeing adherents hemorrhage away.

However, Buddhists are reporting a surge in conversion rates in present-day India as thousands of lower caste Indians seek to escape discrimination. More than 20,000 underwent a ceremony in New Delhi on just one day in 2001. The movement to liberate the so-called "untouchables" began 50 years ago under the auspices of Bhimrao Ramji Ambedkar, himself a convert. Since then an estimated four million people have followed in his footsteps and a further million are poised to switch faiths.

ABOVE: Prayer flags strung across the road lead up the hill toward the Potala Palace, Lhasa, home of the Dalai Lamas until eviction by communist Chinese forces in 1956.

Persecution *of* Buddhists

The history of the hauntingly beautiful Angkor Wat temple in Cambodia was stained in 1975 when it became the site of a massacre by Khmer Rouge soldiers on the equable community of resident Buddhists. It was not the last aggressive act against Buddhism.

Despite their propensity for peace and humility, Buddhist communities all over the world have been subject to appalling prejudice and persecution. The greatest oppression has been felt in Tibet, where Buddhism has largely been driven underground by occupying Chinese forces.

The histories of Tibet and China had been intertwined for many years before the influx of Chinese forces in 1956. Three years later the population of Tibet rose up against its uninvited foreign rulers but was ruthlessly suppressed. Most of the 6,000 monasteries and nunneries across Tibet were closed down; many were completely destroyed by the Chinese. The Dalai Lama, spiritual leader of the Tibetan Buddhists, fled the country as a refugee and settled in neighboring India, where he is still based today. Remarkably, Tibetan Buddhism has not withered or died under the strain of exile. The displaced Buddhists' cause has attracted international attention on a massive scale. Although only 24 years old when he left Tibet, the Dalai Lama has matured into the role of spiritual leader and wise diplomat, winning the Nobel Peace Prize in 1988.

The opening of the 21st century was marked by an appalling act of vandalism against Buddhist monuments, which once again was the subject of international condemnation. Tucked away in a picturesque valley in Afghanistan, the Bamiyan Buddhas were objects of admiration for centuries. Standing at 174 and 125 feet high, these representations of the Buddha were carved out of a cliff face in the Hindu Kush Mountains in the fourth or

fifth century AD. It was a time when the faith was mushrooming in Afghanistan—the country was the stepping stone for the development of Buddhism in the eastern world, including China, Japan, and Korea.

ERASING THE ICONS

Countless travelers along the Silk Route cast their eyes in wonder at these imposing figures, the largest in the world, climbing numerous steps to look out from the top of the largest statue's head. Within a few centuries Islamic forces had swept through the region. The religious face of the nation turned toward Mecca and the Bamiyan Buddhas became monuments to a bygone age. At the beginning of 2001 the radical Islamic government that ruled Afghanistan, the Taliban, ordered the monuments' destruction. Islam finds all religious statues and artwork offensive. The authority for iconoclasm comes from Moses, who destroyed the gold calf made by the Hebrews as he conversed with God at Mount Sinai.

The face and hands of the Bamiyan Buddhas had been the subject of attacks for centuries before the Taliban came to power, as had the frescoes decorating monks' cells in the vicinity. Now tank and anti-aircraft fire was directed at the Buddhas. Holes were drilled in the heads and torsos to house dynamite. Pleas from the international community wishing to preserve or remove the statues fell on stony ground. Ironically, later the Taliban were content for chunks of the Buddhas to be sold to the world's antiquarians.

In 2000, Taliban ministers had allegedly taken axes to an estimated 2,750 ancient works of art in the National Museum of Kabul in pursuit of the same ideology. No other Islamic government, no matter how

ABOVE: From his exile in India, the Dalai Lama remains the spiritual leader of Tibetan Buddhists and continues to seek a peaceful resolution to the secular occupation of Tibet by China.

FACING: Photographed in 1975, the largest of the monumental Bamiyan Buddhas showed the damage inflicted by Islamic militants for more than a century. At this time, restoration work was under way. In 2001, the Taliban ordered the complete destruction of all the Buddhas, in spite of international outrage. Various reconstruction plans are currently under consideration.

devout, has indulged in such cultural recklessness. Buddhism is a missionary religion, yet it has never been spread by force of arms. It is the passive nature of the faith that has left it vulnerable to other religious and political forces.

Jainism—Faith *of* Sympathy

In the long-distant past, 24 heroes—tirthankaras—laid the foundations of Jainism. Little is known about the tirthankaras except that they used considerable mental powers to free the soul. Jainists are notable for their strong belief in the sanctity of all life.

RIGHT: A member of the Svetambara, or "white-clad," sect wears white robes and a mouth guard to prevent him from inhaling and killing insects.

BELOW: A follower of the "sky clad" sect, the Digambaras, squats naked against a wall in Sikar, Rajasthan. His contempt for worldly goods is symbolized by his lack of clothing. His only possessions are a water container and a fan of peacock feathers used to clear his path of insects so he cannot accidentally tread on them.

Jain is derived from *jina,* meaning "conqueror." Yet these are men and women who go to extraordinary lengths not to harm another living thing. They wear masks so flies are not accidentally inhaled. They brush the path in front of them so they don't squash insects.

The last *tirthankara* was Vardhamana Mahavira (599–527 or 540–468 BC), who is today given credit for launching one of the world's most sympathetic faiths. Mahavira was born to parents who already advocated Jainist philosophies. Their duty of faith apparently led them to starve themselves to death so they would cause no further harm to the world. Legend has it that Mahavira married and fathered a daughter before embarking on the unforgiving lifestyle of an ascetic. He cast off all his worldly possessions, even his clothes, for a dozen years before achieving the supreme knowledge he was seeking, called *kevala.* With it came remarkable insight into the human condition.

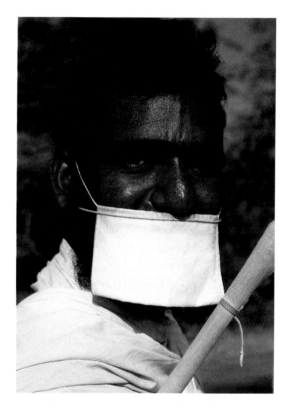

In the remaining years of his life Mahavira and 11 disciples gathered a community of believers and defined the parameters of the religion. According to Jaina tradition his followers numbered 14,000 monks and 36,000 nuns before his death, which occurred close to his birthplace in Patna, eastern India.

Given the proximity of Jainism, Buddhism, and Hinduism, it is not surprising to find common ground. Mahavira probably preceded the Buddha by just a few years and is mentioned in Buddhist scriptures. Like Buddhists the Jains are non-violent vegetarians. As with Hinduism, there is a selection of deities.

However, Jains place a far greater emphasis on non-violence (*ahisma*) than even devout Buddhists. Thus they diverge entirely from Hindus, who pursue animal sacrifice as an integral part of their faith.

THE THREE JEWELS

Jains believe in karma, that actions attach themselves to the psychic body and inhibit the all-important transmigration from earthly being to nirvana. But they view it as a more physical thing, clogging up the soul. The malign activities of karmas are stalled by the adoption of the Jaina code for life: right faith, right knowledge, and right conduct. Yet it is pointless achieving one if it is not in concert with the other two. Only the cultivation of all Three Jewels (different from the Jewels of Buddhist belief) will achieve the inner well-being necessary for karmic release.

Like other faiths, Jainism was soon subject to schism and two parallel sects emerged. The Digambaras are "sky-clad"—naked, in the manner of Mahavira. All they own is a water gourd and a broom made of peacock feathers, used to clear their path. Their begging bowl is the palm of a hand. Once a day, with eyes downcast, they seek sustenance from the community. Having forsaken possessions, they deem themselves one step away from the material world, while still short of a spiritual realm. Digambaras, always male, thrived in southern India.

The Svetambaras are "white-clad," dressed in pale robes, and include women. They are associated with northern and central India. Unlike the Digambaras, they place credence on the 11 Angas ("limbs") and other religiously significant documents that comprise the Jain scriptures. The Digambaras believe all authentic Jain scriptures were lost hundreds of years ago, although they do set store by some commentaries. Members of both sects refrain from washing, for fear of killing bodily parasites or polluting water.

We better know the symbol of the Jain religion as a swastika. Hitler adopted the line representation of the sun and its rays in the middle of the 20th century. Reversed, the religious symbol became the emblem of an entirely different philosophy.

LORD BAHUBALI—A JAINIST SAINT

Prince Bahubali, also known as Gometashvara, fought his prideful brother Bharatha for the inheritance of their father's kingdom. Overpowering Bharatha, Bahubali was about to kill him when his heart filled with remorse at his violent thoughts. Bahubali gave up the kingdom to Bharatha and renounced all wordly things, including clothing. He then performed penances so intense that creepers grew around his body. His story is an example of the inner strength of Jains. The region of Karnataka in southwestern India is home to many monumental statues of Bahubali. This is the largest, near the Jain pilgrimage town of Sravanabelagola. Sculpted from one piece of stone, it stands almost 56 feet high. Pilgrims wash the statue's feet in an annual festival. The most important—Mahamastabikeshba—occurs every 12 years, when Bahubali is festooned with food and sandalwood.

Zoroastrianism—Faith *of* Fire

Once the faith of world leaders, now a religion on the brink of extinction,
Zoroastrianism suffered a dramatic decline in fortunes as Islam swept across Asia.
Often known as Parsis, its followers strive for clarity of thought.

ABOVE: The Ka'aba of
Zoroaster in Naqsh-e-
Rostam, Iran (near the site
of old Persepolis), which
stands in front of King
Darius I's tomb, was built
c.500 BC. Some scholars
believe it was a fire altar.
The tower resembles some
minarets of the first
Islamic era, and indeed
Muslims developed the
concept further to
become the minaret (see
page 44).

BELOW: A Zoroastrian
avoids touching the dead.
Traditionally, corpses are
carried to Towers of
Silence (Dokhmas) where
they are laid bare to
vultures, who pick the
bones clean within two
days. These two towers
stand near Yazd, Iran.

At its peak Zoroastrianism is believed to
have wrought influence over Judaism,
Christianity, Mahayan Buddhism, Greek
philosophy, and even Islam. Today it claims
only about 200,000 adherents, confined
mainly to pockets in Iran and India. The
story of Zoroastrianism's decline is
complicated by doubts over its dates and
deities that are impossible to resolve.

The eras associated with Zoroaster—or
Zathrustra, as he is known in Persian—vary
by a thousand years. He was born some
time before the fifth century BC in a remote
part of Persia and given the name Spitama.
As he fetched water from the River Daitya
for a festival in the ancient Persian religion,
he was taken to the celestial court of Ahura
Mazda, the Lord of Wisdom, where he
experienced a vital revelation. It is not
known if Ahura Mazda already existed in
Persian religion. Ahura Mazda is powerful
but not omnipotent. He is seen as all-
knowing and ever-present but not a creator
god and never to be feared. The emphasis
lies in "a good mind," using rational
thought to dispel ignorance. In opposition is
Angra Mainyu, an evil spirit who can be
overcome with "a good mind."

Like all religious messengers, Zoroaster
underwent rejection and derision, which
ultimately drove him from his community.
However, after converting the influential

King Vishtaspa of Eastern Persia, the infant
faith found fertile territory in which to breed.

Zoroastrian scriptures comprise the
17 songs or *gathas* within texts known as the
Yasna bequeathed by Zoroaster, in addition to
further hymns and a code of conduct together
known as the Avesta. Zoroaster is thought
to have spoken the Avestan language, a
sister of Sanskrit. Later scriptures—the
Pahlavi—set out a more detailed cosmology
and are written in Persian. This indicates
the rudiments of the faith must have spread
considerably over the centuries. It is likely
that mystical elements were embellished
with the involvement of the Magi, the
Persian sages who embraced the religion.

RELIGION OF THE FAITHFUL

For a thousand years Zoroastrianism
powered ahead, not least because it became
the adopted faith of the Persian Empire. At
Persepolis, the lavish city built by Darius I
(c.558–486 BC), the Achaemenid king of Iran,
Ahura Mazda is depicted in stonework.
Although the Achaemenid Empire was
defeated by Alexander the Great, its ultimate
successor between AD 224–636 was the
Sassanid dynasty, which took its name from
a Zoroastrian high priest. With one exception,
the Sassanids were devoted to Zoroastrianism
as a symbol of Persian greatness.

In an early departure from the state
religion, Shapur I acted as patron to Mani
(216–274), a self-styled prophet who
declared that Zoroaster, Buddha, and Jesus
were religiously interlinked. Manichaeanism
had considerable success and was shaping
up as a serious rival to Christianity; it
spread as far as Spain and China. In Persia,
however, it was suppressed by a subsequent
Sassanian king, Bahram I. A devotee of
Zoroaster, Bahram had Mani and his
followers crucified. Manichaeanism was so

undermined in its native Persia that it became impossible to sustain elsewhere.

In 766 Zoroastrians were the victims of persecution. Many fled to India to escape the fierce monotheism of the Muslims. The Hindu name for Persian is Parsi and they are still known by this name today.

In practical terms, the Zoroastrian behaves moderately, believes that fire is sacred, is charitable, marries within the faith, and does not seek to convert others. It is thought that anyone who can leave one religion is not likely to be faithful to the next.

Taoism—*the* Way *to* Confucius

Just as Confucianism is down-to-earth and worldly, so Taoism is enigmatic and spiritual. Taoism founder Lao Tzu (also spelled Lao Zi and Laotse) dwells upon mythology, while Confucius has flesh-and-blood qualities. Yet the thoughts of both men shaped the outlook of millions of Chinese for two-and-a-half millennia.

BELOW: A Sung dynasty statue of Lao Tzu seated on an ox—this is the most popular depiction of the philosopher. The blue ox carried Lao Tzu out of China and into Central Asia so that he could spread his teachings. Lao Tzu was supposed to have been in his mother's womb for 81 years before emerging already an old man. His name literally means "aged child."

The world says that my Tao is vast / And is not like anything else / Because it is great, therefore it is not like anything else. / If it were like something specific, / It would have become trivial long before now.

Taken from the ancient book of *Tao Te Ching*, the stanza above, translated by Thomas H. Miles, is an attempt to solve the riddle of life from an Oriental perspective. The *Tao Te Ching*, the manual of Taoism, is a collection of apparently abstract views that are known equally as well in China as Confucius's *Analects*.

Tao translates to "path" or "road." In English the notion of Tao is best translated as the (correct) Way, but its definition remains elusive. Tao implies harmony, tranquility, effortlessness, and spontaneity. One of the fundamental principles is that if Tao can be spoken about, it is not the Absolute Tao. A keyword is inaction— letting things take their natural course.

Te is another complicated word to translate but probably can best be thought of as "power" or "potential." Together, *Tao Te Ching* becomes "Classic of the Way of Power," a slim book in two parts with a total of 81 chapters.

Clearly, it takes considerable time and intuition to get a handle on this faith/philosophy. Its lack of hard facts even extends to authorship. For centuries Lao Tzu was considered the craftsman behind the *Tao Te Ching* but doubt shadowed this theory from the 19th century. There are no historic co-ordinates within the text to provide further clues—the best guess is that it was written some time between the eighth and third centuries BC. Taoism was expanded by numerous thinkers after the publication of the *Tao Te Ching*, the most prominent being Chuang Tzu (350–275 BC).

MEETING OF MINDS?

Lao Tzu remains an obscure figure. The first written biography appeared centuries after his death. He was apparently born in Honan province and grew up to work in the royal court of the Chou dynasty, which reigned supreme between 1111 and 255 BC.

It was long believed that as an old man Lao Tzu met with a much younger Confucius. The story goes that the former was dismayed by the mannerly ways of Confucianism, while the latter was struck by

Lao Tzu's serenity. Tempting though it is to date Lao Tzu in this way, there are no texts to authenticate the tale, outside of mythology. Confucius was, however, impressed by the theories of Taoism, pondering, "Who can go out without using the door? So why does nobody follow the Way?"

As the Chou dynasty declined, Lao Tzu allegedly took a journey into China's wild west. The guard of a frontier post begged for his teachings in written form and the result was the *Tao Te Ching*. Thereafter Lao Tzu, already a tremendous age, vanished into the mountains and was never seen again. The words of the *Tao Te Ching* have been cherished by the Chinese and pored over by Western scholars after they gained entry into Oriental culture in the modern era.

There was something formed from Chaos.
Born before heaven and earth.

Ultimate and wonderful.
Existing alone without change.
Circulating cyclically without depletion.
It acts like the mother of the world.

Not knowing its name,
I call it "Tao."
If forced to name it,
I would call it "Great."

Taoism adopted mystical practices centuries after the demise of Chuang Tzu. Elements like meditation, feng shui, divination, and temple ritual came to the fore. The Chinese, imbued by the wisdom of Lao Tzu and Confucius, were convinced of the power of the Way. However, its effectiveness was called into question when the cultured Sung dynasty was conquered by the barbarous Mongols in the Middle Ages.

BELOW: During the Chinese New Year Taoist worshippers visit Wong Tai Sin Temple in Kowloon, Hong Kong to burn joss sticks and present offerings.

Confucianism—*a* Civil System

Kong

fu

zi

ABOVE: Three characters that are a familiar sight on temple walls in the East.

Social reformer, sage, sportsman, father, and philosopher. K'ung-fu-tzu or Kongfuzi, better known to the West as Confucius, was all these things and more. But because successors doggedly followed his teachings, China became shackled to its past.

Although he died in 479 BC, Confucius remained very much alive in the minds of the Chinese for centuries afterward, mainly due to the mighty body of written work that was attributed to him. His words were deemed enduring and relevant for generations. Thanks to Confucius and his acolytes, Chinese society

philosophies compelled Confucius to give up his lowly post. He gathered a group of disciples, willing listeners for his ideas. Ironically, his ambition to win a high-ranking government post in which he could radically change the nature of society was never fulfilled. As a "voice of conscience" Confucius was eventually appointed as a

ABOVE: Female dancers in traditional costume perform at Mummyo Shrine at the Sungkyun-kwan Institute of Confucius Studies, Seoul, Korea during Sokchonje, a Confucian spring rite.

was founded on prescribed civility and ran like a well-oiled cog. Politeness and respect were lauded qualities.

Grand Master Kung (Kongfuzi) was born c.551 BC in what is now Shantung province, northeast China. He grew up in straitened circumstances and initially worked as a bookkeeper to finance his family. Soon the lure of teaching his well-observed

minister to King Lu but earned few friends and soon left the job, frustrated.

Although disillusioned, Confucius did not abandon his philosophies and continued the program of self-cultivation that he advocated for everyone. He explained: "When I walk with two others, I always receive instruction from them. I select their good qualities and follow them, and avoid their bad qualities." This earnest pursuit of personal improvement held wide appeal and, by the time of his death, some 3,000 students were in his thrall.

According to Confucius, there were five relationships in society that were sacrosanct. They were between ruler and minister; father and son; husband and wife; older brother and younger brother; and friend and friend. Only the last pairing was equal; the dominance of one partner above another in all other relationships set a hierarchical society, with certain members enjoying deferential treatment.

Confucius introduced safeguards to prevent abuse of the system. In return for civil obedience, the emperor was expected to act benevolently. Corrupt, vicious dictators should be ousted by whatever means open to the people. A humane ruler leading a virtuous people should have no need of a legal system, he said. His own ideal role model was King Wen, the Cultured King, who ruled in the 11th century BC at the head of a regime marked by high moral integrity.

DOMINANCE OF TRADITION

Confucian thought set the agenda for Chinese scholars for centuries. Accordingly, the words taught to schoolchildren in the time of the Han dynasty of the first century AD were repeated to young people in the 20th century, without heed to changing attitudes. Anyone wishing to enter the civil service had to become an expert on the works of Confucius. This singularity of approach kept education within narrow confines and heaped importance on ceremonial ritual rather than scientific advance. Because of Confucius the Chinese developed an abiding love of education but failed to capitalize on it.

Temples were set up to honor Confucius, in which he was known as "The teacher of ten thousand generations," although Confucius maintained a rational approach to supernature and advised men to shape their own destiny rather than rely on faith or divination. When questioned about Heaven and the afterlife, he sensibly replied, "Not know life, how know death?"

CONFUCIUS WAS NOT PERFECT
Confucius was not entirely enlightened and was prone to small-mindedness. He once said that only uneducated women were virtuous and sometimes referred to females as "little people." As revealed in his book, the *Analects*, Confucius complained bitterly if his rice was under- or overcooked.

However, his insistence upon reverential respect for the elderly enhanced the existing practice of ancestor worship.

There's plenty to admire about the teachings of Confucius: "In education there should be no class distinction"; "In the presence of a worthy man, think of equaling him. With a worthless man, turn your gaze within"; "Humaneness is to love others."

ABOVE: This undated portrait of Confucius is widely used in many forms. It originates from a rubbing taken from a stele in the Pei Lin de Sigan-fou, the Forest of Stele.

Shintoism—Way *of the* Kami

The Shinto religion has been a beacon for the Japanese through triumph and adversity. An integral part of everyday life since the earliest times, it was named only in the sixth century, to distinguish between native Japanese religion and incoming Buddhism.

At the heart of the Shinto faith is the concept of *kami*, a broad sweep of sacred or divine beings that includes elements of nature. It is impossible to be more explicit than that. Some scholars insist any further clarification of the word *kami* is a worthless exercise, but further definitions are needed to illuminate its significance. Even Motoori Norinaga (1739–1801), a famous scholar of Shintoism, professed difficulty in fully comprehending the term. He said: "*Kami* signifies in the first place the deities of Heaven and Earth that appear in the ancient records and also the spirits of the shrines where they are worshipped.

"It is hardly necessary to say that it includes human beings. It also includes objects like birds, beasts, trees, plants, seas, mountains, and so forth. In ancient usage, anything whatsoever outside the ordinary, which possessed superior power or which was awe-inspiring was called *kami*."

An early distinction between heavenly and earthly *kami* has long been lost. Some estimates put the number of *kami* at eight million, and growing. The word Shinto, or *Kami no michi*, translates to "Way of the Kami," and in the absence of a true founder it is the *kami* who are revered.

Norinaga re-established a bridge between Japanese mythology and modern Japan via Shintoism. Japanese people might confess to confusion over *kami*, but there is no mistaking the potency of this much-loved tale: Legend says that Japan was united under Emperor Jimmu in 660 BC. He was, it is said, the great-grandson of Ninigi whose grandmother was Amaterasu, goddess and highest-ranking *kami*. Amaterasu dispatched her grandson to Earth with a mirror, a sword, and a jewel, which remain sacred symbols at Shinto shrines. This celestial link established a divinity around the Japanese royal family that endured for centuries.

GATEWAY TO THE SACRED WORLD

The earliest known records for Japanese religious history are the *Kojiki* (Record of Ancient Things), written in Chinese in AD 712. Eight years later came the *Nihongi* (Chronicles of Japan), which incorporated material from the seventh century BC, although its authenticity is doubtful. However, there is no counterpart to the Koran or Bible.

Shinto has been subject to change, influenced by other religions that have infiltrated the Far East. These are primarily Buddhism, Confucianism, and Taoism, although latterly there has been a Christian presence in Japan. Today the Shinto faith is recognized in three forms: Shrine, Sect, and Folk Shinto.

Shrine Shinto emerged when the highly nationalistic and mandatory State Shinto was banned after the Japanese defeat in World War II. It remains closely identified with the Japanese imperial family. Sect Shinto is the umbrella term for at least 13 different movements launched during the Meiji period (1868–1912), when the last shogun was overthrown in favor of the emperor. Each sect has a different priority, for example, faith healing. Folk Shinto is an unstructured system revolving around worship at sacred roadside or agricultural shrines. This may well be the same brand of Shintoism that existed centuries ago.

Every Shinto shrine is marked by at least one *torii*, a gateway symbolizing entry into a sacred world. Mountains are important to Shintoism for being homes of both *kami* and the dead, thus Mount Fuji, the dormant volcano that gives Japan its highest point, is especially significant.

The Ainu people of Hokkaido were hunter-gatherers. They only came under Japanese rule in the 17th century.

HOKKAIDO

Northern Honshu fiercely resisted Japanese expansion until the 12th century.

Akita •

• Wakamatsu

Echigo •

• Ashikaga

• Edo

Suwa •

Kamakura

MT. FUJI ✛

Nara became the first imperial capital in 710 under the Taira clan, where Buddhism was the primary religion. To get away from overt Buddhist influence, the capital moved to Heian in 794. Over the centuries, Shinto belief remained assimilated into Buddhist philosophy, but remained separate, especially in rural areas.

(Heian) Kyoto •

Hinomisaki •

Izumo •

Osaka •

Ise

HONSHU

SEA OF JAPAN

Himeji •

Nara •

Okayama •

Horyu-Ji

Hiroshima •

MT. HAKKEN ✛

Yamaguchi •

• Iki

SHIKOKU

PACIFIC OCEAN

✛ MT. KUJU

✛ MT. ASO

Nagasaki •

KYUSHU

✛ MT. KIRISHIMA

• Kagoshima

Japan between 600–1500
- • main centers with Shinto shrines
- • other important Shinto shrines
- ▢ Northern Fujiwara clan
- ▢ Minamoto Yoritomo clan
- ▢ Minamoto Yoshinaka clan
- ▢ Taira clan

163

The Story *of* Sikhism

Guru Nanak fashioned Sikhism against a backdrop of longstanding religious bigotry and hatred between Hindus and Muslims. He was influenced by the works of Kabir, a preacher who extolled the benefits of both groups.

"I shall follow God's path. God is neither Hindu nor Muslim and the path which I follow is God's." These were the revelatory words of Guru Nanak (1469–1539), the founder of the Sikh faith in northern India. For inspiration, Guru Nanak looked to his teacher, Kabir (1440–1518), which in Arabic

karma and the potency of lyrical verse, he said. However, the caste system and asceticism were awry. With Islam he backed the fundamental tenet—there is only one God and all men are equal before him. By voicing support of both faiths he won the blessing of neither and was run out of his hometown of Varanasi.

He embarked on a personal mission, preaching in small towns and villages around the region. Kabir remained unpopular with those in the hierarchies of the Orthodox religions, but his message struck home among ordinary people. At the time of his death Hindus and Muslims reputedly tried to claim his body—but all they could find was a wreath of flowers.

Kabir's words lived on in his verses and he became the focus of several cults, including the Kabirpanth. Some of his writings were included in Sikh sacred literature, while Kabir's work alone was collected for a book, *Bijak* ("account book"), published by a devotee some 50 years after the preacher's death.

ABOVE: A gilded plaque in the Golden Temple of Amritsar depicts the founder of Sikhism, Guru Nanak, seated between a disciple on the right and the Muslim musician Mardana on the left. Guru Nanak believed that the lyrical quality of music helped to emphasize the nature of his preaching.

means "great." Kabir was allegedly the illegitimate son of a high caste Indian woman who was adopted by a Muslim family. One legend says that he was the product of a divine conception, his mother's pregnancy discovered after a visit to a Hindu shrine. Kabir embraced Islam but also expressed fascination with elements of Hinduism and became a pupil of an eminent ascetic.

Ultimately, Kabir sought to combine the two major faiths in what he called simple union, claiming both possessed concepts that were aspects of the same truth. Hindus were right to believe in reincarnation and

THE FIRST GURU

Facts about the life of Guru Nanak are equally difficult to discern. Born into a Hindu sub-caste of the Khastris in Talwandi, to the southeast of Lahore in the Punjab, he married, fathered two children, and worked in a granary before adopting the life of a wandering holy man. His travels, as well as anecdotes about his childhood, became the subject of "testimonies" written after his death by followers, which were probably embellished to befit a guru's life.

Nevertheless, some bear scrutiny, even today. During a visit to Mecca, Nanak was reprimanded for prostrating himself away from the holy Ka'aba. "Turn my feet in a direction where God is not to be found!" he charged his accusers. His first revelation occurred in Sultanpur, where he worked for an Afghan chieftain. While bathing in a stream, Nanak disappeared. When he emerged three days later he announced, as if in a trance, that there was only one God, who was not Hindu or Muslim.

Sikhism and the Kabirpanth held special appeal for Hindu Vaishnava devotees, Yogis, Buddhist Siddhas, and Muslim Sufis. These groups were prone to rituals that were exhibitionist by nature. When Guru Nanak witnessed these he reprimanded them for neglecting true meditation and contemplation.

He ended his days at Kartarpur, a village built on land donated by a well-wisher. A stream of disciples—or Sikhs—trekked to see him and to worship in the first Sikh temple, which he established there.

True to the socialist-style principles supported by Guru Nanak, the leadership of his new religious movement did not automatically pass to his son, but to the disciple deemed most worthy and most able to bind the faithful together. Guru Angad (1539–52), an obedient disciple to the founder, became the new spiritual leader of Sikhs.

BELOW: Sikhs in Lahore, Pakistan pay homage to Guru Nanak in a crowded room. Images of the gurus are often enshrined in Sikh households. However, Sikhs are monotheistic and use the pictures and Granth Sahib (see pages 168–169) as focal points for their faith, not objects of worship. They do so in the knowledge that the human guru is not on a par with God and that God is the ultimate guru.

The Sikh Gurus

The success of the Sikh movement in its early years was enhanced by the advent of the Mughal Empire in 1526, heralding a golden age of wisdom and culture in northern India. Later emperors, however, were intolerant of the gurus.

Relations between Sikhs and state flourished during the reign of Akbar (1556–1605), the greatest of the Mughal leaders. Deeply interested in spirituality, Akbar interviewed leaders of all major faiths, including the incumbent Sikh, Guru Arjan, and formed a religion of his own by extracting the most appealing aspects of each.

On Akbar's death, Guru Arjan was accused of supporting a rival to the royal successor, Jehangir, and was tortured and killed, becoming the first Sikh martyr. The same fate befell Guru Tegh Bahadur 70 years later, killed on the orders of Aurangzeb, the last Mughal emperor, when he refused to embrace Islam.

In response, Tegh Bahadur's son and successor, Guru Gobind Singh, put the Sikh movement onto a military footing. With the aim of upholding religious freedom for all, Guru Gobind Singh armed Khalsa disciples with five symbols of faith: *kes* (uncut hair), *kangha* (comb), *kara* (steel wristband), *kirpan* (sword), and *kacch* (loose trousers).

Gobind Singh also changed the surnames of all Sikhs to Singh, which means "lion," to emphasize that they were all of one family. Women had the surname Kaur, meaning "princess." Tragically, his own children were martyred by Emperor Aurangzeb.

Gobind Singh declared that the 11th and final guru would be the religious scriptures of the Sikh faith, by this time considerably enlarged since the days of Guru Nanak.

Gobind died in 1708, the year after Aurangzeb.

By the mid-1850s, Sikhs and warriors from the Gurkha hill-tribes of Nepal formed the backbone of the British Army. At this time expansionist Russia was Britain's primary concern, but uprisings of Pathans kept 35,000 men on the notorious Northwest Frontier.

The partition of India in 1947 split the Sikh heartland of the Punjab, leaving the greater portion in Pakistan and the smaller in India.

Kabul

Peshawar

islamabad

Kashmir

Indus

Jhelum

Punjab
to Britain 1849

Chenab

Lahore

Amritsar

Kartarpur

Indus

Multan

Sutlej

Anandpur

Talwandi

Sirhind

Bahawalpur

Rajputana

HIMALAYAS

NEPAL

Indus

Delhi

Ganges

Thar Desert

Mathura

Jaipur

Yamuna

Growth of Mughal Empire by:

- 1526
- 1540
- 1605
- 1707 under Aurangzeb
- British territory by 1846
- — modern border

The swift advance of the Moghuls from the north of the Punjab east and then south benefitted the spread of Sikhism at first. Later Moghul emperors turned against the Sikhs.

THE TEN SIKH GURUS

Guru Nanak (1469–1539)
The author of many hymns, collected in the Granth Sahib. He worked with musician Mardana, a Muslim, and found considerable success in extending his message through music.

Guru Angad (1504–52)
Originally known as Lehna, he impressed Guru Nanak with his sincere humility and cheerful disposition. He penned hymns and developed the *gurmukhi* script, an alphabet of 42 letters, to more accurately reflect the message of the gurus.

Guru Amar Das (1479–1574)
Best remembered for introducing two festivals into the Sikh calendar: Baisakhi is a harvest festival, although the date was later shared to mark the beginning of the Khalsa (see page 171). Diwali is a festival of lights, similar to the celebration held among Hindus. It later became the celebration of Guru Hargobind's release from prison. Guru Amar Das also developed the notion of the *langar*, a community meal open to all following a service at a Sikh temple.

Guru Ram Das (1534–81)
For the first time a relation of the guru was picked as successor. (Guru Ram Das was the son-in-law of Guru Amar Das.) This began an unbroken chain of nepotism. He founded the city of Amritsar and dug the pool by which the Golden Temple now stands. He also contributed to the Granth Sahib and wrote what has become a traditional wedding hymn.

Guru Arjan Dev (1563–1606)
Not only the man who completed the Golden Temple, but also the editor of the Adi Granth, a collection of works by his predecessors.

Guru Hargobind (1595–1644)
The son of Guru Arjan, he finally established cordial relations with his father's persecutor, Emperor Jehangir. He developed a building program for *gurdwaras* (temples) and defined a government based on Sikh religious laws.

Guru Har Rai (1630–61)
The grandson of Guru Hargobind. He studied medicines and established the principle of free medical treatment for all.

Guru Har Krishan (1656–64)
Aged only five when he succeeded his father as guru, he died at eight of smallpox contracted while caring for victims of the disease.

Guru Tegh Bahadur (1621–75)
He was the great-uncle of "the Boy Guru" and was keenly devoted to feeding the hungry. In recognition of his resistance to the wholesale conversion of the region to Islam he was given the name "Brave Sword."

Guru Gobind Singh (1666–1708)
A military man, he was also the writer of hymns that were collected into the Dasam Granth. He died at the hands of an assassin.

ABOVE: Souvenir portraits of the Sikh gurus adorn a local store wall in Amritsar. Such paintings tend to conform to the general Indian delight in bright colors and, in this, often resemble modern iconography of popular Roman Catholic pictures of the saints and the Virgin Mary. However, Sikhs do not pray to icons.

Sikh *Religious* Texts

Unlike any other faith, Sikhism has works from rival religions among its scriptures. The words of eminent Hindus and Muslims sit alongside those of revered Sikhs and are held in the same esteem. There can be no better illustration of how open, equal, and tolerant Sikhism aspires to be.

BELOW: A copy of the Granth Sahib, resting on a special cushioned throne, is read to a congregation.

The primary book of scriptures, which lies central to the Sikh faith, is known by two names: the Adi Granth ("the first book") or the Granth Sahib (the Granth personified). It remains the Guru of Sikhs; thus they turn to it for guidance and wisdom. Such is the respect accorded to the Granth Sahib, it is given a room of its own in temples and homes, just as an honored teacher might be. In the morning it is

attributed to Guru Nanak. There are poems by Hindu and Muslim saints, with a notable contribution from Kabir, as well as the learned words of seven of the gurus (the sixth, seventh and eight bequeathed no writings). The total is nearly 6,000 eloquent exhortations of devotion to God in prose and poetry, interspersed with ethics, mostly written in the *gurmurkhi* script.

The Granth Sahib begins with the Mul

respectfully carried to a canopied, cushioned throne called the Manji Sahib. At night it is carefully wrapped up and stowed away in safety. Before consulting its pages, worshippers remove their shoes, cover their heads, and wash their hands.

The Granth Sahib contains 974 hymns

Mantra, or basic prayer: "There is one God, Eternal Truth is his name, Creator of all things and the all-pervading spirit. Fearless and without hatred, Timeless and formless. Beyond birth and death, Self enlightened. By the grace of the Guru he is known." The same words denote the start of each of the

book's 31 sections.

It is followed by the Japji, or recital, written by Guru Nanak: "There is but one God, whose name is true, the Creator, devoid of fear and enmity, immortal, unborn, self-existent, great and bountiful."

EQUALLY REVERED VOLUMES

The Granth Sahib takes center stage at the *gurdwara* or temple. It is the first object worshippers see when they enter the *gurdwara*, elevated above the members of the congregation, who typically sit on the floor. When it is opened, the devout Sikh waves a *chauri* or fan across it to keep insects at bay, as used for the comfort of high-ranking dignitaries in India. Money and food are offered to the Granth Sahib, just as they would have been to human gurus. These are later distributed in the community.

When they were first given the opportunity to mass-produce the Granth Sahib, Sikhs were confronted with a dilemma. Would owners scattered far and wide keep it in the prescribed manner?

Would there be inappropriate competition for the finest copies? The compromise solution was to make each copy uniform, extending to the same length—1430 pages—and including one key passage on page 939, which sets practices and philosophies for Nanak's followers.

Additional writings important to Sikhs include poetry by Bhai Gurdas, who assisted Guru Arjan in compiling the first Granth Sahib. Bhai Nandlal, a companion of Guru Gobind Singh, left works that go alongside the Granth Sahib, explaining oblique references and elaborating on themes.

The Dasam Granth, poetry by the prolific tenth guru, is written in *gurmurkhi*, Sanskrit, Persian, and other Indian languages, making it hard to comprehend. It is never accorded the same honor as the Granth Sahib, despite the distinguished author.

The onerous duties of possessing a Granth Sahib make it an impractical addition to most normal households. However, the handheld Gutka, which sets out daily prayers, is far more accessible.

ABOVE: The Granth Sahib is treated with utmost respect. Having been removed from its own room, the book is placed on a cushion on a canopied throne (in the photograph, taken in Anandpur Sahib, India the book itself is hidden behind the front of the cushion). It is these lengths that make it difficult for an ordinary Sikh household to own a copy of the sacred book.

Sikh Worship—*the* Gurdwara

All gurdwaras are peaceful places, none more so than the splendid and striking Golden Temple at Amritsar, northern India. The center of Sikh worship, it is one of the greatest holy sites in the world.

Initially, Amritsar seems like any other dusty, noisy, industrial Indian city. But at its heart it breathes tranquility, with a magnificent gold- and copper-clad monument perfectly reflected in the still waters of a picturesque pool. This is the axis of the Sikh faith. Even in the widespread diaspora of Sikhs in the past century, Amritsar has remained the faith's most potent and holy of places.

Guru Ram Das founded the city on a site granted by Mughal Emperor Akbar and began by excavating the "pool of nectar." His son Guru Arjan completed the Golden Temple—also known as Hari Mandir—after the foundation stone was laid by an eminent Muslim, Mian Mir. He ensured everyone had to take a step down into the temple, to indicate it was open to the humblest of people. It became the spiritual home of the remaining gurus.

Marauding Afghan invaders made several attempts to raze the temple during the 18th century. By 1764 Sikhs had restored

it to its former glory. In 1802 it was given its distinctive roof of copper overlaid with gold foil by Ranjit Singh (1780–1839), the so-called Lion of the Punjab who established a Sikh kingdom prior to British subjugation of the region (*see following page*).

Linked by a causeway to the rest of the city, the temple stands in isolation. It is open to all, although everyone must observe the rules of cleanliness by removing shoes, washing feet, and covering heads before entering. There are continuous readings from the Granth Sahib throughout each day, broadcast via loudspeaker.

AT THE GURU'S DOOR

Northern India is dotted with significant sites for Sikh pilgrims. At Sirhind the two young sons of the tenth guru, Gobind Singh, were walled up by ruling Muslims as punishment for refusing to convert from

Sikhism. A *gurdwara*—meaning "the guru's door"—now marks their martyrdom.

The Khalsa army was formed at Anandpur Sahib in 1699. Guru Gobind Singh addressed Sikhs celebrating the festival of Baisakhi at a time when the religion was under pressure from Islam. He asked for one man willing to die for his faith to step forward. The volunteer was taken into a tent from which the guru emerged, brandishing a sword dripping with blood. A further four men came forward and the same thing happened.

The guru then paraded the men, alive and well, before stunned on-lookers. He was, Gobind explained, testing the loyalty and faith of the men. They were to be the first members of the Khalsa, formed not only to defend Sikhism but anyone who was poor or helpless. This event occurred in the *gurdwara* Kesgarh Sahib, although there are a number of other temples in the town.

Gurdwaras have numerous roles. They are, of course, suitable places for meditation and praise, consequently the atmosphere is always contemplative and calm. They also provide temporary accommodation for the homeless, a meal for the hungry, and a social center. Sometimes they are used as clinics or dispensaries.

Marriages and naming ceremonies are held at *gurdwaras*. During a marriage service the pivotal role of the Granth Sahib is emphasized when the happy couple walk four times around the book in a clockwise direction. Without this ritual the wedding is not valid. When a baby is named the book is opened at random and the first verse on the left-hand page is read out. A name is chosen with the same initial as the first word.

There is no holy day for Sikhs and worship is an ordered if informal affair. Music and singing play an important role.

Sikhs use tanks of water for bathing, where possible. Ranjit Singh built a pool at Taren Taran next to an existing *gurdwara*. According to legend, any leper who swims across the tank will be miraculously cured. The Sikh scriptures categorically denies that bathing in a holy pool purifies or ensures salvation, but asserts that it may help to spiritually discipline the mind.

LEFT: The cornerstone of the Sikhs' religious life is the Golden Temple of Amritsar, seated at the center of a small lake. Originally sited in a quiet forest, the lake of Amritsar (its name means "pool of ambrosial nectar") had drawn sages since antiquity. Buddha is known to have spent time meditating on its shores (see page 145). It also drew Guru Nanak, and after his death the lake became a shrine to his followers. Enlarged and its banks laid to stone at some point in the 1570s, the Hari Mandir (Temple of God) was built between 1581 and 1601. Muslims destroyed the temple on numerous occasions, but the Sikhs always rebuilt it more beautifully. During the reign of Maharaja Ranjit Singh (1780–1839), the temple received the gilding and rich marble surrounds it has today.

Persecution *of* Sikhs

During its history Sikhism has spawned numerous sects that have disputed the authority of the faith's perceived orthodoxy. Yet none of the internal divisions has matched the pressure put upon Sikhs by a series of external enemies.

ABOVE: Not to be confused with the Punjab governor, O'Dwyer, General Dyer was the man who ordered British troops to open fire on unarmed Sikhs at Amritsar in 1919.

At first Sikhs were pressed into militancy by the encroachment of Islam. However, the colonial British arrived in the region by the 18th century to furnish the Sikhs with a new enemy.

Sikhism flourished under Marahaja Ranjit Singh (1780–1839) but rivals bickered following his death, weakening the leadership. Consequently the Sikh kingdom in the Punjab was left vulnerable to British empire-builders of the East India Company. After the Sikh Wars of 1845–46 and 1848–49 the Punjab was incorporated into the British realm. The cause of the Sikhs was laid low for half a century. Its resurgence mirrored a general desire for independence held among Indians of all faiths.

The idea of nationalism was refuted by the British. In 1919 lieutenant-governor of the Punjab Sir Michael O'Dwyer presided over one of the bloodiest massacres to stain the history of imperialism. British soldiers opened fire on thousands of peaceful demonstrators in Amritsar, leaving 337 men, 41 boys, and a baby dead. A further 1,500 were wounded, some shot as they tried to flee the attack. The incident sparked a campaign of civil disobedience orchestrated by Mohandas Gandhi, who declared "co-operation in any shape or form with this satanic government is sinful." O'Dwyer survived the political fall-out—to some he remained a hero—but was killed by a Sikh in 1940 who had been serving water at the

fateful demonstration and bided his time before securing revenge.

When India regained its independence in 1948, the Sikhs had a new dispute on their doorsteps. As a significant minority, they had hoped to have a homeland following the partition of India. Instead they found themselves under Hindu government.

BATTLE AT AMRITSAR

Feeling increasingly frustrated and sidelined, elements of the Sikh faith grew ever-more radical in response. Unrest in the region brought army reinforcements to Amritsar in 1984, at the same time as pilgrims were gathering to mark the anniversary of the death of Guru Arjan Dev. The standoff between Sikhs and troops erupted into violence and scores were killed on both sides.

While Sikh extremists holed up in the Golden Temple for a protracted battle, the Indian government initiated Operation Blue Star, in which tanks and artillery were mobilized. By the time the Indian Army gained control of the town, hundreds of Sikhs had been killed. Among the dead were Sant Jarnail Singh Bhindranwale, the leader of the extremists, and numerous unarmed civilians caught up in the battle.

The extent of the casualties and the desecration wrought to holy places inflamed Sikh opinion. Sacred books were destroyed,

the Golden Temple was sprayed by more than 300 bullets, and the Akal Takht, the center of Sikh religious and political authority, was destroyed. Ultimately, Prime Minister Indira Gandhi was held responsible for the bloodshed at Amritsar. Five months later, as she walked from her office to meet actor Peter Ustinov, she was shot dead by two of her Sikh bodyguards. Hitherto faithful servants, the men were tested to the limit by the perceived injustices that had occurred.

One of the men, Beant Singh, was shot by police at the scene. The other, Satwant Singh, who had used his Sten gun on the 67-year-old premier, was tried and hanged. There was intense backlash against Sikhs from Hindus in mourning for Indira Gandhi.

THE DIASPORA OF A FAITH

Globally, there is estimated to be about 20 million Sikhs. While most still live in the Punjab region of India and Pakistan, a great many have dispersed since World War II to form communities as far apart as Indonesia and Canada. The largest concentrations are in Canada—an estimated 400,000—and the United Kingdom—estimated at between 350,000 and 500,000. In a continual act of protest, British Sikhs are fighting for exemptions from British and European Commission laws that enforce the wearing of safety helmets for motorcycle riders and construction workers. They argue that the Sikh's turban is at least as effective as a helmet, a fact often proven during World War II.

Krishna Consciousness

Krishna Consciousness is a faith that came from East to West with immaculate timing. Its moral, peaceful code of conduct appealed to opponents to the arms race and the Vietnam War.

In the mid-1960s increasing numbers of young people were concerned about the lack of spirituality in the Western world, where consumerism is king. A rich vein of discontentment was revealed by the burgeoning hippie movement. Accordingly, the succinct simplicity of the new Krishna religion met wide appeal.

Behind its success was the dynamism of one man, A.C. Bhaktivedanta Swami Prabhupada (1896–1977), who traveled from his home in India to New York to begin a remarkable ministry. Bhaktivedanta grew up in Calcutta, where he became engrossed in devotional Bhakti yoga, also known as

Krishna Consciousness. He studied in detail the words of Chaitanya Mahaprabu (c.1485–1534), who advocated finding God through repetitive chanting, using the words:

Hare krishna, Hare krishna
Krishna krishna, Hare hare
Hare rama, Hare rama.
Rama rama, Hare hare.

As early as 1922, Bhaktivedanta's spiritual master appealed to him to preach the religion in English, at a time when little heed was taken of Hinduism outside India.

BELOW: Perhaps the most familiar sight of "Hare Krishna" devotees is as a group, chanting, playing drums, and small cymbols while walking amid the sidewalk crowds of cities—in this case, London.

Bhaktivedanta was a family man and chose to pursue a career (in the pharmaceutical industry), in keeping with Hindu obligation. As a mark of commitment he began writing and publishing a magazine, *Back to the Godhead*, in 1944, surmounting the difficulties of wartime shortages to do so.

It wasn't until 1950 that Bhaktivedanta renounced his family and business to dedicate his life to preaching. At first he wrote English language books based on the teachings of Chaitanya Mahaprabu. Soon he realized the pressing need to personally extend his mission overseas and he determined to travel to America.

CHALLENGING NEW WORLD

In 1965 he chose the inglorious means of a cargo steamship, *Jaladuta*, to reach Boston, Massachusetts, from India. During the 35-day passage, Bhaktivedanta was dangerously ill, suffering two heart attacks. The frail man was then confronted by the cutting edge of American life where, he confessed, he "did not know where to turn, left or right."

But using a donation from followers, Bhaktivedanta finally moved to New York and rented a shop front. A small band of supporters joined him in worship. The number of converts grew significantly after he led the first open-air *sankirtan* (chanting and dancing) held outside India. The event in Tompkins Square Park amply illustrated the ecstasy of worship available to participants and soon hippies were shaving their hair to join the movement.

In July 1966 Bhaktivedanta initiated the International Society for Krishna Consciousness (Iskcon). Members clad in saffron robes and banging drums or tambourines became a familiar site in busy streets and at airports as they distributed *Back to the Godhead*. At the time of his death in 1977 Bhaktivedanta had opened 108 centers under the Iskcon umbrella and written 51 books. Within 20 years the number of centers had more than doubled, with Iskcon represented in more than 60 countries.

The movement has been subject to accusations of cultism and brainwashing. Yet adherence to its strict life codes—

Krishnas do not gamble, drink, smoke, eat meat, or have promiscuous sex—has helped drug addicts and alcoholics kick their habits. Krishnas are vegetarians active in temples, urban centers, farms, and restaurants, committed to missionary work, but do not seek to eradicate other religions. Since the death of Bhaktivedanta a 30-strong governing body has run the movement.

Most celebrated of the thousands of converts was former Beatle George Harrison (1943–2001). Introduced to Hare Krishna by sitar player Ravi Shankar, Harrison became absorbed by Indian mysticism and wrote a Number One hit single in praise of Hare Krishna, *My Sweet Lord*. In 1973 he donated Bhaktivedanta Manor, Hertfordshire to Iskcon and was believed to have channeled further wealth to the movement through his will.

ABOVE: The founder of Krishna Consciousness, A.C. Bhaktivedanta Swami Prabhupada. In 1969, in celebration of his commitment to the teachings of Prabhupada, Beatle George Harrison produced the "Hare Krishna Mantra" single together with members of the London Radha-Krishna Temple. The mantra reached the number-one position in the European and Asian charts.

The Unification Church

ABOVE: Sun Myung Moon and his wife preside over a mass wedding in Madison Square Garden on July 1, 1982. Moon had been building up to the world's largest wedding in Seoul in 1995; this American event joined 22,000 couples.

On August 25, 1995 the world's largest mass wedding took place in South Korea. The Reverend Sun Myung Moon, founder of the Unification Church, took the vows of 35,000 couples crammed into Seoul's Olympic Stadium. A further 325,000 couples were married via satellite link-up.

Events like the mass wedding have given Sun Myung Moon fame and notoriety in equal measure. Moon and his wife match partners for suitability—there is no room for courtship or romance. Marriages are not consummated for three years; the notion is that this ensures the blood of infants is pure.

Scrutiny of Sun Myung Moon's affairs in the religious, political, and business worlds have resulted in hostile headlines. Yet still church members are at work in more than one hundred countries. They know themselves to be part of the Holy Spirit Association for the Unification of World Christianity. In the eyes of secular cynics they are the Moonies.

Sun Myung Moon was born in 1920 in Korea—then under Japanese domination—into a family of farmers who became enthusiastic Presbyterians. While he prayed on a mountainside during Easter at the age of 15, Moon had a vision of Jesus. Christ implored him to complete the mission begun almost 2,000 years previously and bring peace to mankind.

Moon studied philosophy, theology, and

the Bible before setting down his beliefs, with a program of teachings known as the Divine Principle. After World War II, Moon preached in communist North Korea, where he was jailed for unknown reasons. He was freed from a labor camp by United Nations forces active in the region following the Korean War, having attracted some support for his ideals from fellow inmates.

On May 1, 1954 Moon founded the Holy Spirit Association for the Unification of World Christianity. Long since excommunicated by the Presbyterian Church of Korea, his activities were frowned upon by the South Korean government. Yet the number of disciples continued to grow. In 1971 he significantly expanded his ministry by moving to the U.S., where his appeal for Christian renewal found keen support and his anti-communist sentiments were reflected.

A NEW MESSIAH?

Misplaced public endorsement of disgraced President Richard Nixon turned the tide of feeling against Moon. He was accused of brainwashing the young people joining his church. In 1982 he received an 18-month prison sentence for tax evasion, serving 13 months. Thereafter he continued traveling across America and the world, expounding his message.

In 1992, after serving 40 years "in the wilderness," Moon proclaimed himself the messiah of a new age. Moon and his wife portray themselves as the True Parents of the human race. In a well-worn speech, Mrs. Moon explained that: "The Messiah is the True Parent of humankind. God's original plan was to establish perfected Adam and Eve as the true ancestors of humanity. Satan, however, invaded this ideal and God, ever since, has been working toward the emergence of ideal True Parents through which all humankind can be restored."

The Unification Church is known as much for its wealth and business dealings as it is for

spirituality. It has owned a large number of organizations, including *The Washington Post*. Moon and his family live in a compound furnished with every luxury. In 1998 a book by his former daughter-in-law, Nansook Hong, demolished the carefully cultivated perception that Moon, his wife, and children were imbued with divine qualities.

To mark the 40th anniversary of the Unification Church, Moon announced its new identity: the International Federation for World Peace. But the church still receives bad publicity. In August 2001 it was revealed a Roman Catholic archbishop from Zambia had wed a doctor belonging to the Unification Church from South Korea, to the undisguised fury and astonishment of the Vatican. Following prolonged and secluded discussions with the Roman Catholic hierarchy, the archbishop promised to end his three-month marriage and return to the celibacy of the priesthood.

ABOVE: Reverend Sun Myung Moon and his wife pose happily for a photograph in 1982, only days before he was sentenced to 18 months imprisonment for U.S. tax evasion.

Religious Conflict *in* Asia

With just about every known religion represented on the continent of Asia, perhaps it is no surprise to find it a crucible of conflict. The most startling example of recent times was the war in Afghanistan, initiated by the attack on New York's World Trade Center on September 11, 2001.

As the perpetrators of the attacks on the World Trade Center and the Pentagon came to light, it seemed that Muslims had declared war against the West. In reality, a tiny number of hard-line Islamic fundamentalists were behind the atrocity. Muslims worldwide were loud in their condemnation of the killings, finding no justification for it in the pages of the Koran.

Jihad was the buzzword of the period, believed by many Muslims and non-Muslims to mean a radical assault to further the aims of Islam. An alternative, authentic definition of *jihad* favored by the majority of Islamic scholars is the inner struggle of every Muslim to become a better person. Mohammed exemplifies the essence of *jihad*—he constantly strove to improve himself, to be of greater benefit to his community. This "greater" *jihad* embraces obedience to God and is the crux of Islamic conflict. A so-called "lesser" *jihad* relates to the military option of overthrowing unjust regimes, Muslim or otherwise.

In power, Afghanistan's Taliban regime was disciplined and joyless. Music, television, radio, education for girls, women's employment, and kite-flying were just a few of the things that were banned. Its ministers reduced Islamic law to a means of regulating behavior and dress. Little heed was taken of centuries of culture and humanity that had gone before. Still, extreme Muslims flocked to defend its corner.

THE PRICE OF DEMOCRACY

Why did this outbreak of fundamentalism occur? Strong reservations about American foreign policy had been accruing in the Muslim world, where the U.S. has long been dubbed "the great Satan." America traditionally justified its military activities in countries across the globe as being in defense of democracy and freedom. Critics claim the subtext of U.S. involvement was to buttress its financial interests overseas, particularly when it interfered in the politics of the Middle East, where oil was the crucial commodity. America has been accused of accommodating the worst regimes to maintain stability in the region and preserve its economic hegemony.

Through Muslim eyes, the conflict in Palestine is considerably worsened by U.S.

the region has escalated since the late 1980s—as many as 30,000 people have died in fighting. When trouble flares, both sides are quick to reinforce their borders.

Fundamentalism of a different nature was demonstrated in the Far East on March 20, 1995. Five men boarded a Tokyo subway to release the nerve gas Sarin upon rush-hour

LEFT: Muslims armed with lathis (a quarterstaff) surround the body of a Hindu killed in communal riots in Calcutta, August 24, 1946. Scenes like this became a depressingly familiar sight throughout northern India during the late 1940s, as violence between Hindus and Muslims broke out on many occasions during the partition of British India into Pakistan and India. Hundreds of thousands died on both sides of the religious divide. After a period of uneasy peace, Hindu-Muslim violence erupted again in the 1960s, and has been a constant in Indian political life ever since.

support of an aggressive Israeli regime. However, Muslim governments are typically undemocratic and sometimes repressive. This has also contributed to the frustration of Muslims and highlighted the divide between East and West.

The conflict in Afghanistan overshadowed another long-running dispute in the region, which threatened religious violence in the new millenium. For years Pakistan and India have disputed territory in the Kashmir, a predominantly Muslim area under Hindu rule. Militancy in

commuters. Twelve people died and thousands were injured in the ensuing chaos.

The killers were members of the Aum Shinri Kyo cult, a faith founded by Shoko Asahara featuring elements of Buddhism, Christianity, and a flavor of Hinduism. Those responsible have since received the death penalty. Their aim was allegedly to fulfill Asahara's Armageddon prophecies. Despite the group's outlandish claims about the Christ-like nature of its leader and wide-ranging conspiracies against Japan, there are still at least a thousand professed members.

CHAPTER 7

Australasia

From minor skirmishes with the first penal colony at Port Jackson in 1788, Aboriginal unrest boiled over in several battles during the 1830s. Inevitably, the settlers' superiority in weaponry reduced the Aborigines to a handful of settlements in the north and center by the 1870s.

Ownership of Ayers Rock has been given back to the Aborigines, for whom the famous site has ceremonial significance. It is now known by its Aboriginal name of Uluru.

Map labels:

INDIAN OCEAN
TIMOR SEA
ARAFURA SEA
GULF OF CARPENTARIA
Melville Island
Darwin
Daly
Roper
Ord
Victoria
McArthur
Broome
Fitzroy
Port Hedland
DeGrey
Fortescue
Ashburton
Gascoyne
Murchison
GREAT SANDY DESERT
Tanami Desert
Burketown
Normanton
Norman
Flinders
Cooke
Ca
GREAT DIVIDING
Geraldton
Gibson Desert
AUSTRALIA
MACDONNELL RANGES
Alice Springs
Uluru (Ayers Rock)
Flinke
Simpson Desert
Macumba
Eyre Creek
Warburton Creek
Towr
Menzies
Kalgoorlie
Great Victoria Desert
Oodnadatta
Perth
Freemantle
Esperance
Albany
GREAT AUSTRALIAN BIGHT
Lake Everard
Lake Gairdner
Lake Torrens
Lake Eyre
Warrego
Port Augusta
Port Lincoln
Broken Hill
Port Pirie
Menindee
Adelaide
Darling
Bourke
Balonne
Gwy
1788–1840
1821–36
Port Ma
Port Step.
Wellington 1804–23
Port Jackson (Sydney)
New
Lachlan
Murrumbidgee
Murray
Melbourne
Port Phillip 1802–52
Western Port
Canbera
Bass Strait
TASMAN SEA
Port Dalrymple
Macquarie Harbor 1821–34
Derwent
Tasmania
Hobart 1804–53
Maria Island 1825–32
Port Arthur 1830–77

At the dawn of the 21st century it seemed Australasia was one of Christianity's great success stories. Five out of every six people in Oceania professed to be a Christian of one type or another. This in a region where the faith was unknown just two-and-a-half centuries ago. But one consequence of this religious triumph has been less palatable. The Christian surge has signaled the near-demise of native cults, which had provided a strong centuries-long social framework for adherents.

A 1966 Australian census revealed that just 560 out of a population of more than 80,000 Aborigines claimed to be non-Christian. Significantly, 26,500 people did not reply, ruling themselves out of any religious classification. The situation in Australia mirrors that in New Zealand and the Pacific. A rich and diverse religious life around the region has been subsumed by a foreign culture, albeit one that arrived with the best of intentions.

Missionaries in the 19th century set out from Australia to convert the inhabitants of numerous Pacific Islands. This is ironic, since religion had been neglected or completely ignored in Australia for many years. The first Christian service to take place on its soil was held eight days after crews had landed to claim the colony. For years its parliament was held without religious reference. The first prayers to preface a parliamentary meeting occurred in New South Wales as late as 1862. Even at that time people were worshipping under the umbrella of the Church of England. Only in 1966 did the Anglican Church in Australia

supercede it, with the nation's primate rather than the English monarch at its head.

Catholicism was propagated in Australia largely by Irish convicts sent there by British courts, and its association with the working classes led to a long-standing link between Catholicism and the Australian Labor Party. Immigration since the end of World War II has introduced the full gamut of Christian denominations to Australia (and New Zealand too), as well as Jews and Muslims.

Only with the benefit of hindsight have indigenous religions been celebrated as national assets in Australasia. Fortunately the trend to cherish and protect native customs and beliefs emerged just in time.

Carved spirit-figure posts adorn the end of the roof ridge on many Maori houses.

Maori resistance to European occupation was fiercest in the North island during the First Maori War (1843–48). Fighting broke out again in 1860 but died out by 1870. A peace between Maori and European settlers was formally concluded in 1881.

□ British penal colony and date of operation

region of Aboriginal or Maori unrest

Spirits *of* Dance–Aborigines

In 1770 James Cook and a handful of his crew landed in what became Botany Bay. Botanist Joseph Banks described the natives who greeted him as "one degree removed from the brutes." In fact the Aborigines had a rich sacred heritage that made rival religions appear flat and unimaginative by comparison.

Captain Cook was more receptive toward the Aboriginal tribes. "They may appear… to be the most wretched people on Earth but in reality they are far happier than we Europeans…. They live in a tranquility which is not disturbed by the inequality of condition."

Probably without realizing it, Cook had appreciated the visible benefits of Aboriginal religion, which tailored the naked, painted people of the outback into a

BELOW: With body paint and full ceremonial dress, Aboriginal boys in Arnhem Land, Northern Territory anxiously await their initiation into the adult community by the ritual of circumcision.

The beating heart of Aboriginal religion is the Dreaming. At its most basic the Dreaming is the story of creation. Mythical beings in human or animal form emerged from water holes or caves. These "totemic ancestors" had been in a deep sleep within the world but, once awakened, were able to change form. They molded the bare earth and imparted it with enduring natural assets. From them came mankind.

Rock formations and waterfalls have been personified as earthly remnants of the mythical beings. Although, according to legend, some died and some were transformed, all are imagined as living, vibrant beings.

Aborigines numbered at least 300,000 and had been living on the continent for at least 30,000 years when white settlers arrived in Australia. They were not subject to one central "government" or chief but were scattered in different groupings, thus the interpretation of the Dreaming differed in detail. Certainly it was known by various names, including *altjira, wongar, djugurba,* and *allcheringa.*

The Dreaming and the schedule of beliefs attached to it gave each society a structure, a code of conduct, and an ethereal reward.

contented community. Its potency lay in the force and phenomena of nature, where the faith is rooted. There's myth and magic, art and poetry, and a sense of spirituality equal to any in the world.

It was passed down in a solid oral tradition—written expression did not come to the Aborigines until the 20th century. Given the history of the Aborigines under white rule, it is surprising the notion of the Dreaming survived at all.

SUBJUGATED BY COLONISTS

Hostility between the newcomers and the indigenous population rapidly developed. Whites mostly concluded Aborigines were savages and believed they could be dealt with accordingly. The situation was further exacerbated by competition for land. The colonists were quick to claim the best farming land or areas with significant mineral deposits, regardless of whether these were important hunting grounds for Aborigines or held spiritual importance.

Even those few white settlers who held no animosity toward the natives brought disaster by carrying diseases like smallpox that were hitherto unknown on the continent. Missionaries attempted to annihilate the Aboriginal religion in favor of Christianity. As Aboriginal rights campaigner

Kath Walker observed, the tribes swapped one set of sacred myths for another.

Aborigines were shunted to the squalid margins of Australia's developing society. Only in 1951 were they legally given equal status with whites. As late as 1972 *Newsweek* magazine correspondent Tony Clifton reported "…the most emotionally wearing experience of my life has come just in the last few days—among the Aboriginal population of my native land. Now I have seen how we Australians are condemning a whole race of our fellow citizens to short, brutish, and miserable lives."

Given the relatively newly wielded power of the written word and an overhaul in public attitudes toward tribal culture, new life has been given to Aboriginal concepts. Proof is the ownership of Ayers Rock, the monolithic formation in the Northern Territory held sacred by several Aboriginal tribes, conferred back to them by the government in 1985. Its Aboriginal name of Uluru is now preferred. Religious aspects like body painting and customs including the plucking of a tooth have since become cherished.

ABOVE: Two body-painted boys find fun with a laptop comupter. The lure of Australia's cities has drawn Aborigines away from their homes for many years. Torn from their spiritual background, it has not been a happy experience for many.

A Fierce Spirit—Maori Religion

As early as AD 800 an intrepid band from the Polynesian Islands boarded open canoes and sailed into the unknown. With them they bought yams, dogs, rats, and the framework of the Polynesian religion.

We can only guess at the hardships the Polynesians encountered as they forged through the South Pacific. Their journey came to an end when they arrived at the fertile islands we now know as New Zealand. These were the first Maoris, who lived in relative peace until the arrival of Europeans at the end of the 18th century.

Nature plays a key role in the faith and a range of spirits or *atua* represent the elements. Maori mythology says that Mother Earth and Father Sky were the creators. Their offspring included Rongo, the spirit of farming, Turanga, the spirit of rivers, and Tangaroa, the spirit of the ocean. There was a hero figure linked with light, goodness, and kindness called Tane. In opposition was his brother, Whiro, a dark and dangerous force.

In some Maori traditions there is a supreme being, Io, father of Tane and Whiro. Scholars later cast doubt on the authenticity of this belief, believing he was a late addition in response to Christianity and its concept of a sole creator god. But although Io does not exist for every Maori tribe, it seems unlikely that fierce and formidable opponents of white settlers would have embraced any part of an imposed new religion.

One of the most evident links between the Maoris and their Polynesian forebears is the importance of *mana* in both societies. *Mana* is a supernatural force ascribed to people, places, spirits, and objects. It may be good or evil but always demands enormous respect. Thus it is considered disrespectful to walk across people's legs, pass items over their heads, or stand intentionally higher than others, for this diminishes their *mana*. To offend *mana* is *tapu*—or taboo. Those who break taboos live with the unspoken threat of retribution, which may take the form of an accident, a death in the family, a poor harvest, and so forth. *Tapu* gives bad luck an identity all of its own.

GIFTS AND CURSES

According to one Maori legend, Io prepared three gifts for the human race, presented in baskets. One contained peace and love, the second songs and spells, the third contained help and understanding. He gave them to his son Tane to present to the people of the world. To do so Tane had to climb down the Great Tower of the Overworlds that connected their heaven with Earth.

During the journey Tane was ambushed by his malevolent brother Whiro, who wanted the kudos of delivering the baskets himself. Tane won the titanic fraternal struggle and went on to arm mankind with the gifts of the gods. Not to be outdone, Whiro inflicted them with the unwanted gifts of sickness, crime, and death. The Great Tower was so badly damaged that it could never be used again.

Even at a glance it is apparent that Maori religious culture is rich and robust. Yet it came near to extinction after the arrival of British colonists in 1840. As in Australia, natives fell victim to foreign diseases. The white people were land-hungry and there were a series of conflicts over territorial rights. During this period of unrest a new religion spread among the Maoris. In 1864 Te Ua Haumene, a Maori chief, claimed to have been visited by the angel Gabriel. Te Ua Haumene was so remorseful at the way Maoris had strayed from the path of righteousness that he killed one of his own children. The Maoris, he claimed, were a chosen people.

He presented a faith drawing on traditions from the Christians, Jews, and

Polynesians. Moreover, Te Ua Haumene told his warriors that if they cried "hau hau" (or "hapu hapu") during battle they would be immune to European bullets. Religious fervor assisted in some limited victories in the war against the colonists, but ultimately the Maoris were defeated and the importance of their religion dwindled.

Easter Island—Mystery *in* Stone

In a remote part of the South Pacific lies Easter Island; small, sparsely populated, but enormously significant thanks to timeless treasures stacked on its shores by an unknown people centuries ago.

For years people have pondered upon the army of megaliths standing proudly on the island known to Polynesians as Rapa Nui (Great Rapa) or Te Pito te Henua (Navel of the World). Who carved them? Why were they made? The combined might of modern science and archaeology have failed to find conclusive answers.

At first glance Easter Island seems an unlikely site for such a cache of culture. Formed from three extinct volcanoes, the windy, warm, and wet island covers an area of just 45 square miles. It stands in splendid isolation, some 1,250 miles from its nearest neighbor, Pitcairn Island, and 2,480 miles from the coast of South America.

About 600 statues have been located, of which a hundred are still standing. In height they stand between 10 and 40 feet. They were often decked with a red crown or topknot (*pukao*), adding further height and weight. One of the fallen statues would have stood 32 feet high when upright and weighs 82 tons; its *pukao* a further 11 tons. An unfinished statue has been discovered standing at 68 feet, its back still attached to a rock face. Rows of the statues, or *moai*, were supported on giant stone platforms called *ahus*.

Carbon dating has estimated that the earliest evidence of activity on the island was in the eighth century, although many of the statues date from a later period. Tradition says that the statues, which presumably represented deities, walked across the island to their present sites. Experiments proved that islanders using wooden stakes and rollers would have been able to haul the enormous icons into position.

FALLING FROM GRACE

The statues are made of *tuff*, a soft volcanic rock quarried from one of the volcano craters, called Rano Raraku. Around the quarry lie unfinished statues and primitive though effective tools are scattered on the ground. It is as if the sculptors were suddenly interrupted in their labors and beat a hasty retreat. It seems there was some manner of cataclysm on the island, during which numerous people were killed and *moai* were toppled.

The first European to set foot on the island was Dutchman Jakob Roggeveen on Easter Sunday, 1722. According to his reports, the several thousand inhabitants worshipped the immense statues and also revered fire and the sun. This was not the picture described by Captain

The sun sets over stone statues of heads on the outer slope of Rano Raraku, a soft-stone quarry on Easter Island.

James Cook in 1774, who found the population cut by about two-thirds and the survivors paying little heed to the statues, many of which had been overthrown.

One credible theory says that the islanders, descendents of emigrants from the Marquesas Islands, lived in harmony for centuries in a hierarchical society. This ended when the lower orders rose up against those in command and massacred their masters, burning the bodies in a ditch on the northeastern coast.

Further disasters blighted the island in the 1860s in the form of slave-raiding parties and a smallpox epidemic. The presence of a Christian missionary had already begun to obliterate the native culture. By 1877 the population had plummeted to just 111. Its revival as a farming outpost was assured after Chile annexed it in 1888. Just over a century later it was designated a World Heritage site.

The key to the secrets of Easter Island may be the wooden tablets discovered alongside smaller wooden sculptures in hidden caves. Each tablet bears a form of script that has so far defied all attempts at decipherment. Its use and meanings have long been forgotten, but it is the only known time that Polynesian religion has been set in writing.

Is there a God?

In the modern age, religion has been scrutinized by scientists, philosophers, theologists, anthropologists, archaeologists, politicians, and priests. Yet in an era when so many of life's mysteries can be rationalized it remains impossible to answer one basic question: is there a God? Faith, its focus, and its power remains intangible.

Take the shrine at Lourdes in France, where peasant girl Bernadette Soubirous saw a vision of the Virgin Mary in 1858.

Thousands have visited the town and bathed in the waters of the spring dug by the girl at the Virgin Mary's command. About 7,000 people have claimed a miracle cure. Most instances can be explained away and a board of numerous doctors and

scientists are intent on doing just that. But 66 cases have not been resolved in earthly terms. Put that alongside the bizarre findings of a scientific study—that the sick have a better chance of recovery if they are prayed for—and the existence of God seems more feasible.

But which God? Is it the God who favors long hair and beards or the one who smiles upon a shaven head? Is it the God who is impressed by an ascetic lifestyle or one who takes comfort in family life? Is He offended by birth control and pleased by circumcision? Does He delight in fasting and are plain clothes preferable to bright colors? If everyone in the world is praying to the same God, it seems someone, somewhere has got it wrong.

People don't need a miracle to root their beliefs in God. The Roman Catholic Church believes its membership has passed the one billion mark. There's been renewed interest in Islam, while Judaism has thrived despite being the perpetual subject of violence.

Buddhists have found a rich recruiting ground in India, while Hinduism has no fear of going out of style, despite counting its age in millennia. Cults have come and gone down the ages but religions that have blended simple messages, persuasive literature, and charismatic leadership are well grounded and have the ability to survive.

Religious leaders are trying to counter this and in 2000 there was a host of small-scale, significant events to pave the way for a tolerant future. The Dalai Lama spoke about the need for a variety of religions, Christians apologized to Jews and Muslims for the atrocities committed during the Crusades, the president of the Islamic Conference met with the Pope, and the first Muslim chaplain was appointed at a U.S. university. While rafts of bitter disagreement still exist between the faiths, there is more hope than ever before of reconciliation.

Fundamentally, people turn to religion in the hope of salvation. Fear of the unknown looms just as large for us today as it did for our prehistoric ancestors, and the comfort that faith can provide will be welcomed ever more.

LEFT: A crowd, many with disabilities, attends a religious service at Lourdes, France. Lourdes' reputation as a center for miraculous cures began in the mid-19th century. On February 11, 1858, a 14-year-old sherpherdess called Bernadette Soubirous entered a small grotto near Lourdes to be greeted by an apparition of the Virgin Mary. On a further 17 occasions between then and July 16, Bernadette spoke with the apparition. It became a sensation among the local people. After digging a well at the Virgin Mary's insistence, Bernadette entered a convent, where she died in January 1879, aged 36. Lourdes became a center for pilgrimage, its reputation growing exponentially after several pilgrims claimed to have been cured of their illnesses by the "Lady of Lourdes."

Glossary

Adventists: Christians whose belief in the physical and literal Second Coming of Jesus is paramount.

Ahisma: the principle of non-violence pursued by the Jains.

Angas: "limbs" of Jain scripture.

Asceticism: self-discipline and abstentionism for the purposes of religious advancement.

Atman: in Hinduism, the inner flame or true nature.

Aum Shinri Kyo: Japanese cult responsible for gassing the Tokyo underground.

Autocephalus: a church governed by its own head bishop.

Bab, the: the name given to Sayyid Ali Muhammad, who helped to found the Baháʼí movement, meaning the Gate (to the truth).

Bhikkus: Buddhist monks.

bodhisattva: a notably wise and moral Buddhist.

Bolsheviks: hard-liners among Russian Marxists who engineered a revolution in 1917; forerunners to the Soviet Communist party.

Bon Dieu: Voodoo's high god.

Brahmin: a Hindu priest.

Byzantine: name given to the Eastern Roman Empire.

Caliph: Muslim civil and religious leader, regarded as the successor of Mohammed.

Calvinist: an adherent of Protestant reformer John Calvin (1509–64).

Church of Jesus Christ of Latter Day Saints: the Mormon Church.

Coptic Church: Christian Church of Egypt, founded by St. Mark.

Dalit: the downtrodden among the Hindus, some of whom are known as "untouchables."

Diaspora: dispersal of the Jewish people between 8th–6th centuries BC.

Dianetics: the teachings of Scientology founder L. Ron Hubbard that explain and eliminate engrams, the residue of bad experiences that hold people back and inhibit success.

Dreaming: the Aboriginal Creation beliefs.

guru: teacher or spiritual advisor.

heretic: holder of unorthodox beliefs.

Hinayana: "small vehicle"—the minority branch of Buddhism that believes only in the word of the Buddha.

Hogon: African spiritual leader.

Houngan: Voodoo priest.

Imam: title of various Muslim leaders; in lower case (imam) the leader of prayer in a mosque.

Inquisition: tribunal established in the 13th century by the Church to identify heretics.

ioa: Voodoo spirits.

karma: the belief that every action has consequences that will be reckoned after death.

Mahayana: "large vehicle"—the majority branch of Buddhism that embraces a broad range of philosophy and literature.

mambo: Voodoo priestess.

Monophysites: people who believe that Christ had a single, divine nature rather than a dual nature, human and divine.

Moravian Bretheren: Protestant association formed in Bohemia in 1457, driven out by persecution in 1722.

nave: western part of the church, open to the laity.

Nommos: amphibious aliens known to the Dogon tribe in Africa.

Olympia: Greek village identified as the sanctuary of chief deity Zeus.

oracle: place or person connected with divine prophesy.

patriarch: chief bishop in the Orthodox Church.

Pharisee: member of a Jewish group that recognizes all forms of religious practice, not just its written form.

Pietism: Protestant belief in doing good works, Bible study, and holiness, began by Lutherans as a response to dogmatism in the Protestant Church and influenced the Moravians and Methodists.

Presbyterian: Church governed by elders of equal rank.

Puritans: 16–17th century Protestants who rejected the Church of England for a more disciplined, moral doctrine.

Reducciones: church missions founded by Jesuits in South America.

Reformation: movement that began in the 16th century to reform the existing Roman Catholic Church and ended with the establishment of the Protestant Church.

Sadducee: member of a Jewish group that only recognizes religious practice in its written form; opposed to Pharisees.

Samsara: Sanskrit for "wheel of life," the theory of reincarnation.

Sangha: community of Buddhist believers.

separatists: those demanding separation from a governing power, usually a minority.

Shi'ite: adherent of one branch of Islam, who believes that Mohammed's rightful successors were Ali, the fourth Caliph, and his descendants.

Sunni: someone who follows the Orthodox Muslim faith and believes Mohammed's successors should be elected by the Muslim community.

taboo: forbidden conduct, from the Polynesian word *tapu*.

Talmud: body of Jewish civil and ceremonial law.

Tirthankaras: ancient heroes of Jain theology.

Torah: the first five books of the Old Testament, also known as the *Pentateuch*.

Underworld: a land of spirits and the dead, notably in ancient North and South American beliefs.

White Fathers: Catholic order living in Africa founded in 1868.

Zion: Hebrew terms for the Jewish temple, Jerusalem, or the whole of Israel.

Index

3 Jewels 146–147, 155
4 Noble Truths 144
5 Pillars of Islam 44–45
5 Precepts 144
10 Commandments 14–15
10 plagues 12
12 sons/tribes of Israel 11
13 Articles 18
30 Years War 130

Aaron 12–13
Abbasids 40–41
Abhidhamma 149
Aborigines 181–183
Abraham 10–11, 36, 46–47, 49
Acosta, José de 83
Acre 53
Adena culture 58–59
Adi Granth 168–169
Adventists 66
Afghanistan 152, 178–179
Africa 17, 41, 61, 86–97
Akbar, Emperor 166, 170
al-Basri, Hasan 51
Alexander the Great 103
Ali 39–40
Allah 37
Amaterasu 163
Amazon river 83
America: Central 76–79, 84–85, 96;
  North 56–73, 96, 124, 127; South 61,
  74, 80–83
Amritsar 170
Amun-Ra 92
Ananda 148
Anatolia 104
angels 37
Anglican Church 112–113, 122–123,
  181
Anti-Semitism 20–21
Apep 93
Apostles 30–31
Arabs 20–21
Arizona 59
Arjan, Guru 166
Ark of the Covenant 14–15
Armenia 110
Armenian Church 35
art 88–89, 100
Aryans 134
Asgard 107
Ashkenazim 17
Asia 60, 132–179
Ask 107
Asoka, Emperor 147
astronomy 59, 81, 90–91
Atapuerca 100
Atargatis 104
Athens 118
Augustus, Emperor 104
Aum Shinri Kyo cult 179
Aurangzeb, Emperor 166–167
Australasia 180–187
Australia 61, 182–183
Avesta 156
Avignon 109
Aztec 77–79

Baal 11
Bab, the 52
Baby Doc 85
Babylonians 15
Baghdad 53
Bahá'í faith 52–53
Baha'u'llah 53
Bahubali 155
Baisakhi 171
Bakr, Abu 38
Balfour Declaration 20–21
ball game 76

Bamiyan Buddhas 152
bar Khokhba, Simon 17, 23
Basil II, Emperor 120
Bathsheba 14
Besant, Annie Wood 129
Besht 25
Bhaktivedanta Swami Prabhupada,
  A.C. 174–175
Bijak 164
Black Death 109
Blavatsky, Helena Petrovna 128–129
Bluetooth, Harald 106
Bodhidharma 150–151
Brotherhood of Theologians 119
Bodh Gaya 143
Boleyn, Anne 113
Booth, William 126–127
Bosnia 131
Brahma 134–135
Brahman 134
Buddha 135, 142–145, 148
Buddhism 142–152
Buri 106
Byzantine Empire 34, 110, 120

Calvary 28
Calvin, John 114–115
Canaan 11–12, 14, 23
Canada 61
Carnac 100–101
caste system 140–141
cathedrals 116–117
Catherine of Aragon 112
Catholic Church 20, 35, 84–85,
  109–113, 130, 181
Central America 76–79, 84–85, 96
Chac 77
Chapultepec 78
Chichén Itzá 77
China 147, 150, 152, 158–161
Chou dynasty 158–159
Christ *see* Jesus
Christianity 6, 26–35, 86, 94–95, 98,
  104, 106, 108–109, 130
Christians 30–33, 55, 180–181
Christian Science 70–71
Church of England *see* Anglican
  Church
Church of Jesus Christ of Latter-Day
  Saints 64
Church of the Holy Sepulcher 28, 38
Civil War, English 116, 130
Clermont 110
Confucianism 160–161
Confucius 158–161
Congo 91
conquistadors 77
Constantine the Great, Emperor 33,
  104
Constantinople 34, 53, 111, 118
Cook, James 182
Coptic Church 35, 86
Cortés, Hernán 77
Council of Constance 109
Council of Ferrara-Florence 118
Coyolxauhqui 79
Croatia 131
crucifixion 28
Crusades 54, 110–111
Culhuacán 78
Cuzco 80
Cybele 104

Dalai Lama 147, 151–152
Damascus 39
Dasam Granth 169
David 14
Dead Sea 17
Deecoodah 59
Delphi 102
Denmark 106
dhamma 146
Dianetics 72–73

Diet of Worms 114
Digambaras 155
divination 80
Diwali 139
Dodana 102
Dogen 151
Dogon tribe 90–91
Dog Star 90–91
Dome of the Rock 48
Doyle, Arthur Conan 69
Dreaming, the 182–183
Druids 101
Duvalier, Dr François 85

Easter Island 186–187
Eastern Orthodox Church 118–120
Eddy, Mary Baker 70–71
Edward VI 113
Edward VII 127
Egypt 12, 92–93
Eid-ul-Fitr 45
Eightfold Path 144
Eisai 151
El 11
Elizabeth I 113, 130
Embla 107
England 62, 101, 112–114, 122–125,
  130
engrams 73
Erasmus, Desiderius 113
Eskimos 61
Ethiopia 97
Eucharist 28
Europe 61, 98–131; *see also*
  individual European countries
Exodus, Book of 12

fasting 44–45
Feathered Serpent 77–79
Ferrara-Florence council 118
Finland 101
First World War 125
Five Pillars of Islam 44–45
Five Precepts 144
Four Noble Truths 144
Fox, Catherine/Margaret 68–69
Fox, George 124
France 83, 98, 100–101, 109–110, 115,
  188
Frey 106–107
Fritz, Father Samuel 83
Fry, Elizabeth 125

Gabriel 37
Galileo 111
Gandhi, Indira 173
Gandhi, Mohandas 141, 172
Ganesh 135
Ganges river 138–139
Garvey, Marcus 96
Gaul 98
Gautama, Siddharta 142–143
Gaya river 143
Gemara 23
Genesis, Book of 10–11
Geneva 115
Germany 17, 20–21, 114, 123,
  130
Gethsemane 28
Golden Temple 170–171, 173
Golgotha 28
Goliath 14
Gospels 26–27
Granth Sahib 168–169
Great Schism 109
Great Serpent Mound 59
Greece 102–104, 118–119
Greek Church 35, 118–119
Gregory V 119
Guatemala 76
gurdwara 169–171
Guru Nanak 164–165
Gurus (Sikh) 166–167, 170–171

Hadrian, Emperor 17
Hagia Sophia church/mosque 119
Haiti 84
hajj 46–47
Halakhah 23
Hana Pacha 81
Ha-Nasi, Judah 23
Hari Mandir 170–171
Hasidism 25
Hazor 14
Hebrew Bible 22
Henry IV 115
Henry VIII 112–113
Hero Twins 76
Herzl, Theodor 17
Hicks, Elias 124
Hinayana school 146
Hindus 134–141
Hispaniola 84
Holi 139
Holland 63
Holocaust 21, 67
Holy Office 111
Holy of Holies 15
holy relics 109
Holy Spirit Association for the
  Unification of World Christianity
  176
Horus 92
Houdini, Harry 69
HPB 128–129
Hubbard, L. Ron 72–73
Huguenots 115
Huitzilopochtli 77–79
Huss of Bohemia, John 114

iconoclasm 35
Igbo Ukwu 89
Ignatius of Loyola 82
Imams (Mohammed's successors)
  39
Inca 80–81
India 134, 138, 142–145, 147, 151,
  154, 156, 170–171, 174, 179
Inquisition 111
International Federation for World
  Peace 177
Inti 80
Inuit culture 61
Io 185
Iran 156
Ireland 130
Isaac/Ishmael 10–11, 46, 49
Isis 92, 104
Iskcon 175
Islam 6, 36–49, 86, 130–131
Ismailis 39
Israel 11, 14–17, 21, 54
Itzamna 77

Jacob 11
Jainists 154–155
Japan 150–151, 163, 179
Jehovah's Witnesses 66–67
Jericho 14
Jerusalem 10, 15–16, 27, 110
Jesuits 82–83
Jesus 26–31
jewelry *see* art
Jewish festivals 23
Jews 16–25, 31, 37, 54, 65
Joseph, Akiba ben 23
Joseph of Arimathea 28
Joshua 14
Judaism 6, 10–25, 31, 104
Jung, Carl 7
Jupiter (Jove) 104

Ka'aba 36, 46, 165
Kabir 164–165, 168
Kalamans 144
kami 163
karma 140, 155

Karnak 92
Kay Pacha 81
Khadija 36
Khalsa army 171
Khazars 17
Khokbha, Simon bar 17, 23
Kiev 120
Knights Hospitaller/Templar 110
Knorr, Nathan Homer 67
Knox, John 114
Kojiki 163
Kongfuzi 160
Koran 37, 39, 42–43
Korea 132
Kremlin, the 117
Krishna 135, 139
Krishna Consciousness 174–175
Krishnamurti Foundation 129
Kumbh Mela 138–139
Kung, Grand Master 160
Kushinagar 145

Lake Texcoco 78
Last Supper 28
Lavigerie of Algiers, Charles 95
Livingstone, David 94–95
Lollards 114
Lourdes 188–189
Luther, Martin 114
Lutherans 113, 123; *see also*
    Protestants
Lydenburg 89

Maccabeus, Judas 15–16
Magdalene, Mary 28
Mahabarata 136
Mahaprabu, Chaitanya 174–175
Mahavira, Vardhamana 154
Mahayana school 147, 149
Maimonides 18–19, 23
mana 184
Manichaean Church 98
Manzikert 110
Maoris 184
Mary I 113
Masada 16
Massachusetts 63
Matthopoulos 119
Mauryan dynasty 147
Maya 76–77
Mayflower 63
Mecca 36–37, 41, 47
medicine men 61
Medina 37, 48
Megiddo 12
Menelik II, Emperor 97
Methodists 122–123
Mexico 78
Middle East 8–55, 110–111
Middle Path/Way 144
Midgard 107
Mina 47
Mishna Torah 18, 23
missionaries 31, 82–83, 94–95, 106,
    123, 181, 187
Mithraism 104
Moctezuma II 77
Mohammed 36–38, 42, 47, 50
monasticism 35
Monks Mound 58–59
Moon, Sun Myung 176–177
Moravians 123
Mormons 64–65
Moscow 117
Moses 11–13, 19, 152
mosques 48–49
moundbuilders 58–59
Mount Aconcagua 81
Mount Arafat 47
Mount Moriah 10
Mount Nebo 14
Mount Olympus 102
Mount Parnassus 102

Mount Sinai 13, 46, 152
Mu'awia 40
Muhammad *see* Mohammed
Muslims 37, 39, 55, 98, 110, 178

Native Americans 56, 58–61, 124
Nazareth 27
Nebi Musa monastery 14
Nero, Emperor 33
New York 116, 175
New Zealand 184–185
Nigeria 88–89
Nihongi 163
Nile river 12, 93, 95
nirvana 149, 155
Noah 10
Noble Truths 144
Nok culture 88
Noringa, Motoori 163
Norse 106–107
North America 56–73, 96, 124, 127
Norway 106
Notre Dame cathedral 116–117
Nuri, Mizra Husayn Ali 52

Odin 106–107
Ohio 58, 64
Olcott, Henry Steel 128–129
Old Testament 10
oracles 102
Order of the Star of the East 129
Orthodox churches 118–121
Osiris 92

Pakistan 179
Palestine 17
Pali Canon 148
Pantheon 105
papacy 109
Papa Doc 85
Parr, Catherine 113
Parvati 135
Paul 31
Peace of Augsburg 114
Pennsylvania 124
Penn, William 124
Pentateuch 13
Persia 15, 52, 103–104, 156
Peru 80, 83
Peter I, the Great 120
Pharaohs 92–93
Pidgeon, William 59
pilgrimage 46–47, 108, 138
Pilgrim Fathers 62–63
plagues 12
Polynesia 184, 186
popes: Clement VII 109; Clement
    XIV 83; Gregory VIII 110;
    Gregory IX 111; John Paul II 118;
    Urban II 110; Urban VI 109
Portugal 83
Prabhupada, A.C. Bhaktivedanta
    Swami 174–175
Presbyterians 114
Protestants 113–115, 124, 130
Prussia 83
Puranas 136
Puritans 62, 124
pyramids 92

Quakers 124–125
Quetzalcoatl 77–79
Quimby, Phineas Parkhurst 70
Qur'an *see* Koran

Ra 92
rain god 77, 79
Ramadan 44–45
Ramayana 136–137
Rambam 19
Ramses II 12
Rashi 19
Rastafarians 96–97

Red Sea 13
reducciones 82
Reformation 112–115
reincarnation 138, 140, 146
Renaissance 114
Renovated Church 121
Richard the Lionheart 110
Rinzai Buddhism 151
Roman Empire 16, 31–34, 104–105
Rome 34–35, 109
Russell, Charles Taze 66
Russia 20, 83, 117, 120–121, 127
Rutherford, Joseph 66–67

Sabbath/Shabbat 23, 27
sacrifice (human) 76, 78, 80
saints: Antony 35; Helena 33;
    Paul 31; Peter 35
Saint Paul's cathedral 117
Saint Peter's Basilica 116
Saladin 18, 110
Salt Lake City 65
Salvation Army 126–127
Samsara 140
Sangha 146, 148
Saqqara 93
Sarah (Noah) 10–11
Sassanids 156
Saturn 91
Saul 14, 31, 69
Scientology 72–73
Scotland 114
sculpture *see* art
Sea of Reeds 13
Second World War 21, 121, 125
Selassie, Haile 97
Seljuk Turks 110
Sephardim 17
Serbia 131
Seth 92
Seveners 39
Seymour, Jane 113
shamans 60–61
Sheba, queen of 15
Shi'ite Muslims 39
Shintoism 163
Shiva 134–136, 139
Sikhism 164–171
Sikhs 172–173
Singh, Guru Gobind 166, 171
Singh, (Marahaja) Ranjit 171–172
Sirhind 171
Sirius 90–91
slavery 84, 95
Smith, Joseph 64–65
Society of Friends 124–125
Socrates 102–103
Sodom and Gomorrah 11
Solomon 15
Soto Buddhism 151
Sotor 119
South America 61, 74, 80–83
Spain 17, 40, 83, 98, 100, 130
spiritualism 68–69
Spitama 156
Stalin, Joseph 121
Stanley, Henry Morgan 95
Stations of the Cross 28
stone circles 100–101
Stonehenge 101
Sufism 50–51
sun god 80, 92
Sunni Muslims 39
Sutra Pitaka 148
Svetambaras 155
Sweden 106
Switzerland 114
synagogues 24–25
Synoptic Gospels 27
Syria 104
Syrian Church 35

Taliban 152, 178

Talmud, the 19, 22–23
Tantric Buddhism 151
Tao 150
Taoism 158–159
Tel Aviv 17
temples of Jerusalem 15, 25
Ten Commandments 14–15
Tenochtitlan 78
ten plagues 12
teyolia energy 78
Tezcatlipoca 77–78
Theodosius, Emperor 34
Theosophists 128–129
Theravada school 147, 149
Thirteen Articles 18
Thirty Years War 130
Thor 106
Thoth 92
Three Jewels 146–147, 155
Thutmose 12
Tibet 152
Tibetan Buddhism 147, 151–152
Tlaloc 79
Toltec culture 77–78
Torah 13, 25
Tripitaka 149
Tula 77
Turks 110, 118–119
Twelvers 39
twelve sons/tribes of Israel 11
Tzu, Lao 158–159

Ukraine 121
Uku Pacha 81
Umar 38
Umayyad dynasty 38–40, 51
Underworld 61, 76, 92
Unification Church 132, 176–177
USA *see* North America
Utah 65
Uthman 38–39

Vaishali 147
Valhalla 107
Varanasi 144
Vedas 136–137
Venice 111
Via Dolorosa 28
Vikings 106–107
Vinaya Pitaka 149
Vishnu 134, 136, 138–139
Vladimir, Prince 120
Volunteers of America 127
voodoo 84–85

War of Flowers
Watchtower, The 66
Way of Sorrows 28
Weizmann, Dr Chaim 20
Wesley, John 122–123
wheel of life 140
White Fathers 95
witches 69
World Tree 107
World War I 125
World War II 21, 121, 125
Wycliffe, John 114

Xipe Totec 79

Yathrib 37
Ymir 106
Yom Kippur 23
Young, Brigham 65
Yugoslavia 130

zakat 44
Zen Buddhism 147, 150–151
Zeus 102
Zoe 119
Zoroastrians 156–157
Zwingli, Huldreich 114